Financial Capacity of the Parties

Schriftenreihe der August Maria Berges Stiftung für Arbitrales Recht

Herausgegeben von Dr. Hubertus W. Labes

Band 16

PETER LANG
Frankfurt am Main · Berlin · Bern · Bruxelles · New York · Oxford · Wien

German Institution of Arbitration
(ed.)

Financial Capacity of the Parties

A Condition for the Validity of Arbitration Agreements?

Based on a Conference Organized by the German Institution of Arbitration (DIS) on 29th November 2002 in Berlin

PETER LANG
Europäischer Verlag der Wissenschaften

Bibliographic Information published by Die Deutsche Bibliothek

Die Deutsche Bibliothek lists this publication in the Deutsche Nationalbibliografie; detailed bibliographic data is available in the internet at <http://dnb.ddb.de>.

ISSN 1435-4748
ISBN 3-631-51241-4
US-ISBN 0-8204-6460-0

Printed in Germany 1 2 3 4 6 7

www.peterlang.de

Contents

Preface

*Karl-Heinz Böckstiegel**

The financial capacity of the parties has always been of relevance in many ways for and in arbitration proceedings, be they national or international. However, during the present period in time, due to the grave economic problems in many countries and, as a consequence, a growing number of private persons and enterprises as well as public entities at the local and state level reaching or surpassing the limits of their financial liquidity, it has turned into a much more frequent issue in the practice of arbitration.

Procedurally, in addition to this more general relevance, attention in Germany was particularly drawn to the subject recently by a decision of the German Federal Court of Justice allowing access to the state courts in spite of an arbitration agreement, because allegedly a party lacked the financial means to go to arbitration. This decision which is discussed in detail later in this publication has – for good reason – found critical commentary both in Germany and abroad. It goes far beyond the also much discussed *Gateway* decisions in the United States. This publication illustrates that the decision of the German Federal Court of Justice stands alone in comparison with other countries and it can only be hoped that the decision was due to exceptional circumstances which may not be used as a pretext to disregard the submission to arbitration in other scenarios. Otherwise, the excellent arbitration environment created by Germany adopting the UNCITRAL Model Law some years ago would be jeopardized.

Substantially, many of us have been involved in arbitration cases where the claimant proceeded with his claims, though the respondent did not seem to have sufficient funds to pay any money found to be due in the award, perhaps not even the costs of the arbitration itself. Various reasons may come into play to make such a behaviour a justified business decision:

- The claimant may want to achieve an enforceable award just for the case that the respondent's situation improves and then enforcement will be possible without delay.
- The claimant may need an award as proof of his damage in order to receive payment from his insurance.

* Professor Dr. iur.; University of Cologne.
Chairman of the Board of Directors of the German Institution of Arbitration; Member of the Arbitration Commission of the International Chamber of Commerce; (ICC); President of the London Court of International Arbitration (LCIA) 1993-1997 and Honorary Vice-President.

- If the respondent is a State or public institution claiming immunity against enforcement, getting confirmation of the money or action due by the award may enable the claimant or his home State to apply political pressure.

For the in-house counsel or lawyer drawing up and negotiating contracts, this publication not only identifies and clarifies risks involved in a comparative analysis of the law and practice in major countries, but also tries to indicate means – contractual or otherwise – to avoid or deal with such risks.

The contributions in this publication are based on papers presented at a conference of the German Institution of Arbitration (DIS) in Berlin on 28 and 29 November 2002 which was very well attended both from Germany and abroad. The DIS is grateful to the eminent experts who accepted to speak at that occasion and to update their papers for publication. Our gratitude is also due to the members of the DIS staff, who were responsible for the logistics involved.

Poor Parties and German Forums: Placing Arbitration under the Sword of Damocles?

*Gerhard Wagner**

I. Introduction

In September 2000, the Federal Supreme Court of Germany issued a judgment in a case that involved a contract between a builder and a construction company concerning the installation of heating and sanitary systems into a building and

---

* Professor Dr. iur, LL.M.; University of Bonn.

including an arbitration clause.[1] During the course of performance, the construction company must have had considerable doubts as to the ability of the builder to pay the price for its work and it thus demanded that it be supplied with securities. As the builder refused, the constructor suggested to waive the arbitration agreement in order to have the issue decided in a court of law. Again, the builder disagreed, and the constructor refrained from filing a claim, most probably for reasons of costs. Shortly thereafter, the builder himself turned to a court of law, suing the constructor for damages and claiming that part of the work be deficient. In addition, he declared the arbitration agreement void since he lacked the funds necessary to cover the costs of arbitral proceedings. The defendant constructor motioned the court to dismiss the claim, and the lower courts ruled accordingly. However, the Federal Supreme Court reversed on the ground that the arbitration agreement was "incapable of being performed" within the meaning of Sec. 1032 para 1 German Code of Civil Procedure (ZPO) which for that part is a faithful translation of Art. 8 para 1 of the UNCITRAL Model Law on International Commercial Arbitration.[2]

As will be explained in more detail, this ruling was anything other than a surprise if one considers the case law developed on the issue of impecuniosity under the old code governing arbitral proceedings, in force until the adoption of the Model Law in 1998.[3] For this reason the court probably did not foresee that this decision would cause considerable unrest among commentators.[4] To be fair though, it must be added, that the court also received some support.[5] In addition, most of the critics did not take issue with the doctrine that an arbitration agreement may be rendered unenforceable where one of the parties lacks the funds necessary to pay its share of the filing fee and the advance on costs demanded by the arbitrators. What drew a considerable amount of dissent was the court's holding that impecuniosity of one party rendered the agreement "incapable of being performed" thus making it unenforceable as a matter of

---

1 BGH (14.09.2000) BGHZ 145, 116 = NJW 2000, 3720 = LM Sec. 1032 ZPO no. 11 note *Wagner* = JZ 2001, 258 note *Schlosser*.

2 BGH (14.09.2000) BGHZ 145, 116, 119 seq.

3 For an overview see *Wagner*, Country Report Germany, in: Weigand (Ed.), Practitioner's Handbook on International Arbitration, no. 45 seq.; important cases other than the recent one are BGH (30.01.1964) BGHZ 41, 104, 108 seq; BGH (21.11.1968) BGHZ 51, 79, 81 seq.; BGH (22.02.1971) BGHZ 55, 344, 353 seq.; BGH (10.04.1980) BGHZ 77, 65, 66 seq.; BGH (12.11.1987) BGHZ 102, 199, 202 seq.; BGH (10.03.1994) NJW-RR 1994, 1214, 1215.

4 See infra, footnotes 6 and 7.

5 *Schlosser*, JZ 2001, 260, and also in: Stein/Jonas, Zivilprozeßordnung, 22nd ed. 2002, Sec. 1029 no. 38, Sec. 1032 no. 8; *Münch*, in: Münchener Kommentar zur Zivilprozeßordnung, 2nd ed. 2002, Sec. 1029 no. 59, Sec. 1032 no. 5; *Geimer*, in: Zöller, Zivilprozeßordnung, 23rd ed. 2002, Sec. 1029 no. 83.

law.[6] Very few commentators go even further and reject not only the constructive approach taken by the court but also the underlying principle that inability to pay affects the validity and enforceability of an arbitration agreement.[7]

In the presentation to follow, I will confront both issues, i.e. the substantive problem of the effects impecuniosity of one or both parties has for arbitration agreements, and the technical issue as to the pertinent mechanism to implement whatever effects poverty of a party might generate. In the first respect, the discussion is not confined to cases resembling the recent one just described in which one party refuses to arbitrate, either by calling upon a public court himself or by rejecting the other party's motion to refer the case to arbitration. Quite obviously, impecuniosity most often is only one step away from bankruptcy, and it may be interesting to investigate the consequences a petition for bankruptcy and the installation of a trustee in bankruptcy has for arbitral proceedings and arbitration agreements. With regard to the issue of implementation the concern is with legal technicalities and matters of construction, the central point here being the idea of the Federal Supreme Court to hold the arbitration agreement "incapable of being performed" once at least one of the parties falls into financial distress.

II. The Substance of the Matter: Taking Impecuniosity into Account?

Leaving issues of construction aside for the moment the central question is simple to formulate: May a party lacking the funds necessary to pay for the costs of arbitral proceedings still be held to its agreement to arbitrate or will the agreement be suspended one way or another?

1. Basic Considerations

Under German law, the answer to the question just posed has always been straightforward: The unanimous opinion among courts and commentators is that the impecunious party must not be held to its promise but allowed to beg off the arbitration agreement. The basic argument in favour of this position runs like this: If the impecunious party were held to its agreement, it would be deprived not only of its right to recourse in a court of law but of its right to recourse altogether.[8] Some commentators argue that such a result would even be contrary

---

6 *Wagner*, LM Sec. 1032 ZPO no. 11; *Risse*, BB 2001, Suppl. 6, p. 11 seq.; *Walter*, ZZP 114, 97, 100 seq., and in: *Schwab/Walter*, Schiedsgerichtsbarkeit, 6th ed 2001, chap. 8 no. 11.

7 *Polkinghore/Lehmkuhl*, Dealing with an impecunious opponent, IBA Section on Business Law, Committee D News, March 2002, p. 25 seq.

8 BGH (10.04.1980) BGHZ 77, 65, 69.

to Art. 6 of the European Convention on Human Rights (ECHR),[9] securing the right to fair trial, thought to include the right of access to justice.[10]

Of course, it may be doubted whether Art. 6 ECHR really has any bearing on the issue of parties to arbitration agreements lacking the funds to pay for the proceedings they have agreed to confine themselves to. Still, the result that the agreement must step aside may be justified from a different angle, starting with the interests and intentions of the parties themselves. Ordinarily, of course, neither of the parties will ever think of future contingencies, especially if they are as unpleasant as the prospect of lacking the funds necessary to pay arbitrators. But it is possible to ask what rational parties would have stipulated had they made the issue of impecuniosity one of the subjects of their contract drafting. To pose the question in more precise terms, would a party agreeing to arbitrate future disputes also agree to effectively lose its right if it lacks the funds to pay for the arbitral proceedings? – The answer must be no. A party signs an arbitration clause with an intention to choose a different mechanism of law enforcement. If the agreement was binding even where the party lacked the funds necessary to initiate arbitral proceedings, its effect would not be limited to substituting one law enforcement mechanism for another, i.e. a private tribunal for a public court, but it would foreclose enforcement of the underlying substantive rights in the first place. Made explicit, such an agreement would in fact contain two clauses, one for resolution of disputes through arbitral proceedings where the parties are able to afford them, and another providing for a waiver of the right to enforce otherwise valid substantive claims in case of at least one parties' inability to pay for such proceedings. Rational parties would not agree to anything like that.

As should be noted even at this early stage, the preceding argument is built on the premise that the costs for actions tried in public courts are different from the fees charged by arbitral institutions and tribunals for their services. To be more precise, if the poor party did not fare better in public court with respect to costs, i.e., if the public court was not "cheaper" than the arbitral tribunal, then there would be no sensible reason not to hold the poor party to its bargain and to enforce the arbitration agreement. However, this condition seems to hold in reality as the services of public courts may be cheaper than those of arbitral tribunals for a number of reasons. It may be that the absolute amount demanded by a court is less than the price charged by its private competitor, as is usually the case with small claims which may be tried in German courts at particularly low cost. The fees charged by courts are subject to public regulation, and the

---

9 Stein/Jonas-*Schlosser* (note 5) Sec. 1032 no. 38; MünchKomm ZPO-*Münch* (note 5) Sec. 1029 no. 59; *Fasching*, JBl. 1993, 545, 554.

10 *Jochen Frowein/Wolfgang Peukert,* Europäische Menschrechtskonvention – EMRK-Kommentar, 2nd ed. 1996, Art. 6 no. 63.

pertinent instrument provides for a scale that is designed in such a way to allow for the cost-efficient enforcement of small claims. Another reason to keep in mind is the influence different rules of cost allocation exert on access to justice, an objective central to the recent American decisions on the subject.[11] In a system of judicial administration in which public courts merely charge a modest filing fee and most of the work is done by lawyers who in turn work on the basis of contingent fees, the shift to the world of arbitration most often works to the detriment of a prospective claimant since he now has to pay a considerable amount of money in advance to put the tribunal to work and – equally importantly – bears the risk of having to shoulder the whole cost of the proceeding should he lose his case. Compared to a legal system like that of the United States, generally abstaining from allocating the costs to the losing party and for the very same reason dominated by lawyers working for claimants on a contingent fee basis, a shift to arbitration with a relatively active and expensive court and corresponding rules allowing for fee-shifting necessarily works to the detriment of a poor claimant.

As to the German civil justice system, it certainly allows for fee-shifting and its courts are not that cheap either but still the poor party fares much better in public court, the reason being, of course, legal aid. Generally speaking, under German law, every individual and every legal entity incorporated in Germany is entitled to legal aid, either in the form of a public grant or in the form of a public loan, to be paid back in several instalments where the poor party loses. If legal aid did not exist the difference between public courts and arbitral tribunals would not be dramatic, and cases posing problems for reasons of impecuniosity would be rare. As things stand, however, a poor party may litigate a case in public court at virtually no cost, something certainly unavailable in the area of private arbitral tribunals. Of course, the government could put the whole problem to rest by extending the coverage of legal aid to costs incurred within the conduct of arbitral proceedings. But to my knowledge lawyers working in the field of arbitration have never raised their voices to demand extension of legal aid to arbitral proceedings. Rather, the issue has been brought up by followers of the mediation movement but without success, so far. Given that public budgets are stretched now and will remain so in the future, it seems highly unlikely that these demands will be satisfied and the scope of legal aid be extended beyond proceedings in courts of law. Thus, such a truly amicable solution to our problem does not seem imminent.

---

[11] *Green Tree Financial Corp.-Alabama v. Randolph*, 531 U.S.79, 90 seq.; *Brower v. Gateway 2000, Inc.*, 676 N.Y.S.2d 569, 246 A.D.2d 246, 253 seq. (N.Y.A.D. 1998); *Shankle v. B-G Maintenance Management of Colorado, Inc.*, 163 F.3d 1230, 1233 seq. (10th Cir. 1999); *Phillips v. Associated Home Equity Service, Inc.*, 179 F.Supp.2d 840, 846 seq. (N.D.Ill. 2001).

2. The Nature of the Remedy

a) Neither Sanction nor Act of Grace

The approach developed argues for suspension of arbitration agreements in cases of impecuniosity from the basis of the principle of enforceability of vested rights, well entrenched in the civil justice systems of nations accepting the rule of law. This premise yields important consequences for the nature and scope of the said doctrine. In particular, it neither operates as a sanction nor as an act of grace but is tailored to the objective of making private rights enforceable, either in arbitration or in a court of law. As a consequence, the doctrine works both in favour of the plaintiff and in favour of the defendant, and it is blind to the fact whether the party seeking a release from the arbitration agreement is poor itself or whether it is the other side who cannot afford to pay its way in arbitral proceedings. As the cases decided under the old German arbitration law illustrate, there is a whole range of procedural situations in which the issue of impecuniosity may arise.

A standard scenario for the doctrine providing for suspension of the arbitration agreement to come into play is the one in the recent Supreme Court decision in which the poor plaintiff enforces his rights in a court of law contrary to an agreement to arbitrate the dispute in question.[12] If the defendant then relies on the arbitration agreement, motioning the court to refer the parties to arbitration, the plaintiff may raise a counter-motion not to dismiss for want of the funds necessary to enforce his rights in arbitral proceedings. Given that impecuniosity of the plaintiff is established the court will refuse the motion to dismiss and continue the action brought before it.

As has already been indicated, however, the doctrine also works the other way, in favour of a plaintiff who is not poor and could afford to pay the advance on the costs of the arbitral tribunal but who chooses to sue in public court since the other side, the defendant, is unable to meet his share of the costs of arbitral proceedings. Where the poor defendant invokes the arbitration agreement, motioning the court to dismiss the claim, the rich plaintiff may counter this motion by pleading that the defendant is estopped from relying on the arbitration clause.[13] The reason for a motion to dismiss being held contrary to good faith would of course be the argument that defendant will be unable to fund the arbitral proceedings to be commenced if the court granted the defendant's motion to dismiss.[14] Thus, granting the motion to dismiss would allow the

[12] BGH (30.01.1964) BGHZ 41, 104, 108 ff.; BGH (21.11.1968) BGH 51, 79; BGH (22.02.1971) BGHZ 55, 344; BGH (10.04.1980) BGHZ 77, 65, 66 ff.; BGH (14.09.2000) BGHZ 145, 116.

[13] BGH (12.11.1987) BGHZ 102, 199, 203.

[14] BGH (12.11.1987) BGHZ 102, 199, 203.

defendant to get away scot-free as he would not be answerable in legal proceedings at all, neither in court of law nor before an arbitral tribunal.

b) Irrespective of Fault

A second important point to be mentioned is that the arbitration agreement will be suspended irrespective of the poor party being at fault with respect to its impecuniosity. As the remedy is not meant to sanction the impecunious party it may rely on said doctrine even if its impecuniosity is the result of poor business practice or even negligent behaviour.[15] On the other hand, the Federal Supreme Court was cautious to keep a loophole open for the other side to enforce the arbitration agreement where the poor party had knowledge of its inability to meet the costs of arbitral proceedings but signed up to the arbitration agreement anyway.[16] Although the court has stressed this point, there is not one case in which it has applied this exception and allowed the rich party to insist on the enforcement of the agreement to arbitrate for reasons of good faith. Quite to the contrary, it has held that the mere expectation of the financially aggrieved party at the time of contract formation to earn a profit on the transaction subject to the arbitration clause is sufficient for a good-faith belief in its ability to meet the costs of arbitration if a dispute should arise sometime into the future.[17] It seems that the reason for this reluctance touches upon the very foundation of the suspension doctrine: As dismissal of the action filed with a court of law would deprive the poor party of any means to enforce its legal rights the sanction for carelessly signing an arbitration agreement appears to be drastic indeed. Hence the inclination of the court to apply it in exceptional cases only.

c) Inability to Pay Attorney's Fees

The discussion up to this point is incomplete in one important respect. Although most of the decisions by the Federal Supreme Court concern cases in which the poor party was unable even to pay its share of the costs of an arbitral tribunal this is not the only expense associated with arbitral proceedings. A party to arbitral proceedings is not only obliged to pay the arbitrators but also in need of legal representation by counsel whose services are not available for nothing but will be rendered for payment of appropriate fees only. The decisive factor here is again legal aid which in Germany is not confined to the fees charged by the court but also covers the fees demanded by counsel in return for their services. Thus, the same problem discussed with respect to the charges of the court or the tribunal, reappears when it comes to the costs of legal representation. Again, the poor party fares better in a court of law than in arbitral proceedings since in the

---

15 BGH (30.01.1964) BGHZ 41, 104, 109; BGH (22.02.1971) BGHZ 77, 65, 67 f.

16 BGH (22.02.1971) BGHZ 77, 65, 68.

17 BGH (22.02.1971) BGHZ 77, 65, 68; OLG Hamburg (15.11.1995) RIW 1996, 510, 511.

former scenario the public pays the lawyer whereas in arbitral proceedings the party would have to do without professional advice it cannot afford. Acknowledging that professional legal representation helps to enforce valid legal rights as well as to fend off nonexistent ones and accepting the premise that suspension of the agreement to arbitrate is necessary in order to secure the enforceability of legal rights, it follows quite naturally that the poor party may be granted a release from the agreement if it cannot afford to pay a lawyer itself.

Thus, one might dream up a case in which the poor party is still in command of funds sufficient to pay the advance on costs charged by the arbitrators but lacks the financial means to pay counsel. As of yet, the courts have not decided a case like this but they have made it clear that a reluctant party may only be compelled to arbitrate if it can afford both the costs of the tribunal and to secure the services of counsel to represent it in arbitral proceedings.[18] The only exception concerns cases of a very simple kind, both with respect to the facts and the law, in which professional support does not seem necessary.[19] The rule that the threshold of poverty is fixed at such a level as to include inability to pay for professional legal representation within arbitral proceedings has important ramifications for the option of the solvent party to save the arbitration agreement to which we now turn.

d) Option to Save the Arbitration Agreement

The opponent of the poor party has several options in reaction to the plea for a release from the agreement to arbitrate. One reaction would, of course, be to take issue with the assertion of impecuniosity, disputing the fact that the other side really is as poor as it dresses itself up. This strategy raises important and difficult problems regarding the burden and the standard of proof with respect to the impecuniosity issue which will be dealt with separately.[20] Another strategy is to accept the suspension of the arbitration agreement and to settle with the prospect of litigating the dispute in a public court. At first blush one may think that such acquiescence may be an ill-advised option but reality tells a different story. A creditor and potential plaintiff faces a gloomy prospect once it realizes that it has agreed to arbitrate disputes with a party which is or claims to be unable to pay even its share of the advance on costs demanded by an arbitral tribunal. Without such payment, arbitral proceedings will not be commenced and no award will be rendered. But even if the rich party harboured serious doubts concerning the inability to cover even the costs of arbitral proceedings the question arises as to what can be gained by taking issue with an assertion of poverty. Even if the other side turned out to be less poor than it claimed it would

[18] BGH (21.11.1968) BGHZ 51, 79, 82; BGH (10.03.1994) NJW-RR 1994, 1214, 1215.

[19] BGH (21.11.1968) BGHZ 51, 79, 82.

[20] See infra, III 5.

be highly advisable not to waste precious time arguing over the degree of poverty but to enforce one's rights immediately in whatever forum available. After all, it makes little sense to have convenient and agreeable proceedings before an arbitral tribunal if it turns out later that the other side dissipated its last resources to cover the costs of these proceedings such that it is unable to pay the sum liquidated in the award. Given these prospects, it comes at little surprise that there are cases in which the party who turns to a court of law for relief is not poor itself but believes the defendant to lack the funds necessary for funding arbitral proceedings.[21]

However, there is also another strategy open to the rich party, and that is to take the full costs of arbitral proceedings upon itself. In fact, the solvent party always retains the option to enforce the agreement in spite of impecuniosity of the other side. In this regard, the German law of arbitration is in perfect harmony with Art. 30 para 3 of the ICC-Rules which explicitly provides, firstly, that the parties are liable for the advance on costs in equal parts, and secondly, that each party is free to pay the whole of the advance on costs, should the other party fail to pay its share. It must not be forgotten however, that the option to save the arbitration agreement comes at a high price indeed as the rich party must be prepared to swallow not only the costs of the arbitral proceedings but also to provide the poor opponent with the funds necessary to secure the services of counsel. Hence, it is no exaggeration to say that the rich party may only avoid termination of the agreement to arbitrate if it extends the same financial means to its poor opponent which the latter would receive as legal aid when litigating in a court of law. Quite obviously, a party will only save the arbitration agreement by accepting the full costs of the proceedings if it places a high value on seeing the case tried by an arbitral tribunal instead of the dispute being litigated in court. Such cases will be particularly rare since in situations where a party is unable even to pay for arbitral proceedings its ability to meet the obligations stipulated in an arbitral award to be rendered down the road is doubtful indeed. In such a situation taking on the full costs of the arbitration would amount to the proverbial "spending of good money in order to retrieve money gone for good."

Given the situation just described it bears emphasizing that the option for the rich party to save the arbitration agreement is an option in the true sense of the term, i.e. there is no obligation on the part of the solvent party to exercise it and accept to pay the full costs of the arbitration itself. As the Federal Supreme Court pointed out in a case in which the solvent party was sued by its poor opponent for payment of the full advance on costs demanded by the tribunal, to grant such right would impose an obligation on a private party to extend legal aid for arbitral proceedings which has no basis either in the law of contract or in

---

[21] BGH (12.11.1987) BGHZ 102, 199.

the law of arbitration. To be sure, a rich defendant would be forced to fund arbitral proceedings brought by a poor plaintiff against it, even without the benefit of a court or a tribunal having established that such proceedings are not vexatious but are probable to succeed on the merits. Pursuant to Sec. 114 of the German Code of Civil Procedure even the state will only extend legal aid after a competent court has found the claim or defence to have merit with sufficient likelihood.

In sum then, a review of the options available to the rich party supports the view expressed earlier that suspension of the arbitration agreement is neither a sanction nor an act of grace. Rather, it is a consequence of the insight that neither the arbitral tribunal nor the other party to the arbitration agreement are under an obligation to make the poor party richer than it is. Finally it should be noted that, of course, the arbitral tribunal may avoid termination of the arbitration agreement as well if only by the arbitrators waiving their right to an advance on costs or even their fees altogether. There is nothing in the law precluding such a benevolent act but it is contrary to human nature and thus will be rarely observed in reality.

3. International Cases

Astonishingly – or perhaps not? – the Federal Supreme Court has not dealt with impecuniosity issues in international cases as of yet. All of the judgments in point concern the purely domestic case with one German party suing another German party. Although both the Hamburg and the Hamm Court of Appeal have heard international cases involving impecuniosity these were unproblematic since it was the foreign party who had come to the German courts for the reason of the defendant being unable to pay its share of the costs of arbitral proceedings.[22] If suspension of the arbitration agreement in cases of impecuniosity is accepted to be a well-founded doctrine, as has in fact been argued earlier, then it is also easy to dispose of the scenario in which a poor party of German nationality files a claim against a foreign defendant within a domestic court of law. True enough, suspension of the agreement to arbitrate would deprive the defendant of the benefit of its bargain as the arbitration clause was thought to exclude the possibility that the defendant could become answerable in a German court. However, the question is not whether the foreign defendant suffers but whether the burden placed on the defendant outweighs the benefit to the plaintiff, or rather the detriment suffered by the plaintiff if the arbitration agreement were to be enforced in spite of plaintiff being unable to pay its share of the costs of arbitral proceedings. On the premises developed above the answer must be no as, again, agreement on a special mode of dispute

---

[22] OLG Hamm (15.11.1994) RIW 1995, 681; OLG Hamburg (15.11.1995) RIW 1996, 510, 511.

resolution must not work to the effect of depriving one of the parties of any means to enforce a purportedly valid claim.

The critical scenario is the one in which the foreign party is at once poor and barred from receiving legal aid in Germany or any other country whose courts are competent to hear the case. Such a situation cannot arise with respect to individuals, who are always entitled to legal aid in Germany where the individual is poor but able to find a domestic court competent to hear its case, Sec. 114 ZPO.[23] With respect to corporations however, the matter looks different. As Sec. 116 para 1 no. 2 ZPO stipulates, corporations are not excluded from legal aid but they must be domestic ones in order to be eligible to receive this benefit. It may well be argued that this limitation violates the anti-discrimination provisions of the EC-treaty[24] but as of yet, neither a German court nor the European Court of Justice has decided the issue and declared the discrimination between domestic and foreign corporations in matters of legal aid to be invalid. Also, although Germany still entertains friendly relations with the United States, as evidenced by a friendship-treaty signed in 1954, this instrument explicitly excludes American corporations from receiving what was then legal aid in Germany.[25]

This state of the law has important ramifications for a foreign corporate plaintiff who seeks to walk away from an otherwise valid arbitration agreement for the reason of its impecuniosity. Assuming that there is no other competent court prepared to extend legal aid, the poor party loses nothing if it is held to its bargain and denied a release from the arbitration agreement. Thus, there is no reason to set it aside and to allow the poor party to go to court. Of course, this exception may only be of relevance if arbitral proceedings have been commenced already and the tribunal is then asked to deny its jurisdiction for the reason of impecuniosity. In such a scenario, the arbitrators should continue their proceedings undeterred, which in turn they will be ready to do only if the poor party has already paid its share of the advance on costs and is then unable to secure the services of counsel.

If, in contrast, the party argues a case of the sort just described in a court of law where it is not entitled to legal aid, the fact that the party can afford to pursue its claim there provides ample evidence that it has only dressed up as a

---

23 Cf. the legislative materials, BT-Drucks 8/3694, S. 17; MünchKomm ZPO-*Wax*, 2nd ed. 2000, Sec. 114 no. 1.

24 But see Art. 50 of the European Regulation on Jurisdiction and the Recognition and Enforcement of Foreign Judgments in Civil and Commercial Matters of 22nd December 2000, OJ L 12/01 p. 1, which addresses only a small fraction of the relevant issues. Thus, one might draw the conclusion that European law does not require the member states to place domestic and foreign legal entities on the same footing within legal aid schemes.

25 BGBl. 1956 II, 488, protocol, no. 7 b.

poor party. Again, the impecuniosity defence should be denied. The case would only be different if it were cheaper to process the case in a court of law than through arbitral proceedings and this difference in costs were large enough to make the court accessible to the poor party, but not the arbitral tribunal. As the American cases on arbitration in the field of labour disputes prove this scenario is not at all unrealistic if only with respect to small claims.

4. The Consequences of Bankruptcy for Arbitration Agreements

a) Insolvency and Impecuniosity

It may well be that the learned reader has been wondering once in a while why this article employs the term "impecuniosity" which is a very unfamiliar term in the English language and unknown even to most spelling tools included in current computer programs. Is it not insolvency that the problem here is really about? To be sure, commentators on the latest decision of the Federal Supreme Court essentially treated impecuniosity and insolvency as synonyms, employing one term or another as they saw fit.[26] Others worried about the effects the decision might have for parties to arbitration agreements entering bankruptcy proceedings.[27] As bankruptcy, again, seems to be more or less of a synonym for impecuniosity it looks as if, under German law, arbitral agreements would not survive the opening of bankruptcy proceedings such that the would-be debtor might easily rid himself of an otherwise binding arbitration agreement by filing such a petition. – But not so. In truth, the issues discussed here have less in common with insolvency proceedings than is usually thought. Impecuniosity denotes the situation that a party lacks the financial means to pay its share of the arbitration costs, it does not concern the state of insolvency in which a debtor is unable to pay its creditors and therefore enters a bankruptcy court. Apart from the obvious fact that any poor party may end up in bankruptcy at the end of the day, situations of impecuniosity simply have nothing to do with bankruptcy since they pose a different set of problems for the law of arbitration. In the case of impecuniosity the poor party remains in charge of its affairs, is still entitled to exercise its legal rights, to enter into legal disputes about such rights and to control the resolution of disputes either through arbitration or through litigation. The problem posed by impecuniosity may be put in terms of whether the poor party must settle with the option of either pursuing its claims in arbitral proceedings or dispense with enforcement of its claims altogether or whether it should be allowed to call upon a court of law administering a more or less generous legal-aid program.

---

26 *Polkinghore/Lehmkuhl*, Dealing with an impecunious opponent, IBA Section on Business Law, Committee D News, March 2002, p. 25, 27 seq.

27 *Lachmann*, Handbuch für die Schiedsgerichtspraxis, 2nd ed. 2002, no. 412; *Risse*, BB 2001, Suppl. no. 6, p. 11.

b) The Trustee in Bankruptcy as a Party to Arbitration Agreements

To be sure, the intersection of insolvency and arbitration is plastered with a lot of legal problems as well, but with a set of problems different from the one occurring in impecuniosity situations. Once bankruptcy proceedings have been opened, the debtor loses the authority to enforce its legal rights and to arbitrate or litigate disputes over such rights with the trustee in bankruptcy taking over control. The trustee steps into the shoes of the debtor and now has to decide himself whether to pursue claims already filed with a court of law and whether to initiate or continue arbitral proceedings, Sect. 80, 85 German Bankruptcy Code (InsO). The central question then becomes whether the administrator in bankruptcy also steps into the shoes of the debtor with respect to arbitration agreements such that he is held to arbitrate rather than to litigate disputes within the scope of an arbitration agreement.

In particular one would like to know whether the trustee is bound by an arbitration clause contained in a commercial contract executed by the debtor before entering bankruptcy proceedings. The German courts have always affirmed the binding effect of arbitration agreements in bankruptcy and regarded a trustee as analogous to a successor of the debtor. As it is well-established that the successor is bound by arbitration agreements concluded by its predecessor,[28] the insolvency of a party leaves the arbitration agreement intact.[29] The defendant thus may rely on the agreement in a court of law which the trustee has called upon to resolve a particular dispute falling within its scope. However, it must not be overlooked that bankruptcy law, in Germany as in other countries, classifies claims according to certain criteria for the purpose of applying a different set of rules to each class. In particular, claims of third parties which accrued before the date of filing of the petition may not be enforced against the estate, Sect. 87, 89 InsO. Instead, the creditor has to file its claim with the administrator, allowing the latter to liquidate the assets of the debtor and wait until the hour of distribution of the proceeds has come.[30] Of course, nothing changes if the claim of the third party against the estate falls within the scope of an arbitration agreement. Such agreement substitutes one mechanism of dispute resolution for another but it does not accord a party with priority in bankruptcy over the claims of other creditors. If, however, the trustee disputes a claim in order to exclude it from distribution of the proceeds, the creditor concerned

---

[28] Cf. supra, II 1 e.

[29] RG (8.7.1932) RGZ 137, 109, 110 seq.; *BGH* (28.2.1957) BGHZ 24, 15, 18 (also at BGH (27.02.1957) NJW 1957, 791 and LM § 1040 ZPO no. 2 with commentary *Johannsen*); *BGH* (28.5.1979) NJW 1979, 2567; *RG* (8.7.1932) RGZ 137, 109, 111; *Uhlenbruck*, Insolvenzordnung, 2003, Sec. 85 no. 27; *Thomas/Putzo*, Sec. 1029 no. 14; *Jestaedt*, Schiedsverfahren und Konkurs, Berlin 1985, p. 65 seq.; *Flöther* DZWir 2001, 89, 93.

[30] *Jestaedt* (note 29) p. 106 seq.

retains the option to enforce it. If this claim is subject to an arbitration agreement, the proper forum to seek enforcement is not the court but the competent arbitral tribunal, and bankruptcy law does nothing to change this state of affairs.[31]

Another critical issue is whether claims for recovery of fraudulent conveyances, the Roman actio Pauliana, may be disposed of by arbitration. The traditional answer of the German courts was a clear "no" for the sole reason that the trustee does not succeed to such claims but acquires them in his own right.[32] However, this somewhat formalistic reasoning has lost much of its former appeal, and for good reasons: The legal consequences of a fraudulent conveyance affect the validity and enforceability of contractual rights much like any other defence does and thus it must be determined by the tribunal chosen by the parties at the time they closed the deal.[33] Should the debtor try to evade the sanctions of bankruptcy law by choosing a corrupt arbitral forum or procedure the arbitration agreement should be discarded regardless of the nature of the claim in issue.

c) Arbitral Proceedings Already Under Way

With respect to legal proceedings already begun in the moment the bankruptcy petition is filed, or rather: bankruptcy proceedings opened with respect to the estate of a party to legal proceedings, the German code of civil procedure contains a special provision. Sec. 240 ZPO provides that such proceedings are interrupted and may only be continued at the request of either the trustee or the other party.[34] According to the prevailing opinion of German courts and commentators, this provision is confined to the arena of public courts and must not be extended to proceedings before an arbitral tribunal.[35] As a result, there is neither an automatic interruption of the proceedings as a whole nor of time limits already running. Therefore, in the case of arbitral proceedings already well under way, it is highly advisable for the trustee to assume the position of the debtor as quickly as possible. The arbitral tribunal, on the other hand, should consider that the principle embodied in Sec. 240 ZPO is not a nicety or

---

[31] *Jestaedt* (note 29) p. 123 seq.; *Uhlenbruck* (note 29) Sec. 85 no. 27.

[32] Cf. BGH NJW 1956, 1920, 1921; *Kirchhof*, in: Münchener Kommentar zur Insolvenzordnung, 2002, Sec. 146 no. 37; *Jestaedt* (note 29) p. 77 seq.; Stein/Jonas-*Schlosser* (note 5) Sec. 1029 no. 35; *Flöther* DZWir 2001, 89, 93 seq.

[33] *Uhlenbruck* (note 29) Sec. 85 no. 27; *Hirte*, in: Uhlenbruck (note 29) Sec. 143 no. 66; *Paulus* ZinsO 1999, 242, 244 seq.; see also *Jaeger-Henckel*, Konkursordnung, 9th ed. 1997, Sec. 37 no. 84.

[34] Cf. Sec. 240, 249, 250 ZPO, and Sec. 85, 86 InsO.

[35] RG (7.11.1905) RGZ 62, 24 seq.; BGH, KTS 1966 (21.11.1966), 246, 247; Zöller-*Geimer* (note 5) § 1042 Rdnr. 48; *Jaeger-Henckel* (note 33) Sec. 10 no. 36.

technicality but the central principle of fair trial embodied in Art. 18 Model Law and in Art. 103 para 1 of the German constitution.[36] Thus, the tribunal must not sanction the expiration of time limits but grant an excuse under Sec. 1048 para 4 cl. 1 ZPO, Art. 25 Model Law.[37]

d) Liability for Costs

If the problems discussed so far have done anything, they have sharpened the eye with respect to the issue of costs. Thus, it may be worth asking what the financial consequences are where the trustee ends up losing the arbitral proceedings initiated or continued by himself. The crucial question obviously is whether the estate is liable to reimburse the winning party for the costs it has incurred or whether the latter is relegated to the status of an ordinary creditor in bankruptcy who may hope to receive a small fraction of the face-value of his claim. Although there is no explicit provision dealing with this situation the answer may easily be derived from general principles. It has already been indicated that bankruptcy law draws important distinctions between claims of different nature and origin, and probably the most important distinction is the one between claims against the estate which existed before filing of the bankruptcy petition and claims which grow out of a transaction executed only after the opening of bankruptcy proceedings, i.e. out of a deal struck by the trustee. In the latter case, the creditor enjoys a privilege since he may enforce his claim against the estate at large while the liquidation of assets is still well under way (Sect. 55 para 1 no. 1 InsO). The same principle applies to cases in which the trustee does not enter into a fresh transaction but decides to enforce an executory contract entered into by the debtor before filing for bankruptcy (Sect. 55 para 1 no. 2 InsO). Here, the costs incurred by the other party are a consequence of the trustee's decision to enforce the contract subject to an already existing arbitration clause and thus the winning party may seek reimbursement for costs incurred against the estate at large.[38] Finally, the same result obtains if the trustee decides to continue legal proceedings initiated by the debtor or brought against him by a third party. Again, the opponent's claim for reimbursement should it win the award enjoys a privilege in bankruptcy.[39]

The matter is different where the holder of a claim that accrued before bankruptcy proceedings were opened and which has been contested by the trustee seeks relief from an arbitral tribunal. If the creditor loses, he will have to bear the full costs of the proceedings and receive nothing, and if he wins, he will

---

36 Cf. *Flöther*, DZWir 2001, 89, 90 seq.

37 *Jaeger-Henckel* (note 33) Sec. 10 no. 36.

38 *Uhlenbruck/Berscheid*, in: Uhlenbruck (note 29) Sec. 55 no. 15 seq.

39 *Jaeger-Henckel* (note 33) Sec. 10 no. 119; *Uhlenbruck/Berscheid*, in: Uhlenbruck (note 29) Sec. 55 no. 18 seq.

only be able to collect a – usually small – fraction of the nominal value of his claim through the distribution process. However, he will be allowed to recover the full costs of the arbitral proceedings from the estate since it was the administrator's decision to dispute his claim that forced him into spending money on either litigation or arbitration.[40]

III. Implementation

1. Right of termination vs. Ipso-Iure-Cessation

Given that it is appropriate to allow the parties to walk away from an arbitration agreement otherwise valid and binding in cases of impecuniosity, the problem to be solved next concerns the pertinent legal mechanism. In this respect, two solutions compete with each other. The Federal Supreme Court has endorsed each of them at different times. Under the old German arbitration law the court granted a right of termination to each party seeking a release from the arbitration agreement either because of its own impecuniosity or for the sake of the other party being unable to pay its share of the costs of the arbitral proceedings. As a result, the arbitration agreement was not put to rest by simple operation of the law but only upon a pertinent declaration of a party. It has already been mentioned that the content of the latest decision of the Federal Supreme Court dealing with impecuniosity does not concern the substance of the matter but the mechanism employed to set the agreement aside. The court thought a declaration of termination not to be necessary any longer but held instead that an arbitration agreement was "incapable of being performed" within the meaning of Art. 1032 para 1 ZPO, Art. 8 para 1 Model Law. As is clear from the language of both provisions "incapable of being performed" means something other than invalid but there is no doubt that both are effective means to destroy an arbitration agreement.

What kind of considerations moved the court to abandon the right-of-termination-theory so well entrenched in the old law in favour of the new solution of ipso-iure-cessation? Furthermore, to the extent that reasons for this switch may be given, do such reasons outweigh whatever arguments counsel against the new approach? These questions shall be considered in turn.

2. Interpretation of Sec. 1032 para 1 ZPO (Art. 8 para 1 Model Law)

The court did not give any practical reasons for its switch from a right of termination to the new ipso-iure-cessation theory. Instead, it focused on the interpretation of Sec. 1032 para 1 ZPO. Unfortunately, the court did not even mention that this provision is nothing more than a faithful translation of Art. 8 para 1 Model Law and thus did not care to investigate what it is that the framers of the Model Law had in mind when they drafted Art. 8 para 1 and particularly

---

[40] *Uhlenbruck/Berscheid*, in: Uhlenbruck (note 29) Sect. 55 no. 17.

the pertinent phrase "incapable of being performed". Had the court engaged in such an inquiry and consulted the quasi-official commentary of *Holtzmann/Neuhaus* to the Model Law they would have found out that the drafters were anxious to follow the language of Art. II para 3 of the New York Convention without attaching any specific content to the incapability-clause, leaving its "precise meaning [...] to future development".[41] Whatever one may make of this, there certainly was no pressure exercised by the Model Law or, rather, the objective of international harmonization of arbitration law, to substitute ipso-iure-cessation for a right of termination.

Turning now to Sec. 1032 para 1 ZPO as the progeny of Art. 8 para 1 Model Law, the obvious question is whether the framers of the new German arbitration law had any specific understanding in mind when they implanted the capability proviso into the code. As the former provisions in the ZPO dealing with arbitration were devoid of the "incapable of being performed" clause, it is only through Sec. 1032 para 1 ZPO that the theory of ipso-iure-cessation could have entered German law. It is exactly at this point that the reasoning of the court kicks in.[42] The drafters of Sec. 1032 para 1 ZPO, the court says, refrained from including the right-of-termination doctrine into the new code. Nothing in the legislative materials suggested that the framers thought a declaration of termination for good cause to be necessary for the arbitration agreement to step aside. Hence the justices thought the conclusion to be inevitable that the agreement is rendered "incapable of being performed" in cases of impecuniosity.

It is true, nothing in the explanations given in the Bill of the Reform Act leading to the new code refers to the right-of-termination so readily granted in cases of impecuniosity arising under the old law.[43] It is equally true, however, that the Bill is also silent on the exact meaning of the incapability clause, in fact the Bill ignores this clause altogether and does not even mention the problems posed by impecuniosity. Quite obviously then, the framers of the new law harboured no opinion whatsoever with respect to the effects impecuniosity might have for arbitration agreements – they did not care about the problem at all. Thus, there was no need to substitute ipso-iure-cessation for the traditional right of termination. But even if the framers of the Bill had harboured such intentions it is far from clear whether their motives and intentions should control. In truth, the provisions of the Reform Act were drafted neither by the members of parliament nor by the civil servants in the Justice Ministry but by a commission of practitioners and law-professors installed by the Ministry of

---

41 *Holtzmann/Neuhaus*, A Guide to the UNCITRAL Model Law on International Commercial Arbitration, 1989/94, p. 305.

42 BGH (14.09.2000) BGHZ 145, 116, 119 seq.

43 Bill of the New Arbitration Law, BT-Drucks. 13/5274, p. 37 seq.

Justice and charged with the mission to transform the UNCITRAL Model Law into the German code. This commission published a final report in which the motives behind each suggested provision are explained.[44] Not surprisingly, however, this report is silent on the consequences of impecuniosity too, and there is nothing in it suggesting that the incapability-clause of Sec. 1032 para 1 ZPO was meant to apply in cases of impecuniosity.

3. Was the Court Misled?

One explanation for the switch orchestrated by the court is that the judges presumably were misled by the language they had employed in earlier decisions. When the court laid the foundation of the rule that the parties might walk away from an arbitration agreement in cases of impecuniosity it emphasized that such agreement is rendered "incapable of being performed" if one of the parties lacks the funds necessary to pay its share of the advance on costs asked for by the tribunal. As the code did not contain the incapability-language at this time, why did the court use it? The reason is simple enough: under German arbitration law, the arbitrators and the parties enter into a contract for the service of arbitration obligating the parties to pay the arbitrators for their work in equal shares.[45] Pursuant to a rule of German contract law, i.e. Sec. 273 BGB, a party to a contract may withhold the thing or act it has promised to deliver until the time the other side is ready to offer the price promised to pay as consideration. Applied to the contract for the service of arbitration, failure of the parties to pay the price promised for the work of the arbitrators, i.e. failure to tender the advance on costs, allows the tribunal to remain idle. The same result is obtained under the ICC-Rules of Arbitration which explicitly provide in Art. 30 para 4 that where the parties fail to pay the requested amount as an advance on costs the Secretary General may direct the tribunal to suspend its work and set a time-limit, on the expiry of which the relevant claims shall be considered as withdrawn. Similar provisions are contained in Sect. 25 of the DIS Arbitration Rules and in Art. 24.4 LCIA Arbitration Rules. Thus, it seems that non-payment of the advance on costs really renders the agreement "incapable of being performed" in the true sense of the term.

In truth, however, this train of constructive thought is untenable for several reasons. Technical considerations of minor importance point to the fact that the contract for the service of arbitration imposes mutual obligations on both parties such that Sec. 320 BGB – and not Sec. 273 – provides the rule allowing a party who is not offered what was promised by the other side to withhold its performance as well. But even then, the effect of Sec. 320 BGB is to merely

[44] Bundesministerium der Justiz (ed.), Bericht der Kommission zur Neuordnung des Schiedsverfahrensrechts, Bonn 1994, p. 103.

[45] Cf. *Wagner* (note 3) no. 137 seq. with further reference.

allow the party to remain idle without destroying the underlying contract. Thus, an arbitral tribunal would lose its defence immediately once the parties or only one of them offered to pay the advance on costs in full. In addition, the argument also works if turned around, facing the situation that a party defaults on its share of the advance on costs not because it lacks the necessary funds but simply in order to protract the proceedings. In such case nobody would say that the agreement is "incapable of being performed" although the arbitrators are equally entitled to remain idle and abstain from pushing the procedure forward. As the English Court of Appeal rightly emphasized, nobody would hold a contract for the purchase of land to be "incapable of being performed" for the sole reason that the buyer lacks the funds needed to pay the price.[46] Of course, the same is true under German contract law as it is also well accepted that the mere lack of financial means necessary to live up to one's promise may never affect the validity of contractual obligations.[47] Were it otherwise, contractual obligations would automatically be discharged once a debtor approaches bankruptcy, whilst bankruptcy law is built on the premise that lack of money does anything but relieve a party of its obligations.

Finally, the court may have overlooked that according to its own jurisprudence, suspension of arbitration agreements for lack of funds is not confined to cases in which at least one party is almost broke, not being able to pay its share of the advance on costs. Rather, a party may also abandon the arbitration agreement if it is willing and able to pay the tribunal but lacks the funds to secure the services of counsel. In this instance, it is simply wrong to say that the arbitration agreement is incapable of being performed for the reason that the arbitrators may refuse to begin with their work. The agreement could very well be performed, the critical point being that it should not be performed for reasons of fairness and equality. Thus, the fact that inability of a party to pay attorney's fees entitles it to walk away from an arbitration agreement shows that it misses the point to think about the effects of impecuniosity in terms of breach of the contract for the service of arbitration.

4. Effects of the New Doctrine on Arbitral Proceedings

Another point which might seem a little meticulous at first blush concerns the translation of the new doctrine into the world of arbitral proceedings. Up till now, the German courts have exclusively been confronted with cases in which the issue of impecuniosity was raised before a court of law. Obviously, in such an instance, Sec. 1032 para 1 ZPO applies and the court may refuse to dismiss the action since the arbitration agreement is "incapable of being performed". If the same defence is raised before an arbitral tribunal the tribunal must deal with

---

46 *Paczy v. Haendler & Natermann GmbH*, [1981] 1 Lloyd's Rep. 302, 307 (C.A. 1980).

47 BGH (28.02.1989) NJW 1989, 1276, 1278; *Medicus*, AcP 188 (1988), 489, 501.

it within the framework of Sec. 1040 ZPO, Art. 16 Model Law, both of which do not contain the proviso for arbitration agreements "incapable of being performed". Rather, pursuant to said provisions, the tribunal must continue the proceedings if it can be certain of the "existence and validity" of an arbitration agreement. The obvious question is whether an arbitration agreement "incapable of being performed" under Sec. 1032 para 1 ZPO is non-existent or invalid within the meaning of Sec. 1040 para 1 ZPO, Art. 16 para 1 Model Law. The answer must be yes, as otherwise the defence of impecuniosity would not be available in arbitral proceedings already commenced.[48] It should not go unnoticed, however, that this conclusion virtually destroys the doctrinal foundation on which the reasoning of the court was built, i.e. that the agreement is "merely" incapable of being performed as the arbitrators are entitled to withhold their services until the moneys promised as consideration are tendered. These difficulties could have been avoided easily if the court had stuck with its old rule, i.e. the right of termination. Quite obviously, upon execution of such right, the arbitration agreement is indeed rendered invalid – and not only "incapable of being performed".

5. Burden and Standard of Proof

Up to this point, the discussion was based on the assumption that the poverty of the party that triggers whatever mechanism of termination thought appropriate is uncontested, obvious or at least ascertainable at low cost. Not surprisingly, perhaps, the Federal Supreme Court so far has only been confronted with cases in which the inability of one or both parties to tender the money needed to take the arbitral tribunal to work was undisputed. This is particularly true with respect to the recent case that introduced the theory of ipso-iure-cessation. Here, both parties had already sworn an oath (eidesstattliche Versicherung), stipulating that they lacked the funds necessary to pay even the liquidated claims of judgement-creditors seeking execution.[49] In other cases decided by the court one of the parties was awarded legal aid which in turn established beyond doubt the fact that it was unable to pay for the cost of legal proceedings.[50] However, one might well imagine a situation in which a party raises the impecuniosity defence strategically, in order to renege on an arbitration agreement which has become onerous for one reason or another. It might not even be necessary to assume as much, as the mere possibility to abandon valid arbitration agreements at will, by threatening to plead impecuniosity, may well work as a valuable bargaining chip once relations sour and the prospect of a legal dispute appears on the horizon.

---

[48] *Wagner*, LM § 1032 ZPO no. 11.

[49] BGH (14.09.2000) BGHZ 145, 116, 119.

[50] BGH (21.11.1968) BGHZ 51, 79, 80; BGH (12.11.1987) BGHZ 102, 199, 200.

For all these reasons there is no doubt that the impecuniosity defence has to be handled with considerable care and restraint by the courts in order not to undermine a valid arbitration agreement and to deprive the other party of the benefit of its bargain. So far, the court has been attentive to this risk as is evidenced by its treatment of the only case brought before it in which the poverty of the party concerned was not established beyond doubt.[51] In this kind of situation the court considered that the claimant had suffered serious losses within two consecutive years and that its banks refused to extend credit to it. In addition the judges emphasized that the plaintiff had asked the defendant to pay the total costs of the arbitration proceedings to its counsel as fiduciary, a move which obviously was taken as evidence of good faith. Without saying so explicitly it also seems that the court assumed that the party seeking a release from the arbitration agreement for reasons of impecuniosity is carrying the burden of proof.

Both objectives, i.e. to place the burden of proof on the party seeking a release from the arbitration agreement and to apply a high standard of proof, may be accomplished easily under the right-of-termination-theory. It is a general rule of evidence that the burden of proof must be allocated to the party that has exercised a right of termination, and that the prerequisites for such right must be proven beyond reasonable doubt. Again, it is anything but impossible to impose strict requirements before holding an arbitration agreement to be "incapable of being performed" and to place the burden of proof on the party wanting to walk away from such an agreement. Under Sec. 1032 para 1 ZPO, the defendant generally carries the burden of proof with respect to the valid execution of an arbitration agreement whereas it is for the plaintiff to establish that the agreement is invalid, not binding or incapable of being performed.[52] However, it might still make a difference in practice if the party trying to persuade the court to disregard the arbitration agreement has to build its theory on a subjective right of termination rather than on an objective defect afflicting the arbitration agreement.

6. Having the Cake and Eating it too

Whatever one may think of the preceding analysis, the main concern with the substitution of ipso-iure-cessation of the arbitration agreement and a right to terminate it for good cause is not based on matters of construction or on issues regarding the burden of proof but on the objective of deterring strategic behaviour. The right-of-termination-theory works as a powerful safeguard against strategic behaviour of a party who might successfully petition the arbitral tribunal to discontinue the proceedings for the reason of impecuniosity

---

[51] BGH (10.03.1994) NJW-RR 1994,1214, 1215.

[52] Stein/Jonas-*Schlosser* (note 5) Sec. 1032 no. 17.

only to switch positions in the subsequent proceedings before a court of law, now relying on the arbitration agreement and trying to persuade the court to deny its jurisdiction. True enough, the Federal Supreme Court made it clear in its recent decision that it is still prepared to deter such behaviour by refusing such a motion for reasons of good faith and fair dealing.[53] Astonishingly however, the court went on to apply a lenient standard in the very case brought before it, allowing the plaintiff to insist on the arbitration clause when the construction company raised a claim for payment of the agreed price against it, but then turning to a court of law for enforcement of its own damage claim. Thus, the court allowed the claimant to have both, the benefit of the arbitration clause when it suited its interests, and the assistance of the public courts if it decided that this would help its cause even more. However, it seems unfair to allow a party to an arbitration agreement to have the cake and eat it too. If such party wants to walk away from the agreement for good cause then it should not be allowed to sneak back in at another time and vice versa.

The argument just made also works the other way. Under the old code, the rich party had the benefit of an option whether to accept termination and do without arbitral proceedings or to pay the costs of the arbitral proceedings in full if it entertained a strong interest in having the case tried by an arbitral tribunal. As the rich party enjoyed freedom of choice, the appropriate legal remedy is not one that works ipso iure. To be sure, there is no doubt that the option just described survived the switch from the right of termination to ipso-iure-cessation as the court made it clear that it would not have held the agreement to be "incapable of being performed" if the other party had been willing and able to pay the costs of the proceedings in full.[54] But how can the court know or find out whether the other party is both solvent and willing to swallow the full costs of the proceedings? In a decision made under the old law the court devised a procedure allowing the parties to get onto solid ground. According to this ruling, the poor party had to wait to exercise its right of termination until it had set a time limit for the other party to determine and declare whether it was willing and able to accept responsibility for the full costs of the arbitral proceedings. Only after expiration of this time frame was the poor party allowed to cancel the agreement. Of course, it is not impossible to bring this procedure back to life under the new ipso-iure-doctrine but things have certainly not been made easier. In particular, it is not clear how to identify the party charged with setting the time limit, and it is equally uncertain whether the issue may be brought up at any stage of legal or arbitral proceedings.

---

[53] BGH (14.09.2000) BGHZ 145, 116, 120.

[54] BGH (14.09.2000) BGHZ 145, 116, 119.

7. Conclusion

In sum, the new doctrine introduces some degree of uncertainty into the world of arbitration. True enough, any legal rule allowing a party to walk away from an arbitration agreement in cases of impecuniosity introduces uncertainty und to some extent undermines the character of arbitration agreements as promises. However, the court added further and unnecessary uncertainties by holding the arbitration agreement to be suspended by operation of law. To be fair, these uncertainties may be avoided with some effort, and the court did nothing to indicate an intention to modify the substantive rules governing impecuniosity cases that have been described above. It cannot be denied, however, that it would have made things much easier in this respect if the court had stuck to the old mechanism instead of moving on onto the uncharted territory of ipso-iure-cessation.

IV. Avoiding the Effects of Impecuniosity

1. Overview of the Instruments Available

A final set of issues to be addressed here concerns the options open to the parties signing an arbitration agreement to avoid the effects of impecuniosity, i.e. to somehow armour their agreement such that it will not be set aside if one of the parties falls into financial distress. One elegant solution is to insure this risk with a professional risk carrier, i.e. an insurance company. This option essentially avoids the state of impecuniosity materializing in the first place as it guarantees that there will always be enough money to fund arbitral proceedings initiated by one of the parties to a contract. Of course, the elegance comes with a price tag as the insurance carrier will charge a premium for the assumption of the risk that one party will turn out to be unable to pay the cost of arbitral proceedings if a dispute arises. Be that as it may, I will not go into the insurance option further since it will be the focus of a different contribution.[55] Guarantees will be ignored likewise as they are to be treated analogously to insurance contracts. A third path open in order to avoid the suspension of the arbitration agreement once a case of impecuniosity arises has been mentioned already, i.e. the option for the rich party to take on the full of costs of the proceedings which ordinarily will even have to include the fees of counsel supporting the poor party.[56] With all these issues pushed to the side, the focus here will be on provisions explicitly dealing with the situation of impecuniosity. As such provisions only make sense if they deviate from the rules otherwise applicable they would have to stipulate that the arbitration agreement survives the instance of one or both parties falling into financial distress and continues to be binding even if that works to the effect that a poor claimant is essentially denied the right to enforce its claim by

---

[55] Cf. *Kröll*, 151 seq.

[56] See supra, II 2 d.

initiating legal proceedings against its opponent in a court of law operating a legal-aid-program.

2. Arbitration Agreements and Arbitration Rules

A clause excluding application of the legal framework that has just been explained and – at least partially – accepted could be found in two different types of context. Firstly, one could imagine the parties, or rather: the sophisticated lawyers employed by them, to have thought about the problem up front and to have discovered a distaste for the solution favoured by the Federal Supreme Court. Their reaction could be to address the issue in the arbitration agreement itself. Specifically, one could imagine an arbitration clause reading like this one:

> "All disputes arising out of or relating to this contract or its validity shall be settled ultimately in accordance with the Rules of the German Institution of Arbitration e.V. (DIS) without recourse to the ordinary courts of law, *and regardless whether a party is in a financial position allowing it to pay for the costs of the arbitral proceedings"*.

As this hypothetical demonstrates, it does not take much effort to protect an arbitration agreement from the operation of the impecuniosity doctrine but that does not mean that clauses like this have become popular. It is common knowledge that parties usually do not care much about future disputes and are reluctant to invest scarce resources into elaborating upon custom-made and sophisticated provisions of dispute resolution. Phrased in the language of economics, the transaction costs of devising an idiosyncratic scheme of dispute resolution outweighs the prospective benefits any such scheme may yield for the parties concerned.

It is precisely for this reason that the world of arbitration is dominated by off-the-rack arbitration rules, which in turn may either be free-floating, waiting for some parties to make use of them, or be the creation of an arbitration institution like the DIS or the ICC operating a secretariat which processes incoming claims and functions like the administrator of a private court. Arbitration rules of both kinds could contain provisions derogating from the impecuniosity doctrine. – They could, but do they in practice?

The answer is a strong and unambiguous 'no'. As has already been indicated Art. 30 para 3, 4 of the ICC Arbitration Rules are fully compatible with German arbitration law, and similar provisions are to be found in Art. 41 para 4 UNCITRAL Rules, Art. 24.3 LCIA Rules; Art. 33 para 3 AAA International Arbitration Rules, and also in Sec. 7 and 25 DIS-Rules.[57] All of them confine themselves to problems which have rather obvious solutions. In particular, as no

---

[57] For more references see *Bühler/Jarvin*, in: Weigand (note 3), Part 2, Commentary on Art. 30 ICC-Rules.

arbitrator may be expected to work for nothing and as no law, rule or institution of international commercial arbitration has the power to make a party richer than it really is, it goes without saying that arbitral proceedings cannot get under way if a party defaults on its share of the advance on costs and the other party is not willing to pay the advance in full. The essential question is whether the parties may then turn to a court of law for enforcement of their rights, but the arbitration rules of the major institutions are silent on this issue. To be sure, Art. 30 para 4 ICC-Rules stipulates that the party in default may nonetheless reintroduce its claim at a later time in another proceeding such that one might infer that the arbitration agreement survives non-payment of a party's share of the advance on costs. Even so, as the failure of a party to pay its dues may have all sorts of reasons, an important one being the interest in obstructing and delaying the proceedings, it is impossible to infer that Art. 30 para 4 ICC-Rules excludes the operation of the impecuniosity doctrine. In other words, even though Art. 30 para 4 ICC-Rules allows a party defaulting for whatever reason to reintroduce its claim, this does not mean that an impecunious party or its opponent is barred from turning to a court of law in order to take advantage of the legal aid offered there.

In sum, then, it is no exaggeration to say that discussion of agreements excluding the impecuniosity doctrine, or, what amounts to the same thing, of the pertinent arbitration rules working to this effect, is of purely hypothetical nature. Still, it might be interesting to know whether such exclusionary clauses were valid and binding assuming that they had been included in arbitration agreements or arbitration rules.

3. Consumer Contracts

Under European law, and as far as consumer contracts are concerned, the answer is straightforward. The directive on unfair terms in consumer contracts rejects terms which cause a significant imbalance in the parties' rights and obligations to the detriment of the consumer, provided they have not been individually negotiated. The clause of lit. (q) of the Annex to Art. 3 of the directive cites as an example, a provision "excluding or hindering the consumer's right to take legal action or exercise any other legal remedy, particularly by requiring the consumer to take disputes exclusively to arbitration not covered by legal provisions".[58] There can hardly be any doubt that arbitration agreements which were made to be strictly binding, even in the case where the consumer lacks the funds necessary to commence and entertain arbitral proceedings, will be regarded as unfair in the sense of the directive and its appendix. To be sure, the directive only applies if the consumer is confronted with an arbitration clause on

[58] Council Directive 93/13/EEC of 5.4.1993 on unfair terms in consumer contracts, OJ L 95, 21.4.1993, p. 29.

a take-it-or-leave-it basis, however, this is the standard mode of contracting in cases of consumer transactions. Thus, in business-to-consumer transactions, exclusion of the impecuniosity doctrine simply is a remedy not available.

4. Business Agreements

The directive on unfair terms in consumer contracts is not applicable to business transactions and therefore the matter might be treated differently in this context. However, as far as German law is concerned, caution seems to be good advice. Unlike European law, German law has always treated contracts of adhesion as a phenomenon that affects both the consumer and the business enterprise alike if only one of the parties is confronted with the standard business terms of its opponent on a take-it-or-leave-it basis. As a consequence, the German provisions on unfair contract terms, now to be found in Sec. 305 seq. BGB, apply to consumer contracts and to business transactions alike. Thus, a commercial contract between two firms will be subject to review by the court, provided that the contract terms are boiler plate introduced by one of the parties. The interesting point to note in this context is that the Federal Supreme Court has not confined the scope of review to contractual provisions of a substantive nature, derogating from the substantive law otherwise applicable, but extended it to provisions of a procedural nature, i.e., concerning the mode and process of dispute resolution.[59] In particular, the court has not refrained from reviewing arbitration agreements and holding them to be invalid where it was satisfied that the composition of the arbitral tribunal[60] or the procedure to be applied to resolve the dispute was unfair to one of the parties.[61]

What then, would the Federal Supreme Court think of an arbitration agreement which contained a clause explicitly stipulating that it should survive the impecuniosity of one or both parties unimpaired? Although the answer is a matter of speculation, there is some indication to be found in the decisions which orchestrated the birth of the impecuniosity doctrine in the first place. As has been noted, the arguments presented there may be boiled down to the notion that it is inappropriate and unfair to deprive a poor party of any right of recourse.[62] It is hard to imagine that a court would believe a party to have consciously bargained away its right to enforce its claims in any forum, be it a

---

[59] For a thorough discussion see *Wagner*, Prozessverträge – Privatautonomie im Verfahrensrecht, 1998, p. 131 seq.

[60] Cf. BGH (03.07.1975) BGHZ 65, 59, 64, 65; BGH (15.05.1986) BGHZ 98, 70, 72.

[61] BGH (10.10.1991) BGHZ 115, 324 (= NJW 1992, 575 note *Schumann*, NJW 1992, 2065 = LM Nr. 17 § 127 ZPO note *M. Wolf*); OLG Düsseldorf (01.06.1995) NJW 1996, 400 f.; (23.05.1996) NJW-RR 1997, 372, 373; see also BGH (26.01.1989) BGHZ 106, 336, 339 (= JZ 1989, 588 note *Walter*).

[62] See note 8.

private tribunal or a public court. Most probably, the German courts would invalidate an agreement aimed at isolating an arbitration agreement from the detrimental effects of financial distress. The prediction would be that an exclusion clause would only be accepted if it were bargained for by the parties, but invalidated if part of either arbitration rules of an institutional body or of the boilerplate language in standard business terms. – For practical purposes then, the impecuniosity doctrine of the German law of arbitration is of mandatory nature.

Impecuniosity of Parties and its Effect on Arbitration - From the Perspective of Austrian Law

*Andreas Reiner**

* Dr. iur.; Andreas Reiner & Partner Rechtsanwälte, Vienna.

Introduction

The topic reminds me of the saying: "*It is better to be in good health and rich than to be poor and ill.*" We shall see whether Austrian arbitration law takes a similar, somewhat cynical approach.

The topic is well chosen. The impecuniosity of parties to an arbitration agreement or to a pending arbitration raises a number of questions most of which are interesting from a legal point of view. In addition they arise more frequently than one might think and – although I am rather optimistic by nature – because they may arise even more frequently in the near future.

Before entering upon this topic, I must limit my remarks as follows:
I shall not deal with specific consumer-related questions, but rather only with b2b-arbitration.

I shall not deal with purely practical ways of overcoming problems arising from a party's financial difficulties, such as partial claims, partial awards, reduction of the amount of the deposit (with or without agreement of the arbitrators) and bank guarantees.

Finally, it was my understanding that I should deal specifically with Austrian law rather than present a comparative analysis of multiple legal systems or of international arbitral practice.

I. Inability of parties to pay arbitration costs and its effect on an arbitration agreement

A) The various possible scenarios

1) Impecuniosity of Respondent
   a) Respondent cannot pay its share of the deposit, but can finance its legal defence
   b) Respondent not only cannot pay its share of the deposit, but in addition is unable to finance its defence

2) Impecuniosity of Claimant
   a) Claimant can pay its share of the deposit, but not the share of the Respondent who refuses to pay
   b) Claimant cannot even pay its own share of the deposit
   c) Claimant not only cannot pay its share of the deposit, but in addition is unable to finance its defence

3) Impecuniosity of Claimant and Respondent

B) The main issues

Under Austrian law – as is the case under all other national legal systems of which I am aware – both parties, Claimant and Respondent, are obliged to finance the arbitration (- that is to say, the fees and costs of the arbitrators as well as other costs of the arbitration and fees and costs of any arbitral institution -) in equal shares[1], unless the arbitration agreement or the arbitration rules to which the arbitration agreement refers provides otherwise.

The more difficult questions are:

- What can a party (usually the Claimant) do if the other party (usually the Respondent) fails to comply with its financial obligation to pay 50% of the deposit?
- What can Claimant do if it is unable to pay its own share of the deposit?
- What can a party do if it is unable to finance its defence?

1) What can a party do if the other party fails to comply with its financial obligation to pay 50% of the deposit?

It is a well-recognised principle, even in the absence of any specific provision in the arbitration agreement or in the applicable arbitration rules, that one party may pay the deposit on behalf of the defaulting other party.[2] It is, however, equally recognised, also under Austrian law, that a party is *not obliged* to do so[3], unless the arbitration agreement itself or the agreed Arbitration Rules provide otherwise.[4] The logical consequence is that the party which has paid its share of

---

1 *Fasching*, Kostenvorschüsse zur Einleitung schiedsgerichtlicher Verfahren, JBl. 1993, 545, 550; *Reiner*, ICC-Schiedsgerichtsbarkeit (1989) 149 *et seq.*; *Reymond*, Note sur l'avance des frais de l'arbitrage et sa répartition, Liber Amicorum Jean-François Poudret (1999) 495, 498.

2 Austrian Supreme Court (OGH) July 4, 1935, SZ 17/112 and Feb. 25, 1997, 4 Ob 61/97t concerning (domestic) ad hoc arbitration: "*Der Aufhebungsantrag ist begründet, auch wenn die Antragstellerin den Stillstand dadurch beenden könnte, dass sie auch den auf den Antragsgegner entfallenden Vorschuss erlegt. Dazu ist sie nicht verpflichtet; wenn der Antragsgegner Wert darauf legt, dass das Schiedsgericht über den gegen ihn gerichteten Anspruch entscheidet, so hätte er den ihm auferlegten Vorschuss erlegen müssen.*"
See for instance Art 30 (3) of the ICC Rules; whether it is advisable for a party not to effect substitute payment on behalf of its defaulting opponent, is obviously a different matter entirely.

3 For Austria see for instance: OGH Feb. 25, 1997, 4 Ob 61/97t; *Fasching*, *supra* note 1, at 550 *et seq.*; this is true for the Claimant and – a fortiori – for the Respondent; for a French point of view see *Mourre*, Le droit français de l'arbitrage international face à la Convention européenne des droits de l'homme, Gazette du Palais, Dec. 1 et 2, 2000, 16, 22.

4 Which is certainly not the case under the *ICC-Rules*: "The advance on costs fixed by the Court shall be *payable in equal shares by the Claimant and the Respondent*. However, any party *shall be free* to pay the whole of the advance on costs ..." (Art 30 (3)); see also Appendix III (Arbitration Costs and Fees): "*Each party shall pay in cash its share of the total advance on costs...*" (Art 1(5)); the fixing of separate advances on costs is only an administrative device to avoid a blockage of the arbitration. It is not to be construed as freeing either party from its financial obligation to pay 50% of the deposit.
Under the *Vienna Rules*, the Vienna Court of Appeal in an obiter dictum took the view on Feb. 17, 2000 (not published; by the Supreme Court's order dated June 28, 2000 leave to the Supreme Court was refused) that the parties were jointly liable for the deposits. This

the deposit, if it does not wish to effect payment on behalf of the other party, may rescind the arbitration agreement for breach of contract by the other party.[5;6]

The rule just mentioned is a general rule, applying in a range of situations, including situations in which the reason for the non-payment by one party and/or the non-substitution by the other party is its impecuniosity.

The party in breach of the arbitration agreement cannot avoid rescission of the arbitration agreement by arguing that the other party was entitled to request specific performance[7] and failed to do so.[8]

2) What can Claimant do if it is unable to pay its own share of the deposit?

a) Claimant's impecuniosity shall not lead to a total denial of justice and may therefore justify the termination of the arbitration agreement

As early as 1936 the Austrian Supreme Court[9] had occasion to deal with a Claimant who was objectively incapable of paying arbitrators' fees and expenses. The Supreme Court rightly held that arbitration agreements create a long-term obligation between the parties to which the general principles for

---

view is questionable (at least as long as and to the extent that the arbitrators have not yet begun to work). The matter was quite complex: Two civil engineers (- who went bankrupt subsequently during the course of the proceedings -) had filed a request for arbitration (for approximately € 800.000) against a company which in turn filed a substantial counterclaim in the amount of two and a half times the principal claim. The civil engineers' liability insurance paid the Claimants' and – since Respondent refused to pay for the principal claim, but paid 100% of the (- higher -) deposit for the counterclaim – the Respondent's share of the deposit of the principal claim. Thereafter the insurance company sued the Respondent in Court for reimbursement of the Respondent's share of the deposit for the principal claim on the – surprising – basis of "unjust enrichment". The Court could easily have limited its reasoning to the statement, that Claimants themselves had not complied with their obligation to remit 50% of the deposit for the counterclaim.

5 See also *Schlosser*, Das Recht der internationalen privaten Schiedsgerichtsbarkeit[2] (1989) para. 438 and 442.

6 With regard to the procedure for terminating or setting aside the arbitration agreement see point C/2 *infra*.

7 For instance by requesting a decision from the Arbitral Tribunal (see for instance ICC award March 27, 2001, ASA Bull. 2001, 285 *et seq.* and ICC award 9873 (1999) (not published) as well as ICC award 10526/2000, J.D.I. 2001, 1179 *et seq.* and two other arbitral decisions quoted by *Favre-Bulle*, Les Conséquences du non-paiement de la provision pour frais de l'arbitrage par une partie, Un tribunal arbitral peut-il condamner un défendeur au paiement de sa part de l'avance de frais? ASA Bull. 2001, 227, 233) or a State Court (see for instance Cour d'Appel d'Anvers June 29, 1988, ASA Bull. 2001, 819 *et seq.* and Superior Court of New Jersey, Law Division, Middlesex county, docket n° L 4310-90, quoted by *Jarvin* in J.D.I. 2001, 1183) ordering the other party to pay its share of the deposit.

8 No party can rely on its own non-compliance with any obligation.

9 OGH Sept. 4, 1936, SZ 18/151, commented by *Sperl*.

long-term legal relations must apply. Consequently, such long-term relations may be terminated for important reasons.[10]

The Supreme Court went on to deal with the general principle that no party can be relieved from a (contractual) obligation by reason of its own impecuniosity, but held that this principle cannot apply to arbitration agreements if upholding the arbitration agreement would deprive a party of the possibility of having its case decided by a judge or an arbitrator.[11] "It is impossible that justice be totally denied to a party."

In the given case the Claimant's impecuniosity was stated to have been "unforeseen" at the time of entering into the arbitration agreement, but the legal reasoning was expressed in such terms that it has to be regarded, particularly today in light of article 6 of the European Convention on Human Rights, as applying irrespective of whether the impecuniosity was foreseen or not[12] and even irrespective of whether or not the party is responsible for its own impecuniosity.[13] The principle that the impecuniosity of one party may not lead to a total denial of justice is in my view part of the minimum standard set by Article 6 ECHR.[14] Only in extreme cases a party may be prevented from relying on its own impecuniosity, for instance when a party brought about its impecuniosity through its own fraudulent conduct.

b) The opening of bankruptcy proceedings is no *decisive criterion*

aa) The opening of bankruptcy proceedings does not necessarily amount to Claimant's inability to pay the advance on costs

The mere fact that bankruptcy proceedings have been opened does not necessarily mean that the bankruptcy estate does not have enough assets to pay the advance on costs. Moreover those creditors, who are interested in commencing the arbitration, might be able to finance the advance without running the risk of

---

[10] This approach was approved in particular by *Rummel*, Schiedsvertrag und ABGB, ÖRZ 1986, 146 *et seq.*

[11] This reasoning implies that the impecunious party is better off in the state courts; see point 3 below.

[12] See also *Fasching, supra* note 1, at 554.

[13] This is also the view of Stein/Jonas-*Schlosser*, ZPO[21], § 1025, n° 43.

[14] *Fasching, supra* note 1, at 554; *Matscher*, Schiedsgerichtsbarkeit und EMRK, Liber Amicorum H. Nagel, 235, refers explicitly to the danger that the inoperativeness of an arbitration agreement might lead to a denial of justice; the ICC award 9667/1998 (J.D.I. 1999, 1096 *et seq.*) justified its decision to terminate the arbitration agreement in particular by reference to Art 6 ECHR; see also *Habscheid*, Die Kündigung des Schiedsvertrages aus wichtigem Grund, KTS 1980, 294 *et seq.* and *Mourre*, Le droit français de l'arbitrage international face à la Convention europèene des droits de l'homme, Gazette du Palais, Dec. 1 et 2, 2000, 16, 23.

their own impecuniosity. The Austrian Court practice in granting legal aid[15] to a trustee in bankruptcy confirms this approach: When introducing a claim on behalf of the bankruptcy estate, a trustee in bankruptcy is granted legal aid only if not only the bankruptcy estate but also those creditors who might draw an *important economic advantage* from the (positive) outcome of the proceedings are unable to finance the legal costs[16;17].

bb) The impecuniosity of a party is relevant under Austrian law even in the absence of insolvency proceedings

In Austrian State Courts an impecunious Claimant who declares under oath that he is unable to pay the security for costs requested by Respondent, is exempted from having to provide such security (§ 60 Austrian Code of Civil proceedings). In addition, the same benefit may be granted as part of legal aid under the same conditions as the exemption from Court fees and expert fees as well as the assistance by a lawyer free of charge (§ 64(1) n° 2 Austrian Code of Civil Proceedings). This is interesting because it shows that Austrian law gives more weight to free access to justice than to the other party's purely economic interest in securing its possible cost-claim[18]. I can see no reason not to apply the same principles and values in arbitration.

c) The termination of an international arbitration agreement under Austrian law and Art II (3) of the N.Y. Convention

aa) Which law governs the question whether the impecuniosity of a party renders the arbitration agreement "null and void, inoperative or incapable of being performed"

The N.Y. Convention does not constitute uniform law concerning all aspects of arbitration agreements, but only concerning the form of arbitration agreements. Other questions, such as the setting aside of arbitration agreements for reason of error or fraud are governed by the law or the legal rules applicable to the arbitration agreement. The same applies to the consequences of a party's impecuniosity on the arbitration agreement and that party's entitlement to terminate the

---

15 The introductory remarks to the Austrian law on legal aid (Erläuterungen zum Verfahrenshilfegesetz/BGBl 1973/569, 846 BlgNR 13. GP, 7, July 3, 1973) stress that the objective of that law is the protection of an impecunious party from a denial of justice and explicitly refer to Art 6 ECHR.

16 See for instance: *Riel*, Verfahrenshilfe für die Konkursmasse, RZ 1997, 187 *et seq.*, Innsbruck Court of Appeal (Oberlandesgericht), March 14, 1994, 1 R 334/93, JBl 1994, 770 *et seq.*

17 As to the question what a party in an arbitration can do if it cannot finance its defence, see *infra* point 3.

18 See also: *Czernich*, Die Ausländerprozesskostensicherheit nach § 57 ZPO, ÖJZ, 1998, 251 *et seq.*

arbitration agreement. Consequently, Austrian law as set out above is in no way in conflict with article II (3) of the N.Y. Convention.

Even if the N.Y. Convention did give a uniform definition or request a uniform definition of the terms "null and void, inoperative or incapable of being performed" it is submitted that the principles under Austrian law are an expression of the general principle of fair trial which is inherent in the N.Y. Convention.

bb) The ambit of the national court's jurisdiction under article II (3): prima facie analysis or full review?

The N.Y. Convention does not take position but leaves it to the national court and consequently to the national law of that court whether to proceed to a full review of the question if a party's impecuniosity has rendered the arbitration agreement "null and void, inoperative of incapable of being performed", or whether the state court limits itself to a prima facie analysis.

Austrian Courts would opt for the first alternative, i.e. for a full review of the issue.

The legal situation seems to be identical under the new German Arbitration law.[19]

Swiss law seems to distinguish: If the place of arbitration is within Switzerland, the Swiss courts will limit themselves to a prima facie analysis. If, however, the place of arbitration is outside Switzerland, Swiss courts will proceed to a full review of the issue.[20]

One may dislike the idea of a full review by the national court, but it is fully in line with article II (3) of the N.Y. Convention[21]. The criticism expressed[22] fears that a party in bad faith may seize its own national courts in order to disturb the arbitral process by – falsely – relying on its alleged impecuniosity. By this action the other party would be deprived of having the issue analysed and decided by the arbitral tribunal in accordance with the arbitration agreement. In my view, this criticism is not justified. First of all, such state court proceedings would more likely have to be conducted in the country of the other party (country of the seat or domicile of the defendant) rather than in the country of the

---

[19] § 1032 (1) of the new German CCP does not restrict the Court to a *prima facie* examination, see *Schlosser*, La nouvelle legislation allemande sur l'arbitrage, Rev. arb. 1998, 291, 298.

[20] This was explicitly mentioned in a Court decision dated January 16, 1995 (Swiss Federal Tribunal 121 III 38) and commentaries with regard to Art 7 IPRG and the N.Y. Convention: see: *Patocchi/Geisinger*, IPRG Internationales Privatrecht, ad Art 7 (p. 93) and p. 1425; *Honsell/Vogt/Schnyder*, Internationales Privatrecht, ad Art 7, p. 76.

[21] *Fouchard/Gaillard/Goldmann*, On International Commercial arbitration (1999) 408, at § 674.

[22] For instance by *Emmanuel Gaillard* in his national report of French law.

Claimant. Not all countries allow their nationals to sue any other party in the courts of the Claimant's country. Furthermore, and more importantly, the other party can always file its claims under the arbitration agreement. As long as this party is prepared to pay the requested deposits (which means in practice its own share as well as the share of the (allegedly) impecunious party) the arbitral process will get started. Even if that party has no claims to raise, but wishes to make clear that it should be sued in arbitration and not in the state courts, it could always file a request for arbitration asking for a declaratory award that the arbitration agreement is still alive – in spite of the (alleged) impecuniosity of the other party. Consequently, the party interested in having the arbitration agreement upheld, will be able to get its "day in arbitration".

d) Short comparative review

German law is very similar to Austrian law according to the German Supreme Court's decision dated September 14, 2000[23].

In England the London Court of Appeal had decided in *Paczy vs. Haendler & Natermann GmbH*[24] that an impecunious party may not terminate an arbitration agreement. With all due respect as a non-English lawyer, this decision seems questionable insofar as it ignores the access to justice-aspect. I would rather agree with Schlosser's criticism of this decision[25].

In the more recent *Porzelack* Case[26] the English courts rejected a request for security for costs against an impecunious party on the ground that security for costs can stifle legitimate actions and even lead to miscarriage of justice.[27] I must leave it to our English colleagues to say whether the *Porzelack*-decision overruled the *Paczy* decision in case the upholding of the arbitration agreement would have the same effect.

Only for the sake of completeness I may add that in the *Ken Ren* Case[28] security for costs was rightly granted – in spite of Claimants' impecuniosity –, because the proceedings were financed by a third party which would not have been liable for the reimbursement of Respondent's costs in case of an award against the Claimant[29].

---

23 BGH Sep. 14, 2000, Case no III ZR 33/00.

24 YCCA IX (1984), 445 et seq.

25 *Schlosser*, *supra* note 5 at para. 249 and 442.

26 *Porzelack KG (Germany) vs. Porzelack* (UK) Ltd, [1987] 1 W.K.R. 420.

27 See also *Noah Rubins*, In God we trust, all others pay cash: Security for costs in international commercial arbitration, Am. Rev. Int. Arb., 2000, 362.

28 See for instance RIW 1995, 421; *Sarre*, Security for costs in ICC arbitrations in England, the *Ken-Ren* cases, ICC Bull., Special Supplement (1994) 58 *et seq.*

29 See also *Fouchard/Gaillard/Goldman*, On International Commercial Arbitration 687 *et seq.* who rightly point out that an order for security for costs may be justified when a party appears to have deliberately organised its insolvency.

The *Tolstoy* case of June 23, 1995, in which the European Court of Human Rights[30] upheld a security for costs order against a party which was admittedly incapable of putting up the required sum (£ 124.900) is of little or no relevance to our topic since the concerned party's case had been heard for some forty days (including five days of evidence by the applicant) at first instance before the High Court and the costs to be secured were the likely costs of the other party in the Court of Appeal.

Swiss case law does not seem to be unanimous. In a recent award, a Swiss sole arbitrator granted security for costs against a bankrupt Claimant on the ground that "where a party has gone through bankruptcy proceedings that were suspended due to lack of assets, the other party's interest in security for costs prevails over the first party's interest in unimpeded access to arbitral justice" [31]. The reasoning may have been justified in the given case, but seems questionable as a general rule. In another case reported by Prof. *Reymond*[32], an arbitral tribunal had refused to grant security and had rightly considered that "international arbitration arises in connection with operations of international trade ..., which imply greater risks than domestic trade. Such risks are to be borne by the parties, including, in the view of this Tribunal, the *risk of the other party falling into financial difficulties, up to and including bankruptcy.* (emphasis added). By contrast, it may happen that a party takes certain steps in order to divest itself from its assets so as to be just an empty shell in case it loses the arbitration. Such manoeuvres, contrary to good faith, could justify an order for security for costs."

3) What can a party do if it cannot finance its defence?
In practice, what may happen is that the required deposit for the arbitrators and the arbitral institution is made in full (jointly by both parties or by one party alone), but Claimant does not have sufficient funds to finance its defence (i.e. to pay a lawyer, to pay the fees etc.). The same situation may also arise on the Respondent's side. Even if Claimant is prepared to put up 100% of the deposit, Respondent may still lack the means to finance its defence.

Such a case has never come before the Austrian courts, but in my view the very general reasoning of the Supreme Court of 1936 (see point I/B/2 above) would apply. The arbitration agreement cannot result in a denial of justice, whether for Claimant or for Respondent. Nobody will contest that legal aid is a major cultural and legal achievement and an indispensable element of legal systems in developed societies. It would be an unjustified step backwards to ignore in international arbitration the values on which the concept of legal aid is based. Since there is no system of legal aid in arbitration, arbitration must find other

---

30 Case n° 8/1994/455/536.
31 ASA Bull. 2002, 471.
32 ASA Bull. 2001, 745.

ways and means to protect and uphold those values and policies. One possible way is to reopen the door to the state courts in appropriate circumstances.

The difficulty obviously lies in the application of that policy (avoidance of denial of justice) to a given set of facts. For instance: In arbitration there is no legal obligation to be represented by a lawyer. However, many cases will require the assistance of counsel in order to satisfy the requirements of a fair trial. Even in not too complex cases, considerations of equal treatment (- such as where the other party is represented by one – or sometimes even several – lawyers -) may require legal assistance.

Whenever a party wishes to terminate an arbitration agreement due to its impecuniosity, one obviously has to examine first, as a precondition, whether that party would be better off in the otherwise competent state court: Would it qualify for legal aid? What benefits would it actually be granted? For instance: a company, in order to qualify for legal aid under Austrian law, must furnish evidence that not only the company itself, but also its shareholders are incapable of paying court fees and lawyers' fees. Even a trustee can get legal aid only if he proves that neither the bankruptcy estate nor the creditors having an important financial interest are able to finance the defence.[33] In other terms: a party that would not qualify for legal aid in state courts because its shareholders (- up to the parent company of a group of companies -), the bankruptcy estate or the interested creditors are able to pay the required deposit or to finance the defence, cannot rely on its impecuniosity to terminate the arbitration agreement.

C. Additional (procedural) issues

1) The other party must be given the opportunity to effect substitute payment for the defaulting party

Since under Austrian law a party to an arbitration agreement is not obliged, but entitled to effect substitute payment for the other party, it must be given a fair opportunity to do so. Only after expiration of a reasonable period of time after having been given adequate notice (- or if the other party has clearly expressed its refusal to substitute -) may a party terminate an arbitration agreement and go to the state courts.

Can a party also, in order to salvage an arbitration agreement, offer to pre-finance the other party's defence? The question is probably of a rather theoretical nature, but in very special circumstances, for instance in highly confidential matters (- and provided the arbitration agreement does guarantee confidentiality which, as we know, is not necessarily the case -), a party may be prepared to pay a very high price and even to pre-finance the other party's defence in order to avoid a public hearing in any state court. Such legitimate interests should be

---

[33] See point 2 b) above.

given more weight than the practical difficulties inherent in pre-financing the other party's defence.

2) What is the procedure to be followed?
There is some uncertainty under Austrian law as to the procedure to be followed. Some authors consider that the interested party must first apply for a special court order setting aside the arbitration agreement according to § 583 of the Code of Civil Procedure.[34] Others take the view that the interested party may directly raise its – substantive – claims in the competent state court and may ask the court to rule, as a preliminary point, on the termination of the arbitration agreement.[35] In the 1936 case the Claimant had asked in the state Courts for a declaratory judgement that the arbitration agreement was no longer applicable. The Supreme Court said that many private law provisions are applicable to arbitration agreements and granted the relief without requesting that the special procedure of § 583 be followed.[36]

In 1936 the Supreme Court did not refer Claimant to the special procedure under § 583 and did not deny the request for a declaratory judgement. It seems justified to assume that the Supreme Court would also have accepted the direct filing of substantive claims in the competent state court (- without asking first

---

[34] § 583 (1) and (2) provide as follows:
"(1) If the parties cannot agree on the arbitrator to be appointed by them jointly, the court mentioned in para. 582 shall pronounce the rescission of the arbitration agreement.
(2) The same procedure shall be followed,
1. if named persons are appointed as arbitrators in the arbitration agreement and one of these arbitrators dies, ceases to act consequent upon a challenge for any other reason, refuses to accept office as arbitrator or withdraws from the contract concluded with him because of his appointment; or
2. if an arbitrator who is named in the arbitration agreement or appointed by a party pursuant to the arbitration agreement or by the court pursuant to para. 582 refuses to fulfil the obligations assumed by his acceptance of office as arbitrator, or delays unreasonably in their fulfilment;"
Although this provision only deals with very specific factual circumstances, *Fasching*, *supra* note 1, at 553 *et seq.* and *Backhausen*, Schiedsgerichtsbarkeit (1990) 90 *et seq.* are of the opinion that § 583 of the Code of Civil Procedure must be applied by analogy.

[35] *Rummel*, *supra* note 10, at 146 and *Reiner*, ICC Schiedsgerichtsbarkeit (1989) 159 at note 366.

[36] "*Der Schiedsvertrag regelt gewisse Rechtsbeziehungen zwischen den Parteien. Es ist hier nicht zu entscheiden, ob er durchaus ein privatrechtlicher oder ein öffentlich-rechtlicher Vertrag oder ein Vertrag gemischten Charakters ist. Jedenfalls sind viele Bestimmungen privatrechtlichen Inhalts, und zwar nicht nur Bestimmungen über die Fähigkeit der Parteien, sondern auch die über Zwang und Irrtum auf ihn anzuwenden. Durch den Schiedsvertrag wird ein dauerndes Rechtsverhältnis zwischen den Parteien geschaffen. Darum müssen die Grundsätze zur Anwendung kommen, die sonst für Dauerrechtsverhältnisse Geltung haben.*"

for a declaratory judgement -).[37] The Supreme Court seems to have been more modern in 1936 than some Austrian authors and some Supreme Court decisions are today trying to maintain.

In a more recent decision in 1996 the Supreme Court then explicitly stated that § 583 only deals with the setting aside of arbitration agreements in certain cases, and that it is not to be extended to other grounds for terminating arbitration agreements.[38, 39]

In an international context, Art II (3) of the New York Convention, which does not provide for separate proceedings before a different judge for the setting aside of arbitration agreements as null and void, inoperative or incapable of being performed, must in my view prevail over the special procedure under § 583 of the Austrian code of Civil Procedure.[40]

3) Is the arbitration agreement rendered ineffective only for the present dispute or also for future disputes?

According to the general principle of partial (in-)validity in contract law[41], the arbitration agreement only loses its effect to the extent necessary, that is to say only for the present dispute, but not for any disputes which may arise in the future, at a time when the party in question may have overcome its impecuniosity. This concept of partial (in)validity or partial setting aside is expressly stated in § 583 (3) of the code of Civil Procedure.[42]

---

[37] The French Cour de Cassation allowed a Claimant whose Request for Arbitration had been considered withdrawn by the ICC Court for non-payment of Respondent's share of the deposit, to file its claims in the French State Courts: Cass. civ. 1re, Nov. 19, 1991, Rev. Arb. 1992, 462; in another case an ICC arbitrator was asked to terminate an arbitration agreement pursuant to French Law (Art 1184 Code Civil) which he did by arbitral award, thereby opening the way to the state courts: ICC award 9667/1998, J.D.I. 1999, 1096 *et seq.*

[38] OGH March 26, 1996, 1 Ob 641/95: *„§ 583 ZPO zählt nur einige Fälle auf, in denen das Gericht in einem abgekürzten Verfahren Schiedsverträge außer Kraft setzen kann. Diese Bestimmung hat aber nicht zur Folge, dass die Wirksamkeit eines Schiedsvertrages immer nur durch gerichtlichen Ausspruch und niemals Kraft Gesetzes erlöschen kann, regeln doch die Bestimmungen der §§ 583ff bloß dessen Außerkraftsetzung in bestimmten Fällen, lassen aber die Wirkung von etwaigen anderen Erlöschungsgründen unberührt.“*

[39] Very shortly prior to this decision the Supreme Court had still maintained the view that arbitration agreements are – purely or primarily – procedural agreements with no or little private law character or content; OGH June 13, 1995, SZ 68/112; OGH Feb. 21, 1996, 7 Ob 502/96.

[40] In addition § 583 of the code of Civil Procedure will most likely not survive the intended revision of Austrian arbitration law.

[41] *Koziol-Welser*, Bürgerliches Recht I[12], 157 *et seq.* and 164.

[42] "If the arbitration agreement is concluded with reference to all disputes arising out of a particular legal relationship and the circumstances in which the court is to declare the arbitration agreement as rescinded are such that submission to arbitration of possible

4) What are the consequences of the situation where a party's impecuniosity arises or ceases to exist during pending proceedings?
Once state court proceedings have commenced due to the impecuniosity of one or both parties, it seems that these proceedings must continue, even if, in the course of those proceedings, the impecunious party's financial situation improves to such an extent that it could now afford arbitration.

The more bothersome situation is where, in the course of an ongoing arbitration, a party experiences financial difficulties and for instance can no longer afford an increase of the deposit required by the institution or by the arbitrators, an advance for an expert, or its own lawyer's fees. One can easily see the danger of dilatory tactics or of attempts to frustrate the arbitration, but in very extreme circumstances, if the other party refuses to step in, an arbitral tribunal may have to conclude that the arbitration agreement has become inoperative in the course of an ongoing arbitration.

5) Impecuniosity of one of several Claimants or one of several Respondents?
The impecuniosity of one or several but not all Claimants or of several, but not all, Respondents may lead to a "split" of the arbitral proceedings, unless in view of the applicable substantive law a given claim can only be made by all Claimants or against all Respondents in a single proceeding. In such a situation the remaining Claimant(s) or the remaining Respondent(s), respectively, may be more inclined to effect substitute payment for defaulting parties, but if they decide not to do so, the whole matter may have to be dealt with in the state courts.

6) Impecuniosity of Claimant and Respondent
This situation does not raise any additional or other legal questions, but it increases the likelihood that the arbitration will never be commenced or will not be pursued or that the parties will jointly waive the arbitration agreement.

---

disputes arising in the future is not excluded, the court shall only declare the arbitration agreement of no effect for the case in question."
Another type of „partial" invalidity is found in the *Gateway* decision rendered by the Supreme Court of New York, Appelate Division, August 13, 1998 (Yearbook Com. Arbitration, Vol. XXIVa (1999), pp 343-348). The Plaintiff in this matter, a consumer, argued that the ICC arbitration agreement was invalid because ICC was not a forum commonly used for consumer matters and because the cost of ICC arbitration was said to be prohibitive.
The Court did not vacate the whole arbitration agreement, but only the portion of the arbitration agreement requiring ICC arbitration and gave leave to the parties to seek appointment of an arbitrator pursuant to the Federal Arbitration Act; see also *Schlosser, supra* note 5, para. 442.

II. Effects of the opening of formal insolvency proceedings on arbitration

The complexity of the second subtopic for today arises from

- the tension between general contract law and arbitration law on the one hand and insolvency law on the other
- the fact that parts of the insolvency law raise public policy issues
- the intervention of additional participants, i.e. the receiver and other creditors
- (potential) conflicts of interest
  - between the receiver and the initial debtor (or the debtor's previous management),
  - between creditors and the receiver

  and

  - among creditors.

and

- the fact that a party (for instance a State) or a State entity or a State company may try to hide behind non-legal bankruptcy orders and proceedings.[43]

There are only a few court cases in Austria in that grey area between arbitration and insolvency law and most of them – like the limited legal doctrine – deal with purely domestic-law situations.

I shall *not* deal with debt recomposition proceedings ("*Vergleichsverfahren*") in German terminology, "*Ausgleich*" in Austrian terminology. Unlike bankruptcy proceedings they do not raise very complex questions. The debtor remains in place and continues to act as Claimant or Respondent. Only some of his acts may require the administrator's approval[44].

As a last introductory point I should say a few words on the present Austrian perspective concerning *international bankruptcy*.[45]

Until 1982 Austria followed the *principle of universality* with regard to *moveable assets* and the *principle of territoriality* with regard to *immoveable assets*. All of the moveable assets of the insolvent debtor were to be included in the Austrian insolvency, and the receiver was entitled to take all measures required and necessary to take possession of those moveable assets. By the same token, in case of insolvency proceedings conducted outside Austria, Austria

---

[43] For a practical example see ICC Award 5954/1991 quoted by *Mantilla-Serrano*, International Arbitration and Insolvency Proceedings, Arb. Int., 1995, Vol. 11, No. 1, 51, 58 and *Fouchard/Gaillard/Goldman*, On International Commercial Arbitration (1999) 345.

[44] For an overview of the recomposition proceedings in Austrian Law *(Ausgleich)* see: *Dellinger/Oberhammer*, Insolvenzrecht (2002), 183 to 199.

[45] For a detailed study on the subject, see *Keppelmüller*, Österreichisches Internationales Konkursrecht (1997).

would agree to "extradite" moveable assets located in Austria[46] (- under the condition of (factual) reciprocity -).

In 1982 this position was abandoned in favour of a *purely territorial approach* which could be trumped by bilateral insolvency-treaties.[47] As a matter of fact, Austria did actually conclude a relatively significant number of such bilateral insolvency treaties providing for reciprocal recognition of insolvency proceedings. By contrast, in the absence of an insolvency treaty, Austria refused to give any effect to insolvency proceedings opened abroad and in turn, did not allow Austrian receivers to pursue and to recover assets located abroad.

This new approach and the corresponding court decisions have been constantly and severely criticised by legal scholars[48], but the courts have neither changed their jurisprudence, nor has the legislator taken any action thus far in spite of the fact that the concept of bilateral insolvency treaties was not as successful as initially hoped or expected. The number of bilateral insolvency treaties concluded by Austria (i.e. 4[49]) is relatively high, but it is still insignificant in comparison with the total number of states.

This very limited territorial approach has now been opened up and broadened by EC-Council Regulation no. 1346/2000 of May 29, 2000 on insolvency proceedings.[50]

Furthermore, motivated by the European Regulation and by the obligation to incorporate the provisions of the European Directive on the reorganisation and winding-up of insurance undertakings[51] and of the European Directive on the reorganisation and winding-up of credit institutions[52] in Austrian law the Austrian legislator has elaborated a *Draft Law on International Insolvency (Bundes-*

---

46 §§ 66 and 67 Austrian insolvency Code (*(Konkursordnung,* hereinafter *KO*) prior to the modification of the insolvency law in 1982 (see also note 47).

47 Art II No 92 of the Law which modified the Austrian Insolvency Law (*Insolvenzrechtsänderungsgesetz* – IRÄG 1982, BGBl 370/1982) deleted §§ 66 and 67 (see also note 46 above) and added a new § 180 KO which – with regard to the effect of insolvency proceedings opened abroad – refers to the general provisions of the Austrian law of enforcement (§§ 79 to 82 and 84 *Exekutionsordnung*). These provisions allow recognition and enforcement only on the basis of a bi- or multilateral treaty. See also *Mohr*, Konkursordnung und Ausgleichsordnung (1995) 496 *et seq*.

48 See for instance: *Burgstaller/Keppelmüller*, Universalität oder Territorialität – Wirkt der österreichische Konkurs ins Ausland?, JBl 1996, 285; *Burgstaller*, JBl 2000, 394 (note with regard to OGH Nov. 25, 1999, 2 Ob 316/99 f).

49 With Belgium, Germany, France and Italy; all four treaties have now been replaced by the EC-Regulation 1346/2000 (Art 44).

50 "Any judgment opening insolvency proceedings handed down by a court of a Member State which has jurisdiction pursuant to Article 3 shall be recognised in all the other Member States from the time that it becomes effective in the State of the opening of proceedings" (Art 16.1).

51 Directive 2001/17/EC, dated March 19, 2001.

52 Directive 2001/24/EC, dated April 4, 2001.

gesetz über das Internationale Insolvenzrecht[53]). This Draft is intended to apply to international insolvency proceedings which are not covered by the EU-Regulation and will introduce the principle of universality in Austrian insolvency law.

Insolvency proceedings which have been opened in Austria will have universal scope and will normally encompass all the debtor's assets, wherever they are located. However, if the debtor has the centre of his main interests in a foreign country and if insolvency proceedings have been opened in that country, Austrian insolvency proceedings do not encompass assets located outside of Austria which are subject of these insolvency proceedings opened outside of Austria[54]. Under these circumstances the Austrian insolvency proceedings will be limited to assets located in Austria.

Foreign insolvency proceedings and judgments rendered in such proceedings will be recognized in Austria

- if those proceedings are comparable to Austrian insolvency proceedings
- if the debtor has the centre of his main interests in the country where such proceedings are pending and
- if the Austrian creditors have the same rights as the creditors of said country.

However the foreign insolvency proceedings will not be recognized according to the Draft, if insolvency proceedings with regard to the debtor's assets are already pending in Austria or if the foreign proceedings violate Austrian ordre public[55]. Parallel insolvency proceedings are explicitly admitted.

However until the draft law -which is at the moment[56] still subject to scrutiny- will have entered into force[57], the territorial approach of Austrian law will con-

---

[53] Bundesgesetz mit dem die Konkursordnung, die Ausgleichsordnung, das Insolvenzrechtseinführungsgesetz, das Bankwesengesetz und das Versicherungsaufsichtsgesetz geändert werden (Bundesgesetz über das Internationale Insolvenzrecht – IIRG, JMZ 13.025/37-I.5/2002). The new provisions on international insolvency proceedings will be incorporated in the actual Austrian insolvency code (Konkursordnung) (draft §§ 217 to 245 KO). Those provisions shall also apply on recomposition proceedings (see draft § 78, Austrian code on recomposition proceedings, *Ausgleichsordnung*). With regard to the reorganisation and winding-up of insurance undertakings and credit institutions, new provisions will be also incorporated in the relevant existing laws (Insolvenzrechtseinführungsgesetz, Bankwesengesetz and Versicherungsaufsichtsgesetz).

[54] See § 233 of the draft revision of the Austrian insolvency code.

[55] See § 234 of the draft revision of the Austrian insolvency code.

[56] January 2003.

[57] With regard to the modifications of the Austrian insolvency code *(Konkursordnung)* and the Austrian code on recomposition proceedings *(Ausgleichsordnung)*, the draft law foresees April 19, 2003, as date of entering into force of such modifications.

tinue to apply outside the field of application of the new EC-Regulation (which covers all of the EU-countries except Denmark).

After these introductory remarks, I suggest to deal first with the question of whether arbitration proceedings are suspended automatically or whether they have to be suspended or should not be suspended by the arbitrator in the event of the opening of insolvency proceedings against one of the parties. (For the sake of completeness I might add that parties have a general duty to inform the arbitral tribunal and the other parties of any modification of their legal situation which may affect the case)[58].

A. Automatic stay of arbitration proceedings?

The predominant legal doctrine in Austria takes the view that not only state court proceedings but also arbitration proceedings are suspended *ex lege* by the opening of insolvency proceedings against one of the parties.[59] Interestingly, however, the Austrian Supreme Court, in a quite recent decision in 1999[60] explicitly left open the response to this question, even for domestic arbitration, and simply referred to the fact that legal scholars are not unanimous on the point.

The question of automatic *ex lege* suspension[61] of arbitration proceedings can only arise with regard to arbitration proceedings having their seat in Austria.[62] This follows from the general principle that Austrian law cannot regulate arbitration proceedings having their seat outside this country.

For purely *domestic arbitrations* – without any international link - [63] one might not have an objection to automatic suspension, but the point is of rather limited importance because it is obvious that the only possible solution is to suspend proceedings until the receiver has been able to make up his mind as to whether or not to admit the claim raised in this arbitration against the now-insolvent debtor or whether or not to pursue a claim raised by the now-insolvent party in the role of Claimant. It does not really matter, in my view, whether the suspension occurs *ex lege* or whether it is ordered by the arbitrator.

In *international arbitration* the question is more delicate, because the now-insolvent debtor may have assets outside the countries in which the new EC-

---

58 See for instance ICC award 11130/2001 (unpublished).

59 *Bartisch/Pollak*, Konkursrecht³ (1974), I, 74; Fasching, Kommentar II, 777; *Schubert* in Konecny/Schubert, Kommentar zur KO, § 6 KO at n° 13; contra *Petschek/Reimer/Schiemer*, Das österreichische Insolvenzrecht (1973) 470 *et seq.*

60 OGH Aug. 25, 1999, 3 Ob 348/97 s, JBl 2000, 238.

61 Under Austrian law the bankruptcy court has no power to order the stay of proceedings; in the US, for instance, the situation is different, see van den Berg, The New York Convention (1981) 364.

62 For an example of a US bankruptcy judge's court order having no extra territorial effect on an arbitration taking place in Tokyo, see *van den Berg, supra* note 61, at 364.

63 In a more and more globalised world such cases obviously tend to decrease in number.

Regulation on insolvency proceedings applies (i.e. outside the "territory"), and which are not covered by or included in the insolvency proceedings in Austria[64]. With the entering into force of the new Austrian law on insolvency proceedings this problem is minimized as insolvency proceedings in Austria will in most cases encompass all the debtor's assets. In any event there is a practical need for at least a certain "stay" in order to allow the parties (- and the arbitrators -) to investigate the relevancy or irrelevancy of insolvency proceedings and in particular to ascertain, who will now be acting for the insolvent party (- in order to avoid the risk of a violation of that party's right to be heard -). Furthermore it seems useful to ascertain whether the Claimant may wish to abandon the arbitration against a Respondent who has become insolvent or whether an insolvent Claimant (or its receiver) wishes to pursue an arbitration commenced by the debtor prior to the opening of the bankruptcy proceedings[65].

In view of the need to resolve all these questions which may be more complex and more time-consuming in an international context, and in order to allow the parties the opportunity to express their views on those points, an automatic ex lege stay of international arbitration proceedings seems impossible under Austrian law.

During such period of clarification the resolution of the merits of the arbitration may – in fact – be stayed. In addition, there may be good reasons for an arbitrator, after having heard the parties, to issue a formal order staying the proceedings.

B. Who is entitled to act?

- the insolvent party itself (if it is a natural person) or the previous management of the insolvent party (if it is a legal entity)?

or

- the receiver appointed by the insolvency court?

Under Austrian law the general principle is that the only person entitled to act for an insolvent party is the receiver appointed by the court.[66] In this respect the importance of the revision of the Austrian law on international insolvency be-

---

[64] An automatic *ex lege* stay of international arbitration proceedings is only conceivable and realistic if all concerned laws adapt the universal approach; see Art 20(1) of the draft UNCITRAL Model Law on Cross-Border Insolvency: "Upon recognition of a foreign proceeding that is a foreign main proceeding,

(a) Commencement or continuation of individual actions or individual proceedings concerning the debtor's assets, rights, obligations or liabilities is stayed;

(b) Execution against the debtor's assets is stayed; and

(c) The right to transfer, encumber or otherwise dispose of any assets of the debtor is suspended."

[65] See also: *Brown-Berset/Lévy*, Faillite et Arbitrage, ASA Bull. n°4 1998, 676.

[66] § 3 KO; the exception made by the insolvency law for the debtor's "personal" rights (§ 6(3) KO) is of no practical relevance in (international) commercial arbitration.

comes particularly apparent. Until the entering into force of such law, problems may arise, due to the territorial approach. Presently the receiver is not entitled to act with regard to those assets belonging to the debtor that are located outside the territory. The same is true for the enforcement of the claims of the insolvent party with regard to the assets of other parties where those assets are located outside the territorial limits imposed on the Austrian receiver by Austrian law.

Depending on the factual location of such assets (- a point that the arbitrator will have to clarify with the parties -) the arbitrator may be required to deal with the receiver *and* with the bankrupt party itself (or with the former management, as the case may be).[67]

In all of these situations it is legally possible

a) for the receiver to give power of attorney to the bankrupt party itself (or to the former management or their respective lawyer)[68] or

b) for the former management or the bankrupt party itself to give power of attorney to the receiver.

The universal approach foreseen in the new Austrian law on international insolvency will therefore enlarge the receiver's competence and facilitate the arbitrator's task when confronted with a bankrupt party.

C. Does the arbitration agreement survive?

There is neither a clear-cut "yes" nor a clear-cut "no" answer to this question.

1) Cases in which the arbitration agreement indisputably survives

It is undisputed that an arbitration agreement, which was entered into by the now-insolvent party prior to the opening of the insolvency proceedings, survives

- with regard to the enforcement of preferential third party rights against the insolvent debtor (or the estate), such as a supplier's claim for the return of goods that were delivered under retention of title ("*Aussonderungsansprüche*") and as to claims related to mortgages validly granted prior to the opening of the insolvency proceedings ("*Absonderungsansprüche*")[69];

---

[67] As long as Austria follows the territorial approach it is impossible from an Austrian point of view to deal with the powers of the former management or the receiver as an issue of "capacity" in the sense of Art V (1) lit a of the New York Convention and § 595 (1) n° 1 of the Austrian Code of Civil Procedure.

[68] This happened for instance in the ICC case 6057/1991 (J.D.I. 1993, 1016) between a Syrian Claimant and a French Respondent who went bankrupt in the cause of the arbitration. Although the arbitral tribunal sitting in Syria took a territorial approach it did note in the award that the French receiver had confirmed the attorney's power to continue to act for the bankrupt company.

[69] *Fremuth*, Schiedsverfahren und Konkurs, Zur Bindung des Masseverwalters an Schiedsvereinbarungen des Gemeinschuldners, ÖJZ 1998, para. II.

- with regard to claims between shareholders of a company or partners of a partnership[70];
or
- with regard to claims of the initial debtor which the receiver wishes (to continue) to pursue on behalf of the estate against third parties[71];
and
- with regard to all contracts which the receiver assumes on behalf of the estate and which therefore become fully binding on the estate as if they had been newly entered into by the receiver.[72]

2) What is not covered by the arbitration agreement?
It is equally uncontested in Austrian law that an arbitration agreement entered into by the now-insolvent debtor does *not apply* to disputes arising out of the receiver's special right to contest the validity of certain agreements, payments etc. made by the debtor prior to the institution of insolvency proceedings, for instance in case of collusion between the initial debtor and its counterpart. Such rights do not arise under the agreement containing the arbitration agreement, but are granted to the receiver (- and not to the initial contract party (= the initial debtor) -) ex lege by the insolvency law.[73] This applies – a fortiori – if and to the extent that the receiver is entitled under the bankruptcy law to contest even final and binding decisions, rendered prior to the opening of the bankruptcy proceedings against the debtor.[74]

3) Does the arbitration agreement apply to a creditor's claim which has been duly raised in the insolvency proceedings but which has not been admitted by the receiver?
This is the difficult issue having practical importance.

a) What is the normal procedure in a domestic case without an arbitration agreement:
The immediate effect of opening insolvency proceedings is that legal proceedings filed against the debtor are interrupted *ex lege*. The Claimant then has the

---

[70] OGH April 17, 1996, 7 Ob 2097/96z, ZIK 1997, 60.

[71] *Fremuth*, *supra* note 69, para. II.

[72] The receiver can also conclude new arbitration agreements. Until recently the receiver needed prior approval by the creditors' committee if the value of the matter exceeded ATS 500.000 (= € 36.336,--). Since amended in 2002 (BGBl I Nr. 75/2002), this has no longer been the case.

[73] *Fremuth*, *supra* note 69, para. III; see also ICC Partial Award 6697/1990, Rev. Arb. 1992, 135, note by P. Ancel, concerning a bankrupt Luxemburg Claimant: "The only disputes which are excluded are those which have a direct link with the bankruptcy proceedings, namely those disputes arising from the application of rules specific to those proceedings."

[74] *Konecny*, Bekämpfung vollstreckbarer oder festgestellter Konkursforderungen, JBl 1995, 409 *et seq.*.

possibility of giving notice of its claim to the insolvency court ("*Anmeldung der Forderung im Konkursverfahren*"). The receiver may then either admit these claims, totally or partially, or he may contest them, totally or partially. The same right to contest other creditors' claims is granted to each other creditor .[75]

If a creditor's claim is not contested, the notification of the claim becomes final and the registration of this claim in the corresponding claims-register ("*Eintragung im Anmeldeverzeichnis*") becomes a "title" that is enforceable against the estate (- but of course only up to the relevant ratio according to the general rule providing for equal treatment of all creditors -).

If the receiver contests a creditor's claim, a certain time limit is granted to the creditor

- to pursue the state court proceedings the creditor had initiated prior to the commencement of the bankruptcy proceedings; in this case, the proceedings simply continue with the following two modifications:
- the *initial debtor is replaced by the receiver*

and

- the request for a court decision *ordering the debtor to pay* is *replaced* by a request for a *declaratory judgement*

or

- if no court proceedings had been commenced prior to the opening of the bankruptcy proceedings, the creditor must now commence such proceedings for a declaratory judgement against the receiver in the bankruptcy court.

b) Are the receiver and the other contesting creditor(s) bound by the arbitration agreement?

If the initial debtor had agreed to arbitration, the obvious question arising is

- whether the claim must be raised (anew) in the bankruptcy court[76]

or

- whether the receiver and the creditor are entitled/obliged to commence arbitration (-or to continue an arbitration commenced prior to the commencement of bankruptcy proceedings-) (if the (alleged) claim is contested by the receiver or one or more other creditors)[77]

---

[75] See § 105 (5) KO and *Konecny* in Konecny/Schubert, Kommentar zur KO, § 105 at n° 7 and § 106 at n° 33.

[76] This is the predominant view in Austria; see *Schubert*, *supra* note 75, § 7 KO at n° 10; *Konecny*, *supra* note 75, § 110 KO at n°6 and § 113 KO at n° 7; *Petschek/Reimer/Schiemer*, Das österreichische Insolvenzrecht (1973) 583; *Fremuth*, *supra* note 69, para. IV.

[77] *Sobalik*, Das Klagebegehren im Prüfungsprozess (§§ 110 *et seq.* KO), ÖRZ 1979, 189; *Fasching*, Schiedsgericht und Schiedsverfahren im österreichischen und internationalen Recht (1973) 28.

aa) Is the claim still arbitrable?

The continued validity of the arbitration agreement cannot be denied on the grounds of non-arbitrability. Disputes between creditors of the former debtor and the receiver concerning the validity of such creditors' claims are capable of being "settled"[78] which – still today – is the relevant test for arbitrability under Austrian law.[79; 80]

bb) Violation of the right to be heard?

Under Austrian law a claim filed in bankruptcy proceedings may be contested by the receiver and/or by one or more other creditors. No matter who contests a claim, whether it is a) only the receiver, b) only one or several creditors or c) the receiver and one, several or all creditors, the proceedings have to be conducted against all parties who have contested the claim (§ 110(1) KO). Consequently they all become parties to the proceedings and as such are necessarily given the right to be heard.

If the receiver and/or one, or several, or all creditors choose *not to contest* a given creditor's claim, they – implicitly – admit and accept this claim and waive their right to contest it. The fact that the effects of such an arbitral award are then extended to them by operation of law (§ 112(1) KO) therefore poses no problem whatsoever (whether under Art 6 ECHR or under any other rule or principle).[81]

---

[78] Konecny, *supra* note 75, § 110 KO at n° 51.

[79] It goes without saying that the answer is the same under the more modern definition of arbitrability which Austria will most likely adopt in the not too distant future, according to which any and all "economic" claims are arbitrable; see *Oberhammer*, Entwurf eines neuen Schiedsverfahrensrechts (2002), § 582 of the draft revised Austrian Code of Civil Procedure.

[80] This does not seem to be a universally recognised rule. The New York Court of Appeal for instance decided in a reinsurance matter between Arda, a Bermudan corporation and the Superintendent of Insurance of the State of New York for an insolvent New York insurance company named Nassau that under the law of New York the arbitration clause is not capable of performance and settlement under the laws of New York (Art II New York Convention). The Court may have been influenced not only by "New York's strong public policy" in insurance matters, but also by the fact that both insurance companies were owned and controlled by the same people. (Yearbook Comm. Arb'n XVII, 1992, 666).
Presumably due to such public policy considerations, Art 20(2) of the Draft UNCITRAL Model Law on Cross-Border Insolvency refers to national law to govern "the scope, and the modification or termination, of the stay and suspension referred to in paragraph 1 of this article." (see note 64 above). Possibly for similar reasons Art 1(2) of the Council Regulation (EC) No 1346/2000 on insolvency proceedings excludes from its scope "insolvency proceedings concerning insurance undertakings".

[81] I agree with *Deixler-Hübner*, Die Nebenintervention im Zivilprozess (1993) 207, that creditors who chose not to contest another creditor's claim cannot thereafter request to be admitted as intervening parties ("*Nebenintervenient*") in proceedings commenced by the

cc) Are the receiver and any contesting creditors legal successors of the initial debtor?

There is no unanimous view on this point.

Some authors argue – very formalistically – that at least the creditors' right to contest the claim is new since it arises by law (- and therefore not from the underlying legal relation between the initial parties -).

Others take the opposite view and argue that the receiver and such creditors are simply (partial) legal successors of the initial debtor and are therefore bound by the arbitration agreement.

In my view one has to look at the substance of the rights relied upon. For what reasons and on what basis may the receiver and/or creditors contest the claim?

To the extent the receiver as well as the contesting creditors can only have those rights which the initial debtor had at its disposal, their rights are not "new". The only change – arising by operation of law – is that the initial debtor is now replaced by the receiver and/or by those creditors who also wish to contest the claim in question. This is a case of legal succession.[82] Therefore not only the receiver, but also all of the other creditors who wish to contest a claim are bound by the arbitration agreement, as they are bound by any other contract clause[83] (– concerning payment, concerning the specifications of equipment to be delivered, concerning the guarantee period etc –), whether they like such clauses or not.[84]

---

receiver and/or other creditors who have chosen not to admit the claim, but rather to contest it. To admit such creditors as intervening parties would also be unfair for cost-reasons, because in the event of success the intervening party would be entitled to reimbursement of its legal costs, while if it lost, it would not have to pay (or to participate in the payment of) the successful creditor's legal costs; contra *Konecny*, *supra* note 75, § 110 KO, at n° 13, and *Fremuth*, *supra* note 69, para. IV C.

The legal situation in the case of proceedings for the setting aside of a limited liability company's shareholder meeting is different, because such proceedings are conducted against the company (Art 42(1) of the Austrian Law on Limited Liability Companies) and because the law specifically allows each shareholder to intervene in the proceedings (§ 42 (5) leg. cit.).

[82] Contra Konecny, *supra* note 75, § 113 at n° 2.

For German insolvency law which is at least with regard to the position and rights of other creditors very close, if not identical to Austrian law, see *Flöther*, Auswirkungen des inländischen Insolvenzverfahrens auf Schiedsverfahren und Schiedsabrede (2001) 84 *et seq.*, who considers the creditor to be an "alter ego" of the initial debtor.

The same result was reached by an ICC arbitral tribunal (place of arbitration: Germany) in a case between a Japanese Claimant and a Swedish Respondent, ICC Interim Award 7337/1996, Yearbook Comm. Arb'n XXIV (1999) 149 *et seq.*

[83] *Flöther*, *supra* note 82, at 90.

[84] Unless a given clause (- at least in theory this could apply (also) to an arbitration clause -) or the contract as a whole can be attacked by the receiver, for instance, for collusion

dd) Unequal treatment with regard to the constitution of the arbitral tribunal?

Obviously, there can be no such problem, if there is only one Respondent, either the receiver, (– which is the most frequent situation –) or only one creditor.

But even if the claim is contested by the receiver *and* by one or more creditors or by two or more creditors only, the situation is quite different from the well-known Dutco-situation, since those several Respondents are nothing more than legal successors (or an "alter ego"[85]) of one initial debtor.[86]

The legal situation is particularly easy if the arbitral tribunal has been constituted prior to the opening of the bankruptcy. The plurality of Respondents who thereafter replace the initial debtor cannot affect the validity of the constitution of the arbitral tribunal. The situation is in no way different if a Respondent dies and is replaced by several heirs. The – multiple – Respondents cannot now contest the validity of the constitution of the arbitral tribunal, even if they now have different interests. The same applies if a company is split into two new legal entities. They are also both legal successors of the initial company.

The same solution must apply if the arbitration has not commenced prior to the opening of the bankruptcy proceedings (against the initial debtor only), but after the opening of the bankruptcy proceedings against several Respondents[87].

ee) Economic arguments

The nullity or inoperativeness of the arbitration agreement is not only less attractive in legal terms, but would be inefficient and uneconomical because it would result in a waste of all (– or at least most –) of the time and money invested in arbitration proceedings, where they were started but not finalised prior to the commencement of the bankruptcy proceedings.[88;89]

---

between the initial debtor and the third party. As has been set out in point C/2 above, such disputes do *not* fall under the arbitration agreement.

[85] See *supra* note 82.

[86] Even if one were to apply the *Dutco*-philosophy, this would not necessarily render the arbitration clause null and void or inoperative. Normally, it is possible in such circumstances to save the arbitration agreement by adapting the rules for the constitution of the arbitral tribunal, for instance by appointing a sole arbitrator or by having all three arbitrators appointed by the arbitral institution; for ICC arbitration see Art 10 of the ICC Rules 1998.

[87] The receiver *and* at least one other creditor *or* against at least two other creditors.

[88] For this very reason § 113 KO says that a creditor who had commenced legal proceedings prior to the opening of the bankruptcy, and whose claim has been contested by the receiver, may resume those legal proceedings in the court where they had been commenced and is not required to start new proceedings in the bankruptcy court.

On those considerations of procedural efficiency see *Schubert*, *supra* note 75, § 7 at n° 55 and *Konecny*, *supra* note 75, § 113 at n° 2. The receiver and other contesting creditors have to accept such proceedings from where they were at the time of the opening of the insolvency proceedings and are bound by procedural acts taken by the initial debtor. In the same sense: *Sobalik*, Das Klagebegehren im Prüfungsprozess (§ 110 *et seq.* KO), ÖRZ

ff) Additional reasons for the survival of the arbitration agreement in an international context

(i) Article II of the New York Convention

Article II of the New York Convention imposes on its member states the obligation to recognise the validity of arbitration agreements which fulfil the formal requirements of the Convention.

Since the type of disputes we are talking about is arbitrable, and since the right to be heard is fully respected and equal treatment is given, there is no reason to assume that the opening of bankruptcy proceedings in itself would render the arbitration agreement "null and void, inoperative or incapable of being performed"[90].

Under the New York Convention, Austria is therefore obliged to recognize the validity of the arbitration agreement.

(ii) Why differentiate between international jurisdictional clauses and arbitration clauses.

Although Austrian law (§ 111 (1) KO) provides for the exclusive jurisdiction of the bankruptcy court for the type of disputes we are discussing here, international jurisdictional clauses are held to be valid under the EC-Regulation 44/2001 of December 22, 2000 on jurisdiction and the recognition and enforcement of judgements in civil and commercial matters.[91]

According to article 1 (2) lit b the Regulation does not apply to bankruptcy or related proceedings[92] but this exclusion is construed narrowly and applies only

---

1979, 189 *et seq.* and *Klicka*, Zur Fortsetzung eines nach Schluss der Verhandlung durch Konkurs unterbrochenen Zivilprozesses, RdW 1991, 107; contra *Konecny, supra* note 75, § 113, at n°2, except in the presumably rare case that procedural act is to be qualified as an act of collusion between the initial debtor and its "opponent" in the proceedings. In practice, it should be possible to deal with such issues in the pending arbitration, but if not, they must be raised in separate proceedings in the bankruptcy court (see point C/2 above and *supra* note 84). Such presumably very rare cases do not justify setting aside the arbitration agreement.

89 This argument does, however, not justify to give effect to the arbitration agreement only if the arbitration has been commenced prior to the opening of the bankruptcy proceedings, as seems to be the prevailing opinion under Dutch law, see *Vesna Lazic*, Arbitration and Insolvency Proceedings, Claims of ordinary bankruptcy creditors, vol. 3.3. Electronic Journal of Com. Law, Dec 1999, point 4.3.2.2.1.

90 See also *Flöther, supra* note 82, 54 to 57; *Mantilla-Serrano*, International Arbitration and Insolvency Proceedings, Arb. Int., Vol. 11, No. 1, 1995, 51, 69.

91 This regulation has replaced the Brussels Convention.

92 "The regulation shall not apply to:
(a) …
(b) bankruptcy, proceedings relating to the winding-up of insolvent companies or other legal persons, judicial arrangements, compositions or analogous proceedings;
(c) …"

to disputes arising under the relevant bankruptcy proceedings or which are intimately related to them. The exclusion applies, for instance, to disputes regarding the order of priority according to which certain claims are admitted and satisfied in bankruptcy proceedings. It also applies to rights granted by law to the receiver which the initial debtor did not have, such as the right to contest an agreement entered into or a payment made by the debtor prior to the opening of the bankruptcy proceedings where such agreement or payment violates the principle of equal treatment of the creditors (see point C/2 above). The exception in article 1 (2) lit b of the EC-Regulation 44/2001 does *not* apply to ordinary commercial disputes regarding claims in which the receiver's legal position (whether as Claimant or as Respondent) is no different from the initial debtor's legal position.[93]

I can see no good reason to uphold international jurisdictional clauses but not to uphold (international) arbitration clauses.

(iii) Increased risk of procedural inefficiency in an international context
In an international context there are even stronger practical arguments in favour of the survival of the arbitration agreement than in a purely domestic context.

International arbitration is often more expensive than domestic arbitration, so that more money would be lost if an arbitration, commenced prior to the opening of the bankruptcy proceedings, cannot be pursued thereafter. But even if the arbitration has not started before the institution of bankruptcy proceedings, it can be quite burdensome to litigate an international dispute in state courts for most of the reasons frequently cited as arguments in favour of international arbitration (flexibility of the proceedings, language of the arbitration, no appeal etc.).

(iv) As a Claimant the estate wishes to avail itself of the New York Convention
The bankruptcy estate and the receiver do not always act as Respondent[94]. As Claimant, the receiver obviously wishes to obtain an arbitral award which is a far more international title than a decision of any state court in the world. Obviously, the legal fate of the arbitration agreement cannot depend on whether the receiver acts as Claimant or as a Respondent. Such a differentiation would amount to a blatant violation of the principle of equal treatment of both parties.[95]

---

[93] See *Konecny, supra* note 75, § 110 KO at n° 7; *Kropholler,* Zivilprozessrecht[5] Art 1, par. 33 *et seq.*; *Schlosser,* EuGVÜ, Art 1 at para. 21.

[94] One even gets the impression from the decisions rendered and from the articles written on the subject that receivers act at least as frequently in the role of Claimant in arbitrations as they do in the role of Respondent.

[95] *Petschek/Reimer/Schiemer, supra* note 76, for instance take the view that as a Claimant the receiver can rely on the arbitration agreement (page 470), but that he is not bound to it as a Respondent (page 583). In the *Casa v. Cambio* case (ICC Partial Award 6697/1990, Rev. Arb. 1992, 135, note by *P. Ancel*) the arbitral tribunal relied at least implicitly on this idea

D. *What does an international arbitrator have to bear in mind (- from an Austrian law perspective -) when confronted with the insolvency of one of the parties?*

As shown in the chapter C above, the arbitration agreement will survive in many instances. We have also seen that there is no automatic ex lege stay of pending arbitrations. We now have to see how an arbitral tribunal is to proceed if Austria is involved

1) because bankruptcy proceedings are opened in Austria against one of the parties or
2) because bankruptcy proceedings are opened outside Austria, but within the territory of the EU regulation against a debtor who has assets located in Austria or
3) because bankruptcy proceedings are opened outside the territory against a party which has assets in Austria.

1) Opening of bankruptcy proceedings in Austria

a) No assets located outside the *territory in which the European Regulation on Insolvency proceedings applies (the territory)*;

There are no specific problems

- if *neither the insolvent party (as Respondent) has any assets located outside the territory in which the European Regulation on Insolvency proceedings applies (the territory)*;

nor

- *if the bankrupt debtor or the receiver (as Claimant) wishes to enforce rights against assets located outside the territory.*

aa) The initial debtor (or the former management) will no longer be entitled to act in the proceedings. The initial debtor(s) role and position will be taken over by the receiver.

---

of equal treatment of the parties in order to reject a bankrupt Luxemburg Claimant's request to decline jurisdiction over Respondent's counter-claim: "[the tribunal] should examine whether Cambior's request for provisional measures falls within the exclusive jurisdiction of the courts of Luxembourg, as claimed by Casa, which argues that the public policy provisions adopted in the context of administration proceedings have a substantial influence on the dispute, to the extent that they render it non-arbitrable...[T]he fact that one of the parties is subject to bankruptcy proceedings is not itself sufficient to render a dispute non-arbitrable per se. The best proof of this is that, despite the fact that it was placed under administration, Casa did not hesitate to request arbitration on the basis of the arbitration clause appearing in the contract which it had signed with Cambior many years prior to being placed under administration.", see also *Fouchard/Gaillard/Goldman*, On International Commercial Arbitration 355.

bb) The receiver as Claimant is bound by an arbitration agreement entered into by the debtor

cc) Claims against the now bankrupt debtor will have to be notified in the bankruptcy proceedings and the arbitral tribunal should suspend the arbitration in order to allow the receiver (- as well as other creditors -) to consider the claim, to admit it or to contest it.

dd) If a claim raised against the initial debtor (the receiver) is contested by the receiver and/or other creditors for reasons on which also the initial debtor could have relied, the arbitration agreement remains valid, but both the Claimant and the arbitral tribunal will have to take into account

- the principle of equal treatment of creditors

as well as

- the prohibition of individual enforcement measures.

Consequently, Claimant will have to modify its claim as follows:

- The claim should now be directed against the receiver.

- A payment claim should be modified to a claim for declaratory relief (principle and amount of the claim) and the arbitral tribunal must admit such modifications or amendments of the claim.

ee) Even if the parties have not agreed on and the arbitrators have not ruled on the application of substantive Austrian Law, the arbitral tribunal will have to "take into account" Austrian insolvency law concerning the termination or continuation of contracts[96], concerning a creditor's right to compensate and other substantive issues.

Violations of any of the above international public policy principles will entail sanctions if the place of arbitration is in Austria: by the setting aside of the award and, if the place of arbitration is outside Austria: by the refusal to recognise and enforce such an award in Austria.

b) Assets located outside the territory

If a party against which bankruptcy proceedings have been opened in Austria has *assets outside the territory in which the EU regulation applies*, the arbitral tribunal will have to ascertain whether that other country or those other countries

[96] Irrespective of the place of arbitration.
The same approach was adopted in the ICC Award 10025/2000 (unpublished; place of arbitration Switzerland, Austrian chairman) involving a Slovenian bankrupt Claimant. Although the contract provided for Swiss substantive law, the Arbitral Tribunal "took into account" Slovenian bankruptcy law ("*Tatbestands-*" bzw. "*Reflexwirkung*").

would recognise the Austrian insolvency proceedings. If they do, there is no problem. If they do not, then the arbitral tribunal will have to try to find ways and means to render a decision which can ultimately be enforced in those other countries as well. One way of doing so would be to deal with the receiver *and* with the initial debtor (or with former management) and to do whatever is required to render an award which none of them could attack successfully. The award might include not only a declaratory decision, but also a payment order. The payment order would be required for those countries which do not recognise the Austrian insolvency proceedings. In all other countries, the payment order could not be enforced, but the declaratory decision would be recognised.[97]

2) Opening of bankruptcy proceedings outside Austria, but within the territory of the EU regulation against a debtor who has assets located in Austria

This scenario does not raise any specific problem because it is fully covered by the EC Regulation.

3) Opening of bankruptcy proceedings outside the territory

Exactly the same problems set out in point 1 b) above may arise and the same solutions should be applied in a situation where bankruptcy proceedings are opened outside the territory which are not recognised in Austria[98], and where the debtor has assets in Austria against which the debtor's creditors wish to enforce their claims.

Conclusions

No arbitrator or counsel can exclude the possibility of having to deal with parties that are neither rich nor healthy, but rather who are poor and ill. Nevertheless, it should always be possible to find the right answers, if one applies the following principles:

1) The parties' right to be heard must be respected and the parties must be treated equally.

2) No arbitration agreement shall lead to a denial of justice because of a party's true impecuniosity.

---

[97] In fact, the interested party might, from the outset, limit its request for recognition and enforcement to the declaratory part of the award.

[98] Austria has not concluded any insolvency treaty with any country outside the EC-Regulation. Consequently, under the present territorial approach, Austria does not and cannot recognize any insolvency proceedings opened outside the territory. The situation will change under the new law which will abandon the territorial approach in favour of the principle of universality.

3) Do not overestimate the frequency and/or gravity of problems that may arise out of a party's (alleged) impecuniosity or its insolvency.

4) Adopt a pragmatic approach and maintain flexibility in order to be able to adapt the solution to the very specific circumstances of a given case. Solutions which may be useful in domestic arbitration, may not be appropriate in an international context.

5) Arbitrators must aim for amicable and efficient legal cooperation with the bankruptcy courts and their respective bankruptcy laws.

6) Arbitrators must aim for the greatest possible recognition and efficiency for their awards.

7) Arbitrators must take advantage of and maintain their autonomy, allowing them to deal properly with situations of fraud and, for instance, to disregard fraudulent bankruptcy proceedings.

Impecuniosity of Parties and Its Effects on Arbitration: A French View

Emmanuel Gaillard[*]

In its decision of September 14, 2000, the German Federal Supreme Court of Justice (*Bundesgerichtshof* (*BGH*)) decided that the impecuniosity of a claimant had rendered the arbitration agreement it had entered into "incapable of being performed" within the meaning of Section 1032 I of the German Code of Civil Procedure.[1] In this dispute concerning claims for damages and for additional payment under a construction contract, the BGH held that the respondent's arbitration objection was therefore unjustified and that the trial court had correctly confirmed its jurisdiction regarding the dispute at issue.[2]

The result arrived at by the BGH is not new. In fact, the same court had repeatedly confirmed its view that an arbitration agreement could not be successfully invoked to object to the jurisdiction of a national court in cases where a

---

* Professor of Law, University of Paris XII; Partner of Shearman & Sterling, Paris; Head of the International Arbitration Group of Shearman & Sterling. The author wishes to thank *Joachim Knoll*, an Associate of Shearman & Sterling (Paris) in the International Arbitration Group, for his assistance in preparing this article.

1 Section 1032 I of the German Code of Civil Procedure, based on Article 8 of the UNCITRAL Model Law, provides:
"A court before which an action is brought in a matter which is the subject of an arbitration agreement shall, if the respondent raises an objection prior to the beginning of the oral hearing on the substance of the dispute, reject the action as inadmissible unless the court finds that the arbitration agreement is null and void, inoperative or incapable of being performed."

2 BGH, September 14, 2000 – III ZR 33/00 (OLG Dresden); see *e.g.* JZ 5/2001, p. 258.

party is impecunious.[3] However, the court had previously based its decisions on the fact that the arbitration agreement had been terminated for grave cause (*"Kündigung aus wichtigem Grund"*). In its latest decision, the court changed this position in that it no longer requires such termination, the arbitration agreement being, *ipso jure*, "incapable of being performed".

While the decision brings back memories of a ruling made by the Austrian Supreme Court in 1936, which held that when one party, through no fault of its own, became unable to make an advance deposit for the costs of the arbitration, the arbitral tribunal was entitled to determine that the arbitration agreement was void,[4] the position taken by the BGH is far from being commonly accepted internationally. Similar claims do not appear to have succeeded in many other jurisdictions.[5] Nevertheless, several commentators in Germany seem to welcome the result reached by the BGH, and to only criticize the court's changed view that a termination of the arbitration agreement is no longer required.[6]

It is my pleasure to provide some thoughts on this decision and on the question of the effects of impecuniosity of parties in international arbitration in general from the point of view of a French international arbitration practitioner. To introduce this perspective – under which the decision reached by the BGH must frankly be considered as rather disturbing - I would first make a few preliminary remarks on some of the main principles and policies of French arbitration law.

One of the crucial characteristics of French law is its very strong pro-arbitration bias, which has been formed by both the legislator and the French courts and which goes far beyond the one adopted by legal systems, such as that in Germany, which have based their arbitration law on the rather conservative UNCITRAL Model Law.[7] Several aspects of this policy adopted by French law will have a decisive impact on the question at issue. For instance, French arbitration law obtains a large degree of flexibility by applying different rules to domestic arbitration and to international arbitration. Further, applying a "substantive rules method", it follows rules as to the assessment of the validity of an arbitration agreement and as to the principle of competence-competence that are significantly more in favor of international arbitration than those applied in other jurisdictions, both in a procedural and a substantive sense. This policy is obvi-

---

[3] BGHZ 41, 104 (January 30, 1964); BGHZ 51, 78 (November 21, 1968); BGHZ 77, 65 (April 10, 1980); BGHZ 102, 199 (November 12, 1987).

[4] *Oberster Gerichtshof* (Austrian Supreme Court) SZ 18/151, September 4, 1936.

[5] For some cases of a similar nature that have been decided by Indian courts, see *W. Laurence Craig, William W. Park, Jan Paulsson*, International Chamber of Commerce Arbitration 270 *et seq*. (2000).

[6] See *e.g. P. Schlosser*'s note, 5 JZ 260 (2001); *G. Walter*'s note, 114 Zeitschrift für Zivilprozess 99 (2001).

[7] Obviously, French law is not the only one that followed such strong line in favor of international arbitration. Other jurisdictions, such as Switzerland, the Netherlands, and Belgium have followed the same trend in many respects.

ously further confirmed by the well-known decisions of French courts recognizing and enforcing arbitral awards that have been set aside in their country of origin.[8]

It is against this background of a jurisdiction that has chosen to clearly favor international arbitration – to an extent that is by no means always approved by commentators from other jurisdictions[9] - that my views on the effects of the "impecuniosity of parties" on arbitration, which substantially differ from those expressed by the BGH, should be seen.

I. The Notion of "Impecuniosity of Parties"

Before addressing its effects on international arbitration, some preliminary remarks should be made on what "impecuniosity" is (*A.*), and on the ways in which it can affect "the parties" in an international arbitration (*B.*).

A. "Impecuniosity"

"Impecuniosity" is obviously a rather vague term. While Black's Law Dictionary does not refer to it at all, the American Heritage Dictionary only gives very little guidance by defining "impecunious" as "lacking money; penniless". Does "impecunious" in the current context mean that a party is "too poor to afford arbitration"? If so, how does this apply to individuals and to companies? Is an individual too poor to arbitrate if it is too poor to perform its vital functions if it goes to arbitration? Is a company too poor to arbitrate if it cannot continue its activity and at the same time arbitrate?

What seems clear is that the "impecuniosity" of a party needs to be distinguished from its bankruptcy. While the bankruptcy of a party can be easily assessed on an objective and legal level, "impecuniosity" appears to act on a more subjective and factual level. The distinction between the two is crucial in light of the rather clear rules that have by now been established for cases of bankruptcy in the context of international arbitration. As will be discussed in more detail below, the distinction is particularly important from a French perspective, given that French courts have held that parties cannot rely on concepts like impossibility, hardship, or *force majeure* to escape their contractual obligation to pay a sum of money, where the sole reason not to do so is their financial situation, as long as they are not bankrupt.[10]

---

[8] See note 41 below.

[9] See *e.g. Jean-François Poudret, Sébastien Besson*, Droit comparé de l'arbitrage international (2002) (on the question of the enforcement of arbitral awards set aside in their country of origin, see pp. 962 *et seq.*); *Otto Sandrock*, To continue nationalizing or to denationalize? That's the question now in international arbitration; publication forthcoming in the 12 The American Review of International Arbitration No. 3-4 (2001).

[10] See *e.g.* Cass soc., February 20, 1996, *Ms. Chabrier v. Assoc. Perspectives*, in which the *Cour de Cassation* summarized and confirmed the French case law in this respect: "En re-

This being said, a whole number of elements will need to be taken into account in assessing whether, in the context of international arbitration, a party that is not bankrupt can rely on its financial difficulties to escape an arbitration agreement. These elements, which shall merely be put out for discussion at this point, include the following:

- It could be argued that a party having a good claim cannot possibly be impecunious. After all, a strong claim can be an asset which may enable an otherwise poor party to initiate arbitration proceedings, either by borrowing money with the help of a pledge of claim, or possibly by means of a contingency agreement with its legal counsel, where such agreement is legally feasible.
- The assessment of the effects of the impecuniosity of a party may well depend on the kind of arbitration at issue. The effects in the context of ICC arbitrations[11] can well be different from those in AAA, DIS, or ICSID arbitrations. Similarly, the situation for arbitrations held with their seat in France may be different from ones having their seat in the USA or in Germany.
- The time at which the impecuniosity of a party is assessed may be decisive. If one considered the question of the impecuniosity of a party as one regarding the validity of the arbitration agreement, it would seem that the status of the parties at the time of the arbitration agreement is the relevant one. This would leave open the question to what extent subsequent events that may affect the parties' financial situations have to be taken into account. If, on the other hand, one considered the question as

vanche, des difficultés économiques (Cass. soc., 28 avr. 1986, D. 1987, Jur. P. 474, obs. *J.-P. Karaquillo*), la perte d'un marché (Cass. soc., 27 nov. 1990, n° 87.40407) ou la liquidation judiciaire d'une entreprise (Cass. soc., 20 oct. 1993, Bull. Civ. V, n° 240; RJS 1993, p. 724, n° 1225; Dr. soc. 1993, p. 970) [...] ne constituent pas des cas de force majeure."; see *also Philippe Malaurie, Laurent Aynès*, Cours de Droit Civil – Tome VI: Les Obligations 485 (10th edition, 1999) ("L'événement doit être irrésistible; c'est la condition principale; s'il pouvait être surmonté, bien que l'exécution eût été difficile et onéreuse, le débiteur serait responsable de n'avoir pas exécuté: *il n'existe pas de force majeure financière.*") (emphasis added).

11 See *Yves Derains, Eric A. Schwartz*, A Guide to the New ICC Rules of Arbitration 319 (1998) who explain: "Occasionally, it is the Claimant party that is unable to pay its share of the advance on costs. From time to time, the Court is, thus, requested by Claimants pleading indigence to accord them special treatment by, for example, fixing the advance on costs at a lower level than it normally would based on the Cost Schedules. As a general matter, no matter how much the Court may sympathize with such requests, it has not considered it appropriate to try to take account of the parties financial circumstances in fixing the amount of the advance on costs."); see *also W. Laurence Craig, William W. Park, Jan Paulsson, supra* note 5 at 270; see also Award in ICC Case No. 9667 of 1998, 127 Journal du Droit International 1096 (2000), and *D. Hascher*'s note.

an issue of performance, the financial situation of the party would only be assessed at the time when the party brings its claim, so that events subsequent to the arbitration agreement would clearly be taken into account.

- A party may be impecunious as a result of bad economic decisions it made. It may, on the other hand, find itself in this position for reasons entirely beyond its own influence and fault. In light of this, should the reasons for the impecuniosity of a party be examined in assessing its effects on the arbitration?[12]
- Possibly most importantly, the question of who is to be the judge over the cause of a party's impecuniosity and its effects, and on the basis of what rules of law such decision is made, is crucial. Is it the party itself, the national judge, or the arbitral tribunal that decides upon these questions?

All this goes to show that the question of impecuniosity is by far not as simple as it may seem on its face. The answers to all of the questions set out above can have a decisive impact on the effect such impecuniosity can have in arbitral proceedings. Most of them will be discussed in more detail below.

B. Impecuniosity "of Parties"

Clearly, a distinction has to be made depending on which of the parties invokes its impecuniosity. Very different kinds of issues arise depending on whether it is the potential claimant or the respondent who claims to be impecunious.

Where a claimant who has accepted to sign an arbitration agreement and who allegedly has a good claim invokes its incapacity to pay its lawyers, the arbitrators, and possible administrative fees, it seems, at least at first sight, that its intention is quite simply to get out of the arbitration agreement it has originally signed. Similarly, a respondent should obviously not be entitled to successfully argue that it is too poor to be sued in arbitration. Fortunately, in such case, the claimant can normally still sue an impecunious respondent, but it will likely have to finance the entirety of the procedure, at least by way of advances on fees and costs.[13] In cases where the respondent has a counterclaim, the respondent turns to be claimant in respect of the counterclaim and the first proposition applies, *i.e.* it should not be allowed to escape its arbitration agreement by arguing that it is impecunious. It should be noted in this respect that, normally, a respon-

---

[12] The BGH merely explains in this respect that the limits of a party's right to invoke its impecuniosity lie in its reliance being vexatious, contrary to good faith, or unethical, within the meaning of Sections 226, 242, and 826 of the German Civil Code.

[13] See *e.g.* Article 30 (3) of the 1998 ICC Rules of Arbitration.

dent who does not pay for the costs of the arbitration can still appear and be heard in the arbitration, but its counterclaims will not be heard.[14]

Finally, it should be noted that the evaluation of the effects of the impecuniosity of one party should differ considerably depending on who raises the impecuniosity. In one case, a party invokes its own impecuniosity and argues that, as a result, it should not be forced to arbitrate. In the other case, the party not being impecunious argues that the impecunious party should be bound by the arbitration agreement, but that the constellation is unfair since even if it wins in the arbitration, it will very likely never recover the awarded sum and nevertheless pay the entirety of the costs of the arbitration. Obviously, the latter is one of the main arguments for a request for security for costs,[15] if not, to make the stakes even higher, a security for claims.

---

[14] On this question, see *e.g. Yves Derains, Eric A. Schwartz, supra* note 11 at 319; *W. Laurence Craig, William W. Park, Jan Paulsson, supra* note 5 at 264; *Stephen Bond*, ICC (Topic 2: Refusal by a party (a) to make advance deposits for the costs of the arbitration, and (b) to submit a statement of defence), in: ICCA Congress Series No. 5, p. 120, 121 (*A. J. van den Berg* ed., 1991); *J. Gillis Wetter, Charl Priem,* Costs and Their Allocation in International Commercial Arbitrations, 2 The American Review of International Arbitration 249, 325 (1991); *Michael Bühler,* Costs in ICC Arbitration: A Practitioner's View, 3 The American Review of International Arbitration 117, 147 et seq. (1992); *Claude Reymond,* Note sur l'avance des frais de l'arbitrage et sa répartition, in: Etudes de procédure et d'arbitrage en l'honneur de Jean-François Poudret 495, 499 (1999).

[15] See *e.g. Otto Sandrock,* The Cautio Judicatum Solvi in Arbitration Proceedings or The Duty of an Alien Claimant to Provide Security for the Costs of the Defendant, 1997 Journal of International Arbitration 17, 34, who lists as one of the instances that are recognized as special circumstances justifying a *cautio judicatum solvi* the case where "the claimant is too poor to finance the advance deposit for the fees of the arbitrators out of his own pocket, but must avail himself of the financial aid of a third person"; see also *Noah D. Rubins,* La garantie des frais de justice en arbitrage, 2000 International Business Law Journal 380, 382, who explains: "Le besoin d'un cautionnement des frais de justice découle de l'objectif de certains systèmes consistant à remettre la partie gagnante en l'état et ce, en contraignant son adversaire au paiement des honoraires, frais de justice et autres dépens supportés par la partie gagnante à raison de sa requête ou de sa défense. [...] Si du fait de leur résidence à l'étranger, de leur impécuniosité ou du transfert de leurs actifs hors du ressort de la juridiction saisie, les plaignants ne peuvent être atteints par un jugement, cet objectif est contrarié". The author would submit, however, that the mere fact that a party is suffering financial difficulties or is the subject of bankruptcy proceedings is not sufficient, in itself, to form the basis of a request for security; see Fouchard Gaillard Goldman On International Commercial Arbitration ¶1256 (*E. Gaillard* and *J. Savage* eds., 1999); *Michael O'Reilly,* Costs in Arbitration Proceedings 80 *et seq.* (1995); *Catherine Li,* Evaluating the Various Non-Litigation Processes for Resolving Disputes: The Cost-Effectiveness Approach, 18 Journal of International Arbitration 435, 439 (2001); on the issue generally, see *Andreas Reiner,* Les mesures provisoires et conservatoires et l'Arbitrage international, notamment l'Arbitrage CCI, 1998 Journal de Droit International 853, 892 *et seq.*

These preliminary remarks being made, we shall now turn to the main question at issue, being whether, from a French perspective, a party can rely on its impecuniosity to avoid an arbitration agreement.

II. Can a Party Rely on its Own Impecuniosity to Avoid the Arbitration Agreement?

The type of situation that gave rise to the decision of the BGH was a case where a party relied on its own impecuniosity to avoid the arbitration agreement. Before examining the French approach to this question, it might be helpful to give an example that transposes the situation into an international context.

A large French company enters into a contract with a small German company. Their contract, which is to be performed in Germany, contains an ICC arbitration clause with Paris as the place of arbitration. The German company gets into financial difficulties and addresses the German courts,[16] asking them to declare the arbitration agreement "incapable of being performed", on the basis that it cannot afford the arbitration. In view of the decision of the BGH, and the lack of any statutory distinction between domestic and international arbitration, should the German courts follow this request? Now take the reverse case: a large German company contracts with a small French company to perform a task in France. The contract contains an arbitration agreement. The French company then gets into financial difficulties and addresses the French courts asking them to declare the arbitration agreement invalid (or alternatively addresses the French courts with a claim of its own), while the German company insists upon the validity of the arbitration clause and initiates arbitration proceedings.

In trying to examine how a French court would decide, we shall first consider how the issue would be characterized procedurally (*A.*) and what rules of law would be applied to decide upon the question of the validity of the arbitration agreement (*B.*). We shall then assess the merits of the issue (*C.*). Finally, we shall consider what the practical consequences of the German case law would be (*D.*) and what policy considerations should, in our view, impact upon the decision (*E.*).

A. The Procedural Characterization of the Issue

The first main aspect to be taken into account in assessing the current question is that in France, an alleged invalidity of an arbitration agreement would almost undoubtedly not be examined by the national courts in the first place. Rather, as one result of the strong pro-arbitration bias of French law, it would be for the ar-

---

[16] Which it can under Article 5 (1)(a) of the EC Council Regulation No. 44/2001 of December 2000 on Jurisdiction and the Recognition and Enforcement of Judgments in Civil and Commercial Matters ("A person domiciled in a Member State may, in another Member State, be sued: in matters relating to a contract, in the courts for the place of performance of the obligation in question.")

bitral tribunal to examine this question on the basis of its competence-competence.

Article 1458 of the New French Code of Civil Procedure provides that a court, in a case where a dispute has not yet been submitted to the arbitral tribunal, must declare that it lacks jurisdiction, unless it finds that the arbitration agreement is "manifestly null". Accordingly, the court is to carry out only a *prima facie* review of the existence and validity of the arbitration agreement.[17] Based on the competence-competence principle, it is, at this stage, exclusively up to the arbitral tribunal to carry out an in-depth analysis of the existence and validity of the arbitration agreement and, if necessary, to render a separate award on jurisdiction in this respect.[18] Only if one of the parties subsequently brings an action to set aside such award or to have it enforced in France would French courts have to examine the validity of the arbitration agreement in depth.[19]

Section 1032 of the German Code of Civil Procedure, on the other hand, following the wording of Article II (3) of the New York Convention and Article 8

---

[17] For a discussion of this principle and for references to French case law on this clause, see Fouchard Gaillard Goldman On International Commercial Arbitration, *supra* note 15 at ¶672; see also *e.g. Antonias Dimolitsa*, Separability and Kompetenz-Kompetenz, in: ICCA Congress Series No. 9, 217, 238 *et seq.* (1999); for a similar position taken under Swiss law (in cases where the place of arbitration is in Switzerland), see *Tribunal Fédéral*, April 29, 1996, *Fondation M. v. Banque X*, 1996 ASA Bulletin 527, 1996 Revue Suisse de Droit International et de Droit Européen 586, and *F. Knoepfler*'s note. The *Tribunal Fédéral* held in this case that "[t]he arbitration agreement at issue has every appearance of being valid, without any manifest sign, the obviousness of which would point to a prima facie examination, of elements which would allow it to be qualified as null and void, inoperative or incapable of being performed." However, see also the different position taken by the *Tribunal Fédéral* in a case where the place of arbitration was in a foreign country, stating that a mere *prima facie* examination of the arbitration agreement by the court was not sufficient since it was "at odds with the court's duty to examine its own jurisdiction exhaustively before deciding on the merits, as well as with the possible effect of a decision by a court not to hear the merits." *Tribunal Fédéral, Compagnie de Navigation et Transports S.A. v. MSC Mediterranean Shipping Company S.A.*, 1995 ASA Bulletin 503, and *J.-F. Poudret*'s and *G. Cautier*'s note at 383.

[18] Particularly in complex disputes, where the examination of the merits of the case can be very time-consuming, such awards on jurisdiction are certainly preferable in that they avoid unnecessary loss of time and costs. For a more detailed discussion of this issue, see *Emmanuel Gaillard*, L'effet négatif de la compétence-compétence, in: Etudes de procédure et d'arbitrage en l'honneur de Jean François Poudret 387 (Lausanne, 1999); Fouchard Gaillard Goldman On International Commercial Arbitration, *supra* note 15 at ¶677 *et seq.*

[19] As the *Cour de Cassation* confirmed in its *V2000* decision, without even referring to the hypothesis of the arbitration clause being patently void, the arbitrators must "apply the arbitration clause subject to the subsequent review by the courts in order to verify their own competence, particularly as regards the arbitrability of the dispute"; Cass. 1e civ., May 21, 1997, *Renault v. V2000 (formerly Jaguar France)*, 1997 Revue de l'Arbitrage 537 and *E. Gaillard*'s note; 1998 Revue Crit. DIP 87 and *V. Heuzé*'s note.

of the UNCITRAL Model Law, allows courts to hear the merits of a dispute without referring it to arbitration, if they find that the arbitration agreement is "null and void, inoperative or incapable of being performed". While this is not clear from the wording of the clause, it seems accepted that German courts, in assessing the existence and validity of the arbitration agreement under Section 1032 of the German Code of Civil Procedure, are not limited to a *prima facie* examination of the arbitration agreement, but that they may fully address the question of the agreement's effectiveness.[20]

From a French perspective, such practice, which obviously substantially weakens the negative effect of the competence-competence rule, is most unfortunate. In any event, it seems obvious that the position taken by French courts on the question at issue is likely to be very different from that adopted by German courts. In all likelihood, French courts would not initially address the question of the effect of the impecuniosity in detail, but refer it to the arbitral tribunal and only potentially examine it in detail in the context of an action to set aside an award rendered by the arbitral tribunal, or to enforce a foreign award in France.

B. The Rules of Law Applicable in Deciding upon the Validity of the Arbitration Agreement

The second question to be addressed is what rules of law French courts would apply in deciding upon the validity of an arbitration agreement. In this respect, the particularity of French law is that French courts do not apply the choice of law method, but rather apply substantive rules of international law in order to decide upon the validity of an arbitration agreement. In two series of decisions starting in the late 1980s, French courts have established that, in an international context, "the arbitration agreement has a validity and effectiveness of its own", and that its validity should be autonomous of any national law and should only be governed by the very limited requirements of international public policy:

> "in the field of international arbitration, the principle of the autonomy of the arbitration agreement is of general application, as an international substantive rule up-

[20] See *e.g. Peter Schlosser*, La nouvelle législation allemande sur l'arbitrage, 1998 Revue de l'Arbitrage 291, 300; *Klaus Peter Berger*, Germany Adopts the UNCITRAL Model Law, 1 Int'l Arb. L. Rev. 121, 122 (1998); it should be noted that Section 1040 III 2 of the German Code of Civil Procedure further quite significantly limits the principle of competence-competence of arbitrators, giving the courts a chance to review the arbitral tribunal's decision on its own competence, thus giving the national courts the "last word" as to the jurisdiction of the arbitral tribunal, even in the absence of a proper award on jurisdiction made by the arbitral tribunal (Section 1040 III 2 provides: "If the arbitral tribunal considers that is has jurisdiction, it rules on a plea referred to in subsection 2 of this section in general by means of a preliminary ruling. In this case, any party may request, within one month after having received written notice of that ruling, the court to decide the matter. While such a request is pending, the arbitral tribunal may continue the arbitral proceedings and make an award."); see on this subject *G. Walter*'s note, 114 Zeitschrift für Zivilprozess (2001) 99, 103.

> holding the legality of the arbitration agreement, quite apart from any reference to a system of choice of law, because the validity of the agreement must be judged solely in the light of the requirements of international public policy"[21]

Finally, the French *Cour de Cassation* endorsed this substantive rule method in its now famous *Dalico* decision in which it held that:

> "by virtue of a substantive rule of international arbitration, the arbitration agreement is legally independent of the main contract containing or referring to it, and the existence and effectiveness of the arbitration agreement are to be assessed, subject to the mandatory rules of French law and international public policy, on the basis of the parties' common intention, there being no need to refer to any national law."[22]

This position adopted by French courts did not remain uncriticized, even within France. Commentators argued that in reality, the arbitration agreement could not be entirely independent of national law or that the view that an autonomous arbitration agreement necessarily had its "own effectiveness" was not tenable.[23] However, such views appear to ignore that the fact that the validity of the arbitration agreement is examined solely by reference to the French conception of international public policy merely means that it is no longer affected by the idiosyncrasies of local law. In fact, by exclusively taking into account the

---

[21] CA Paris, December 17, 1991, *Gatoil v. National Iranian Oil Co.*, 1993 Revue de l'Arbitrage 281; for an English translation, see 7 Int'l Arb. Rep. B1 (July 1992); for references to the entire series of decisions and commentaries, see Fouchard Gaillard Goldman on International Commercial Arbitration, *supra* note 15 at ¶436.

[22] Cass. 1e civ., December 20, 1993, *Comité populaire de la municipalité de Khoms El Mergeb v. Dalico Contractors*, 121 J.D.I. 432 (1994), and *E. Gaillard*'s note; 121 J.D.I. 690 (1994), and *E. Loquin*'s note; 1994 Revue de l'Arbitrage 116, and *H. Gaudemet-Tallon*'s note; 1994 Rev. Crit. DIP 663, and *P. Mayer*'s note; While taking a very different theoretical route, the U.S. Court of Appeals for the Third Circuit, in interpreting Article II(3) of the New York Convention, arrived at a similar result in *Rhône Méditerranée Compagnia Francese di Assicurazioni e Riassicurasioni v. Achille Lauro* (712 F. 2d 50 (3d Cir. 1983) and IX ICCA Yearbook Com. Arb. 474-482 (1984)): "We conclude that the meaning of Art. II section 3 which is most consistent with the overall purposes of the Convention is that an agreement to arbitrate is 'null and void' only (a) when it is subject to an internationally recognized defense such as duress, mistake, fraud or waiver [...] or (b) when it contravenes fundamental policies of the forum State. The 'null and void' language must be read narrowly, for the signatory nations have jointly declared a general policy of enforceability of agreements to arbitrate."

[23] See *e.g. Pierre Mayer*, L'autonomie de l'arbitre international dans l'appréciation de sa propre compétence, in: Collected Courses of The Hague Academy of International Law, Vol. 217, Year 1989, Part V, ¶110; *H. Gaudemet-Tallon*, note following CA Paris, March 26, 2001, 1991 Revue de l'Arbitrage 456, 469. For an analysis of the criticism expressed against the French case law in this respect, see Fouchard Gaillard Goldman on International Commercial Arbitration, *supra* note 15 at ¶438-441.

French legal system's view of the fundamental requirements of justice in an international context, it is particularly suited to international arbitration.

For this reason, French courts are significantly more hesitant to declare an arbitration agreement invalid than German courts that apply the choice of law method in determining the applicable law to his question.[24]

C. The Merits of the Issue

Having shown that French courts would be very unlikely to decide upon the validity of the arbitration agreement before the arbitral tribunal, and that the test they would apply in this case would be restricted to the very limited requirements of international public policy, we shall now address the question whether, under this test, French courts would consider the impecuniosity of a party to be a sufficient ground to render an arbitration agreement invalid, be it in the context of the enforcement of a foreign award, or in a procedure for the annulment of an award rendered in France.

The BGH made its decision on the basis that, in its view, the respondent could not successfully invoke the arbitration agreement since it was "incapable of being performed" within the meaning of Section 1032 I of the German Code of Civil Procedure, based on the argument that the claimant would not have been able to advance the costs of the arbitration, and that these costs could not have been covered otherwise. The court further set out that there had been no reason to believe that the respondent in the arbitration would have been ready to advance the costs of the arbitration and the claimant's lawyers' fees, particularly in light of the fact that, like the claimant, the respondent was impecunious and had executed an affirmation *in lieu* of oath to that effect. Finally, the respondent's employer's liability insurance would only have covered the costs incurred by the respondent in the arbitration, and not those incurred by the claimant.

Different from Section 1032 of the German Code of Civil Procedure, the French New Code of Civil Procedure provides in its Article 1458:[25]

---

[24] See *P. Schlosser*'s note, 2001 JZ 260, who argues that it would be "rather bold" to develop a uniform law to be applied to the question of the validity or the nullity of arbitration agreements which could derogate from the national law, and which would not be subject to the control of a supra-national court instance. On this question generally, see *Antonias Dimolitsa, supra* note 17 at 217, 242 ("Depending on the extent to which the autonomy principle is recognized in their legal systems, the courts will apply conflict of laws rules for this purpose in order to determine which law is applicable to this question, or alternatively proceed with a certain notion of the effectiveness of the arbitration agreement in international trade, whether or not this has become a *règle matérielle*"); *Abhishek M. Singhvi*, Article II (3) of the New York Convention and the Courts, in: ICCA Congress Series No. 9, 204, 214 (1999).

[25] Article 1458 applies to both domestic and international arbitration; see Cass. 1e civ., June 28, 1989, *Eurodif v. République Islamique d'Iran*, 1989 Bull. Civ. I, No. 255; 1989 Revue de l'Arbitrage 653, 2d decision.

> "When a dispute which has been referred to an arbitral tribunal by virtue of an arbitration agreement is brought before a court, the latter must rule that it lacks jurisdiction to hear the dispute.
>
> If the dispute has not as yet been referred to the arbitral tribunal, the court again must rule that it lacks jurisdiction, unless the arbitration agreement is manifestly null."

As was explained above, based on the substantive rule method, French law is extremely liberal with regard to international arbitration agreements and, consequently, the test to be applied by the courts under Article 1458 is a very strict one.[26]

Tracing the language of Section 1032 of the German Code of Civil Procedure and of Article II(3) of the New York Convention, three possible grounds might be imaginable in an attempt to escape an arbitration agreement, namely that the arbitration is null and void, that it is invalid or inoperative, or that it is incapable of being performed. The likely view of French courts on these three options shall now be examined in turn, on the basis of the above-described policy adopted by French courts, as well as the principles applied in interpreting the New York Convention, as described by one of the most eminent commentators as: "[h]aving regard to the 'pro-enforcement bias' of the Convention, the words should be construed narrowly, and the invalidity of the arbitration agreement should be accepted in manifest cases only."[27]

First, it might be contended that the impecuniosity of a party could render the arbitration agreement null and void, implying that it was never valid. In this context, the classic argument would be to raise an alleged lack of arbitrability of the issue. However, none of the classic types of dispute that may potentially be considered as non-arbitrable, such as for example consumer disputes, labor disputes, or disputes involving family law, are at issue in the current case. Also, no issue of bankruptcy – in which arbitrability considerations may in fact become relevant – arises in the discussed situation where the impecuniosity of the party has not led to a bankruptcy situation. Further, no other generally accepted grounds for the nullity of an arbitration agreement, such as lack of consent, duress, fraud, undue influence, or non-compliance with the formal requirements

---

26 See *e.g. Philippe Fouchard*, La coopération de Président du Tribunal de grande instance à l'arbitrage, 1985 Revue de l'Arbitrage 27, who explains that an arbitration agreement is only manifestly null where "this nullity is obvious, indisputable and unable to be called into question by any serious arguments"; see also CA Paris, December 7, 1994, *Société V 2000 v. Société Project XJ 220 ITD et al.*, 1996 Revue de l'Arbitrage 245 and *Ch. Jarosson*'s note.

27 *Albert Jan van den Berg*, The New York Arbitration Convention of 1958 – Towards a Uniform Judicial Interpretation 155 (1981); see also the above mentioned decision by the U.S. Court of Appeals for the Third Circuit in *Rhône Méditerranée Compagnia Francese di Assicurazioni e Riassicurasioni v. Achille Lauro*; 712 F. 2d 50 (3d Cir. 1983) and IX ICCA Yearbook 474-482 (1984).

for the arbitration clause apply in the current case.[28] For instance, in my experience, arbitral tribunals in France[29] as well as French courts would not grant a request to invalidate an arbitration agreement in a case where one party argues that in signing the agreement it had made a mistake, that it had already been in a bad financial situation, that it therefore needed the contract very badly and thus signed the arbitration clause, in other words that it was under some kind of duress.

The second possible contention, following the grounds set out in Section 1032 of the German Code of Civil Procedure, would be to argue that the arbitration agreement is inoperative, meaning that it has subsequently lost its validity, such as for example by a change of circumstance, the occurrence of a resolutory condition, the expiry of a contractually agreed deadline for the validity of the agreement, the termination of the agreement by mutual consent, or, most relevantly in the current case, as a result of the termination for grave cause by one of the parties.[30] The latter is the approach that had been adopted by the BGH before the reform of the German arbitration law, which came into force on January 1, 1998,[31] when it had already repeatedly confirmed that an arbitration agreement may be rendered invalid as a result of the impecuniosity of one party. However, as was mentioned above, at that time, the court had made it a condition for such result that the arbitration agreement had been terminated for grave cause,[32] on the basis that it was not reasonable and acceptable to hold a party bound by this agreement.[33]

Again, I would not agree with such view. Despite the fact that it has also been argued by other commentators that an arbitration agreement is "inoperative" in cases where the parties have implicitly or explicitly revoked the agreement,[34] I am convinced that French courts would not allow a party to escape an arbitration

---

28 See for these examples *van den Berg, supra* note 27 at 156.

29 For a summary of arbitral case law on the question whether an arbitration agreement exists or is valid, see *e.g. Antonias Dimolitsa, supra* note 17 at 245-248.

30 See *e.g. G. Walter*'s note, 114 Zeitschrift für Zivilprozess (2001) 99, 101.

31 Gesetz zur Neuregelung des Schiedsverfahrensrechts, v. 30.12.1997 (BGBl. I S. 3224).

32 BGHZ 41, 104 (January 30, 1964); BGHZ 51, 78 (November 21, 1968); BGHZ 77, 65 (April 10, 1980); BGHZ 102, 199 (November 12, 1987); for a detailed discussion of the termination of arbitration agreements for "grave cause", which is based on the good faith provision in Section 242 of the German Civil Code, see *Walther J. Habscheid*, Die Kündigung des Schiedsvertrages aus wichtigem Grund, 41 Konkurs-, Treuhand-, und Schiedsgerichtswesen 285 (1980).

33 The view that the impecuniosity of a party can justify the termination of the arbitration agreement for grave cause has been widely welcomed in German commentary; see *e.g. G. Walter*'s note, 114 Zeitschrift für Zivilprozess 99, 102 (2001); *Jörg Risse*, Undurchführbarkeit der Schiedsvereinbarung bei Mittellosigkeit des Klägers, 56 Betriebs-Berater, Beilage 6, 11 (2001).

34 See *e.g. van den Berg, supra* note 27 at 158.

agreement by attempting to unilaterally terminate such agreement on the basis of its financial difficulties. As was mentioned above, under French law, as long as a party is not bankrupt, it cannot rely on a lack of money alone in order to escape its contractual obligations.[35]

Finally, it has been submitted – and this is also the approach now adopted by the BGH – that the impecuniosity of a party could render the arbitration agreement "incapable of being performed". Again, I do not agree. Cases of arbitration agreements that are "incapable of being performed" are cases where the purpose of the agreement cannot possibly be achieved anymore, for instance because the arbitral tribunal has already declared that it does not have jurisdiction, because the chosen arbitrator is not available or because the chosen arbitral institution does no longer exist.[36] As van den Berg rightly states in his comment on Article II (3) of the New York Convention, the impecuniosity of a party does not render an arbitration agreement "incapable of being performed":

> "The words 'incapable of being performed' would seem to apply to those cases where the arbitration agreement cannot be effectively set into motion. This may happen where the arbitral clause is too vaguely worded, or other terms of the contract contradict the parties' intention to arbitrate. It would also apply to cases where the arbitrator named in the agreement refuses to accept his nomination, or the appointing authority designated in the agreement refuses to make the appointment of the arbitrator. [...] The possibility of a lack of financial resources to satisfy an award must be deemed *not* to render an arbitration agreement incapable of being performed within the meaning of Article II(3).[37]

In my opinion, the approach followed by French courts in this respect would be rather similar to the one adopted by the English Court of Appeal in *Haendler & Natermann GmbH v. Janos Paczy,*[38] in which it was held:

---

[35] It has even been argued that this rule constitutes a general principle of private law; see *Jörg Risse*, *supra* note 33 at 11; see also Article 6.2.1. of the UNIDROIT Principles of International Commercial Contracts 145 (UNIDROIT ed., 1994), which provides that the mere fact that the performance of the contract becomes more onerous, *i.e.* that it entails a higher economic burden for one of the parties does not suffice to assume that there is "hardship"; for a reference to this principle in arbitral case law, see Final Award in ICC Case No. 8486 of 1996, XXIV ICCA Yearbook Com. Arb. 162, 167 (1999).

[36] For examples for these cases in German law, see *e.g. Münch*, in: Münchener Kommentar zur Zivilprozessordnung 1077 (2nd edition, 2001) Vol. 3, commentary on § 1032, note 4.

[37] *Van den Berg*, *supra* note 27 at 159; *van den Berg* further emphasizes that, in any event, "doubts should be resolved in favour of arbitration." This interpretation seems to be accepted, also by German commentators: see *e.g. G. Walter*'s note, 114 Zeitschrift für Zivilprozess (2001) 99, 101; *Jörg Risse*, *supra* note 33 at 11.

[38] December 3-4, 1980, 1981 Lloyd's Law Reports 302; IX ICCA Yearbook Com. Arb. 445 (1984). In this case, the impecunious claimant brought an action before the High Court in London, despite the existence of an arbitration agreement, with the help of a legal aid certificate it had obtained. The claimant stated that legal aid would not be available for arbitration proceedings, and that it would be unable to otherwise meet the costs of ICC arbitra-

> "In my judgment, on the true construction of these words, 'incapable of being performed' relates to the arbitration agreement under consideration. The incapacity of one party to that agreement to implement his obligations under the agreement does not, in my judgment, render the agreement one which is incapable of performance within the Section any more than the inability of a purchaser under a contract for purchase of land to find the purchase price when the time comes to complete the sale could be said to render the contract for sale incapable of performance. The agreement only becomes incapable of performance in my view if the circumstances are such that it could no longer be performed, even if both parties were ready, able and willing to perform it. Impecuniosity is not, I think, a circumstance of that kind."

In summary, French courts would, in my opinion, adopt a position that is very different from, if not contrary to, that adopted by the BGH. They would be most unlikely to find any merit in the contention that an arbitration clause should be declared null and void, invalid, or "incapable of being performed" because one of the parties is impecunious.

D. The Practical Consequences of the German Case Law

In addition to the strictly legal assessment of the question at issue, an argument that an arbitration agreement should be rendered invalid as a result of the impecuniosity of a party should be rejected from a point of view of the practical consequences this would have.

It seems quite likely that, as a consequence of the decision of the BGH, the years to come will see a number of parties arguing that since they cannot afford to arbitrate, they have a right to ignore the arbitration agreement they entered into, and that instead they should be allowed to go to their own courts. Similar attempts have repeatedly been carried out in the past, fortunately in vain: at one point, it was very fashionable to attempt to escape an arbitration agreement by arguing that such agreement was invalid because the underlying contract was invalid. These attempts have consistently been rejected, based on the principle of the autonomy of the arbitration agreement.[39] Later, it became fashionable to try to achieve the same goal by arguing that the dispute was not arbitrable, and that the national law of a party prevented that party from arbitrating, for example based on the fact that it was a public entity. Again, these attempts were consistently rejected in the context of international arbitration.[40]

---

tion. The defendant successfully applied for a stay of the High Court proceedings. The Court of Appeal had to decide upon the appeal against the High Court's later decision not to remove this stay of the proceedings.

[39] See Fouchard Gaillard Goldman on International Commercial Arbitration, *supra* note 15 at ¶389 *et seq.*

[40] For a detailed discussion of this issue, see Fouchard Gaillard Goldman on International Commercial Arbitration, *supra* note 15 at ¶534-558; see also *Claude Reymond*, Souveraineté de l'Etat et participation à l'arbitrage, 1985 Revue de l'Arbitrage 517.

The practical consequences of allowing such tactics in the case of the impecuniosity of a party are unthinkable. To take an example, say a large German contractor is carrying out an infrastructure project in Serbia. The parties not only include an arbitration clause in their contract, but they also agree to enter into arbitration agreements with their local sub-contractors, providing for ICC arbitration in Vienna. Disputes under a sub-contract arise and the sub-contractor, having its own claims against the German contractor, announces that it cannot afford to go to arbitration in Vienna and that it will therefore bring its claims before its own local courts. The local courts may follow the German example and conclude that due to the impecuniosity of the sub-contractor, the arbitration agreement was incapable of being performed. Protracted litigation may arise on this sole issue, detracting the parties from processing on the merits of the case. However, with the arbitration agreement having been declared invalid by the Belgrade courts, the German contractor will be left with very little protection.

Another example may serve to show further difficulties which the German case law would provoke if applied in international arbitration. A small German sub-contractor enters into a sub-contract with a large French company for a project to be performed in Germany. The sub-contract contains an arbitration agreement providing for ICC arbitration with the seat of the arbitration in Zurich. Both parties have claims against each other. While the sub-contractor claims that the main contractor has not paid the amount owed for a certain service, the main contractor claims damages based on the allegation that the sub-contractor has not performed the sub-contract. The French contractor brings its claims in front of the arbitral tribunal, having paid the entirety of the advances on costs, and the arbitral tribunal proceeds with the arbitration. At the same time, since it claims not to be in a position to pay the advances on costs for its counterclaim, the German sub-contractor successfully brings an action before German courts. Later, after an arbitral award and a court decision in Germany have been rendered – both of which are likely not to be entirely consistent – the French contractor requests to have the award enforced in France. Thus, the French court will have to decide whether it enforces the award or whether it gives preference to the decision of the German court which invalidated the arbitration agreement, based on the impecuniosity of the German sub-contractor. In light of the case law rendered in the *Hilmarton* and *Chromalloy*[41] matters, it is

---

[41] *Cour de Cassation*, June 10, 1997, *Société OTV v. Société Hilmarton*, 1997 Revue de l'Arbitrage 376, and *P. Fouchard*'s note; US District Court, District of Columbia, July 31, 1996, *Chromalloy Aeroservices v. République arabe d'Egypte*, 1997 Revue de l'Arbitrage 439; CA Paris, January 14, 1997, *République arabe d'Egypte v. Société Chromalloy Aeroservices*, 1997 Revue de l'Arbitrage 395, and *P. Fouchard*'s note; see also *P. Fouchard*, La portée internationale de l'annulation de la sentence arbitrale dans son pays d'origine, 1997 Revue de l'Arbitrage 329; *E. Gaillard*, The Enforcement of Awards Set Aside In The Country Of Origin, 14 ICSID Review 16 (1999); *J. Paulsson*, Rediscovering

submitted that French courts would most likely enforce the arbitral award, thus ignoring the decision rendered by the German courts.

E. The Policy Underlying the German Case Law

The main reasoning adopted by the BGH in invalidating the arbitration agreement at issue is that, otherwise, the mere lack of money would lead to a party losing its fundamental right to judicial relief. In this respect, the court refers, though only indirectly, to Article 6 of the European Convention for the Protection of Human Rights and Fundamental Freedoms.[42] In other words, where a potential claimant does not possess the required financial means to carry out the arbitration proceedings, and where no other legal and financial help is available, the claimant should not be put in a position where it could not obtain any judicial relief whatsoever.[43] Further, the BGH and the commentators attempt to justify the results reached under both the old and the new law by arguing that the disadvantages faced by the respondent are mitigated given that the respondent may still insist on the agreed arbitration procedure by advancing the costs – including the other side's lawyers' fees – for such proceedings.[44]

While, on their face, these policy arguments may seem rather convincing, their effects are disastrous in that they entirely ignore the reasons why parties in international business agree to have their disputes settled by way of arbitration in the first place. It should be remembered that an abandonment of the arbitral competence, while significant in any event, is even significantly more harmful

the N.Y. Convention: Further Reflections on Chromalloy, 12 Mealey's International Arbitration Report 1 (1997, No. 4).

42 Article 6 I provides: "In the determination of his civil rights and obligations or of any criminal charge against him, everyone is entitled to a fair and public hearing within a reasonable time by an independent and impartial tribunal established by law. [...]" See also *Jörg Risse*, *supra* note 33 at 11; for a discussion of the policy considerations under German law before 1980, see *Walther J. Habscheid*, *supra* note 32 at 285; for a discussion of the applicability of Article 6 in international arbitration, see *Robert Briner*, *Fabian von Schlabrendorff*, Article 6 of the European Convention on Human Rights and its Bearing upon International Arbitration, in: Law of International Business and Dispute Settlement in the 21st Century – Liber Amicorum Karl-Heinz Böckstiegel 89-109 (2001).

43 See *Gerhard Walter*'s note, 114 Zeitschrift für Zivilprozess (2001) 99; *Peter Schlosser*, Das Recht der internationalen privaten Schiedsgerichtsbarkeit 342 (2nd edition, 1989); *Schlosser* particularly refers to the above-mentioned decision of the English Court of Appeal in *Haendler & Natermann GmbH v. Janos Paczy*, which, in his view, would leave the claimant in that case devoid of any judicial relief.

44 See *e.g. Jörg Risse*, *supra* note 33 at 11; see also the earlier decision in BGHZ 77, 65 (April 10, 1980).

in international situations, given that international arbitral awards are often far easier to enforce than court decisions.[45]

Particularly in the context of a notion as 'soft' as the one of "impecuniosity", national courts should not offer parties a way to escape the arbitration agreement they entered into. It should remain the absolute last resort for parties to arbitration agreements to resort to national courts, be it based on specific grounds that the arbitration agreement was void or on the general ground that justice had not been done, which should be reserved for cases in which forming the arbitral tribunal is genuinely impossible, and not merely more onerous.[46] The mere impecuniosity of a party does not require such recourse, but could much better be dealt with at the end of the arbitration, by the arbitrators themselves, namely in the context of the allocation of the costs of the arbitration.

It is therefore submitted that, in international arbitration, the approach which a French court would most likely take when faced with an alleged invalidity of an arbitration agreement due to the impecuniosity of a party, is clearly preferable to that adopted by the BGH. The test applied by French courts is whether *prima facie*, there is a valid arbitration agreement before it transfers the case back to arbitration. Hardly any costs are incurred in this procedure which consists of only one motion, without the possibility to appeal the decision. It has often been argued that one of the reasons why arbitration is today the preferred means of settling disputes in international business is that its costs are lower than those for domestic litigation. While this is not true in every case, it certainly must be true in the current case. As was shown in the examples above, by refusing to arbitrate, an impecunious party risks ending up in three different litigations in three different countries, with or without obtaining legal aid for these steps. Undoubtedly, one single arbitration procedure would be less costly than a similar chain of litigations. Thus, from a practical standpoint, it would seem that an impecunious party is well advised to simply follow the arbitration it had agreed to, and to incur the related costs, rather than to incur unnecessary litigation costs in up to three different countries.

The BGH currently has before it an appeal on points of law brought against a decision by the Berlin Court of Appeal[47] confirmed that an arbitration agreement was "incapable of being performed" within the meaning of Section 1032 of the German Code of Civil Procedure because the claimant could not advance the costs of the arbitration procedure and the costs were not otherwise covered. From the perspective of a French practitioner of international arbitration, it can

---

[45] See on this issue also *E. Gaillard*, Laws and Court Decisions in Civil Law Countries (Topic 2: Refusal by a party (a) to make advance deposits for the costs of the arbitration, and (b) to submit a statement of defence), in: ICCA Congress Series No. 5, 105 (1991).

[46] The author's view thus remains as set out in *E. Gaillard*, *supra* note 45 at 104, 105.

[47] *Kammergericht Berlin*, Beschluss vom 13.08.2001, Az.: 2 W 8057/99 (92 O 116/99 LG Berlin).

only be hoped that the BGH will take this opportunity to review its case law on the validity of arbitration agreements and to arrive at a solution that is more suited for international arbitration.

Finally, however, we believe that the real and practical answer lies yet elsewhere, namely in a reasonable approach taken by both parties and arbitrators to arbitrations in which one of the parties is impecunious, bearing in mind the following:

Arbitrators should, and do, award the costs of the arbitration, including the arbitrators' fees, the institutional fees, and the attorneys' fees to the winning party,[48] so that the winning claimant that was in financial difficulties does not have to bear the costs of such a procedure.

Parties in international arbitration have to recognize that an arbitral tribunal of three arbitrators is by far not always necessary. To adopt a model with one sole arbitrator may well increase efficiency and speed, and obviously reduce costs. Parties should take the time to consider this option when drafting the arbitration agreement, more so than they currently do.

Finally, in light of the increasing importance and popularity of international arbitration, legislators should consider modifying their legal aid systems to make legal aid available in the context of international arbitration.

---

[48] For references to arbitral case law adopting such approach, see Fouchard Gaillard Goldman On International Commercial Arbitration, *supra* note 15 at ¶436; *Michael O'Reilly*, *supra* note 15 at 32 *et seq.*; *Eric A. Schwartz*, The ICC Arbitral Process – Part IV: The Costs of ICC Arbitration, 4 ICC International Court of Arbitration Bulletin 8, 20 *et seq.* (May 1993); *Michael Bühler*, *supra* note 14 at 117, 139 *et seq*; *Catherine Li*, *supra* note 15 at 435, 437 *et seq.*; for the position under the UNICTRAL Arbitration Rules, see *Stewart Abercrombie Baker*, *Mark David Davis*, The UNCITRAL Arbitration Rules in Practice – The Experience of the Iran-United States Claims Tribunal 213 *et seq.* (1992); *Pieter Sanders*, Commentary on UNCITRAL Arbitration Rules, II ICCA Yearbook Commercial Arbitration 172, 214 *et seq.* (1977).

Insolvency in Arbitration - Swiss law

*Laurent Lévy**

The term "bankruptcy" describes any organized proceedings to realize and liquidate the assets of a debtor among his creditors, following the declaration of his insolvency by a court or a State agency[1].

The characterization "bankruptcy" requires at least the reunion of the following elements:

A judge (possibly a State agency) will acknowledge the insolvency of a debtor and hand down a judgement (or decree) adjudicating bankruptcy.

- A collective procedure will follow and involve all the assets and liabilities of the debtor (under limited exceptions such as personal belongings of an individual person and under the reservation of the limited territorial effects

---

* Doctor-at-law, Paris, Attorney-at-law, Schellenberg Wittmer, Geneva, Switzerland.

1 Council of Europe 5 June 1990 Convention; "Collective insolvency proceedings which entail the partial or total divestment of a debtor and the appointment of a liquidator" (Art. I.1 European Community Council Regulation N° 1346/2000 of 29 May 2000.

of a bankruptcy judgement (so-called territorial rather than universal effect of bankruptcy).

- The "dispossession" (or "divestment") of the debtor results in the taking of the possession by the trustee (or receiver) of the property of the bankrupt debtor at the time of the adjudication bankruptcy (according to Article 1.3b of the Istanbul Convention, the "dispossession" of the debtor is defined as the transfer to a trustee of the powers to manage, to control and to dispose of the bankrupt debtor's property)[2].
- From one jurisdiction to another, the bankruptcy proceedings will vary. For instance, bankruptcy may be voluntary or involuntary. The act of bankruptcy (i.e. the act which makes a person subject to bankruptcy) may be the inability to meet one's liabilities as they mature or insolvency (i.e. the condition of a person whose assets would not be sufficient to discharge all the liabilities). Likewise, in some countries, bankruptcy is limited to traders, while, in others, it may concern any person. The effects of bankruptcy proceedings will also be diverse and may include civil and criminal penalties, the winding up or restructuring of a bankrupt corporation, etc.

In fact, bankruptcy proceedings purport to achieve several objectives, such as the (partial) satisfaction of the creditors, the reorganization and survival of an undertaking and of the employments, the penalties against the debtors, etc.

The insistence on either of those goals rather than the others is a political and social choice: of necessity, the balance will not be the same in all jurisdictions.

The interests at stake (national economy, public order and ethics, etc.) affect the bankruptcy procedure with public policy considerations. The equal treatment of the creditors ("*par conditio creditorum*"), the exclusive and mandatory jurisdiction of the bankruptcy judges, stay of certain legal remedies against debtors and other kind of moratoria may in certain jurisdictions raise public policy considerations.

Thus, arbitration and bankruptcy are of heterogeneous natures: arbitration is predicated on party autonomy and privity. Bankruptcy proceeds from official and collective considerations. Hence, the hard core of bankruptcy proceedings will be beyond the reach of any arbitrator. However, in most jurisdictions, arbitrators may adjudicate civil and commercial disputes in spite of one of the parties being bankrupt. Prior to studying the consequences of bankruptcy proceedings on the admissibility of arbitration (II) and the arbitration

---

2 In Switzerland, bankruptcy strictly speaking and a form of composition involving the abandonment of all or some of the debtor's assets to his creditors would qualify as bankruptcy under such definition (*Konkurs* and *Nachlassvertrag mit Vermögensabtretung*). The so-called ordinary composition proceeding (*Nachlassvertrag*) and the deferral of bankruptcy (*Konkursaufschub*) would not qualify.

proceedings itself (III), one will mention some effects of undeclared insolvency under Swiss law (I)[3].

I. Undeclared Insolvency and Arbitration under Swiss law

The insolvency of a party, whether declared or not, may produce effects under the applicable substantive law. For instance, in indirect agency, the agent's insolvency may allow the principal to exercise the rights acquired by the agent directly against a third party and *vice versa*[4].

The insolvency may also generate procedural effects.

On September 14, 2002, the German Supreme Court (*Bundesgerichtshof*) handed down a judgment which may be summarized as follows[5]. The parties (owner and contractor) had entered into an arbitration agreement. The owner refused to provide security for the completion of the works and refused to waive the arbitration agreement, i.e. to permit the contractor to file an action before a State court. Subsequently, the owner himself sought damages against the contractor before a State court (*Landgericht* Dresden), where the contractor raised the arbitration-exception. The *Landgericht* and, upon appeal, the *Oberlandesgericht* Dresden held the claim to be inadmissible but the *Bundesgerichtshof* reversed. The Supreme Court relied on Section 1032 German Code of Civil Procedure. *("A Court before which an action is brought in a matter which is the subject of an arbitration agreement must dismiss the action if the respondent raises an exception prior to the beginning of the oral discussion on the merits unless the Court finds that the agreement is null and void, inoperative or incapable of being performed").*

In its parts of relevance here, Article 1032 German Code of Civil Procedure corresponds to Article 8.1 UNCITRAL Model Law. The UNCITRAL legislative history (and for that matter the construction of Art. II.3 New York 1958 Convention) does not bring forth any hint confirming the interpretation of the

---

3 Recent contributions concerning insolvencies in arbitration. Switzerland: *Brown-Berset, Lévy*, Faillite et arbitrage, Swiss Arbitration Association Bulletin (BASA) 1998, p. 664; France: *Fouchard*, Arbitrage et faillite, Revue de l'arbitrage 1998, p. 471; Germany: *Eberl*, Das Schiedsverfahren in der Insolvenz, No 10, 2002, p. 393, Insolvenz und Vollstreckung (INVO); Comparative approach: *V. Lazic*, Insolvency proceedings and commercial arbitration, Kluwer T.M.C., Asset Instituut, The Hague, 1998.

4 See Art. 401 (3) Swiss Obligation Code; Art. 3: 302 and 3: 303 Principles of European Contract Law. Other example: if a party to a bilateral contract becomes insolvent, the other party may terminate this contract or suspend its own performance; see Art. 83 Swiss Obligation Code, Art. 7.3.3 and 7.3.4 UNIDROIT Principles of International Commercial Contracts.

5 Case III ZR 33/00, Betriebs-Berater, (55), 46, 2330 and comment by *J. Risse*, Annex 6, 11. This landmark decision is new in that, since the 1997 Arbitration Act (which amended Section 1032 German Code of Civil Procedure), it has become unnecessary for a party to terminate the agreement (for good cause, namely its insolvency) prior to filing an action before the State Court, Juristenzeitung 2001, p. 258, Comment *P. Schlosser*, Neue Juristische Wochenschrift 2000, 50, p. 3720.

Bundesgerichtshof (see *Holtzmann-Neuhaus*, A Guide to the UNCITRAL Model Law, Kluwer 1994, pp. 302 and ff.).

In a case where the claimant is financially unable to conduct arbitration proceedings and the respondent is unable or unwilling to bear the claimant's costs in arbitration, the claimant may file its claim before the municipal courts, because the arbitration agreement has become inoperative ("undurchführbar"). The German Supreme Court holds that there is a compulsory inability to carry out the arbitration agreement in order to avoid the deprivation of a party to seek legal redress in front of any jurisdiction (either a State court or an arbitral tribunal).

The insolvency of a party may thus have an influence on the arbitration agreement (A) and the cost of the arbitration (B).

A. *Insolvency and arbitration agreement*

Will the insolvency of a party affect the arbitration agreement? In Switzerland, there are some texts to this effect (1), but the principle answer is negative (2).

1. Domestic arbitration

In domestic arbitration, Article 30 of the March 27, 1969, Intercantonal Arbitration Convention provides[6]:

> "The arbitral tribunal may order an advance of foreseeable costs and may make the procedural processes dependent thereon. It shall determine the apportionment of such advance.
>
> If one of the parties does not advance the sums required of him, the other party may elect to make an advance of all the costs or to forego the arbitration. If he chooses the latter course, the parties shall no longer be bound by the arbitration agreement in respect of the dispute in question."

Several Swiss arbitration institutions know of similar rules[7].

It follows that an insolvent party may face the voidance of the arbitration agreement if the other party does not advance the arbitration costs. In such an instance, the municipal courts will recover their jurisdiction over the "dispute in

---

6 In international arbitration, Art. 176 Private International Law Act (PILA) of December 18, 1987 permits the parties to exclude in writing the international arbitration provisions of the PILA and to agree to the exclusive application of the Intercantonal Arbitration Convention. In practice, it seems this provision remained unused and is likely to be repealed.

7 For instance Art. 55 of the Zurich Chamber of Commerce, Art. 19.4 of the Regulation 150 of the Swiss Engineers and Architects. See also Art. 55 of the Arbitration Rules of the Basle Chamber of Commerce (May 4, 1995): "Failure to pay the advance of costs. If a party does not pay the advance of costs required of it, the other party may elect to advance all the costs or to waive the arbitration. If it chooses to waive, then the arbitral tribunal is empowered to declare that the parties are not bound anymore by the arbitration agreement in respect of this dispute". As to the way the arbitration costs should be borne when claimant refuses to pay the respondent's share of the advance on arbitration costs, Cantonal Court Graubünden, May 15, 1996, BASA, 1988, p. 66.

question": the arbitration agreement will remain existing and binding as to any other disputes falling within its ambit.

In such situation, the insolvent party may file a claim directly before a State court. The other party would be estopped from raising an arbitration exception unless it is able and willing to advance all the costs of the arbitration.

2. International arbitration matters

The Private International Law Act (PILA) does not make any mention of advance of costs and failure to pay it. If a party refuses or is unable to pay his share of the advance, a Swiss Court would declare the arbitration agreement inoperative or incapable of being performed[8].

Upon an arbitration exception, Article 7 (b) PILA and Article II.3 New York Convention of June 10, 1958 do provide that a Swiss Court shall decline its jurisdiction unless it finds that the arbitration agreement is null and void, inoperative or incapable of being performed[9].

A Swiss court would hold that insolvency is not an excuse for failing to perform one's obligations. The insolvency of a party should not deprive the other party of the jointly accepted advantages of arbitration (neutral *forum*, celerity, agreed language, etc.). In fact, in international commercial matters, one may expect that both parties will not enter into an arbitration clause without some knowledge about the other parties and their own financial status: insolvency is not unforeseeable and not an excuse to evade an arbitration clause.

The answer should remain the same in the case of a party unable to pay the advance of costs because of foreign exchange control legislation.

Swiss courts may, however, accept to entertain their jurisdiction if they find that the non-insolvent party is relying abusively on the arbitration agreement, that is only as a means to deprive the insolvent party of any possibility to obtain redress in front of any jurisdiction. The impossibility of a party to obtain any legal aid in an arbitration would not be in itself sufficient to make the arbitration agreement moot: a situation of clear abuse by the other party would be required, a *venire contra factum proprium* or a predatory conduct to deprive the other party of the means to obtain the financing of the arbitration (for instance, propagating rumours around the other party to frighten away potential financial backers).

---

8 *Contra*: *A. Bucher*, Berner Festgabe 1988, pp.144-145. In arbitration, in such instances, the respondent is barred from relying on an arbitration agreement in proceedings before a Municipal Court if the claimant is insolvent because the arbitration agreement is incapable of being performed (German Federal Court (BGH) 14.7.2000, NJW 2000, 50 p. 3720 n°12. Accord : *Lalive/Poudret/Reymond*, Le droit de l'arbitrage interne et international en Suisse, Payot 1989, ad Art. 182, n°17 p. 359).

9 To determine whether an arbitration agreement is valid under Art. II.3 New York 1958 Convention, the Swiss judge will refer to Swiss conflicts of law rules, namely to Art. 178 PILA if the seat of the arbitration is in Switzerland.

Confronted with the same issue (a party unable to pay its advance of costs), Swiss arbitrators should not either declare the arbitration agreement incapable of being performed. If the other party does not make the payment of the full advance, the arbitral tribunal may only order the termination of the arbitral proceedings. The validity of an arbitration agreement is governed by Article 178 (2) PILA: "*As regards its substance, an arbitration agreement shall be valid if it conforms either to the law chosen by the parties, or to the law governing the subject matter of the dispute, in particular, the law governing the main contract, or if it conforms to Swiss law.*"

It is Article 178 (2) PILA which governs the issues arising during the performance of the arbitration agreement, such as the impossibility to carry it out. The afore-cited Article 7 PILA and II.3 New York 1958 Convention are applicable only before municipal courts. Thus, an arbitrator sitting in Switzerland would lack any legal basis to allow an insolvent party to renege on an arbitration clause. As a matter of fact, this arbitrator might even order the insolvent party to pay some security for costs, which confirms *a fortiori* that he will not hold the arbitration agreement inoperative or incapable of being performed.

B. Insolvency and costs of the arbitration

Article 183 PILA empowers the arbitral tribunal to order provisional or protective measures unless the parties agreed otherwise. Swiss arbitrators are thus empowered to order security for the costs of the arbitration, including the reasonable legal expenses of the other party.

The scope of this provision is as wide as conceivable and suggests a distanciation from the prior restrictive approach of Swiss arbitration towards security for costs. A serious potential risk of non-enforcement of a future award on costs may appear as a sufficient ground for security for costs, which seems a somewhat too liberal approach[10]. Is it possible to order a security for costs against an insolvent party? The dilemma is well-known: The insolvent claimant may be deprived of any possibility to assert its rights if it cannot post a security. Conversely, the other party has a legitimate right not to engage into an arbitration without a reasonable assurance not to suffer any harm if it prevails. The Swiss position seems to be that it is possible to order a security for costs against an insolvent party. In a Zurich Chamber of Commerce arbitration, an arbitrator did not hesitate to grant an order for security for expenses against a claimant who had been adjudicated bankrupt and whose bankruptcy proceedings had been stayed due to the lack of any assets[11].

---

[10] See *Markus Wirth*, BASA 2000, p. 36.

[11] Order of November 20, 2001, BASA 2002 (3) p. 467 (471 N°15-19). See also BASA 1999, pp. 59, 63 ff.

II. Bankruptcy and Admissibility of Arbitration

The adjudication of bankruptcy and liquidation proceedings will result in the dispossession of the debtor, the commencement of liquidation (or reorganization) proceedings and court interventions. This change of the debtor's situation brings up issues of standing (A) and subject matter arbitrability (B).

A. Standing

Insolvency proceedings raise issues of capacity (does the estate have capacity to enter into an arbitration agreement?) (1) and of personal scope of the arbitration agreement (is the estate bound by an arbitration agreement into which the bankrupt debtor had entered?) (2).

1. Capacity and authority

Under Swiss law, the capacity of a party to enter into an arbitration agreement is in principle governed by the rules of law with which the case has the closest connection (Art. 187 (1) PILA) rather than by the law applicable to the arbitration agreement. It follows that the *lex concursus* will govern this matter. If Swiss law is applicable, the estate will have the capacity to enter into an arbitration agreement. The trustee will have the necessary authority provided he is authorized by either the creditors' committee or the second assembly of the creditors[12].

Likewise, the *lex concursus* will determine whether the estate has the capacity to be a party to an arbitration (Art. 187 (1) PILA). Thus, the solution is the same as under Article V.1a New York 1958 Convention and the European conventions on bankruptcies[13].

At any rate, as an international arbitrator is not integrated into any legal system, he will not have to give any priority to the laws of the seat of the arbitration: in particular, the territoriality or universality of a bankruptcy is not an issue in international arbitration. A judge holds his power from a State and will make his decisions according to the laws of such State and on such State's territory. The arbitrator has no *lex fori* and holds his powers from an agreement: he will thus take into consideration a bankruptcy judgment but will not research whether the effects of such judgment should be conditioned to recognition or *exequatur*.

The capacity of the debtor will also be determined according to the *lex concursus* (Art. 187 (1) PILA). In general, dispossession is not a matter of

---

[12] See Art. 237 (3) (3) + 253 Federal Act of April 11, 1889 on debt collection and bankruptcy, "LP".

[13] Art. 7, 9, 10 and 11 Istanbul Convention and Art. 4, 2c and 18 Brussels Convention of 29 May 2000.

capacity but rather of *locus standi* (power to legally act with respect to claims and other rights or liabilities in the ownership of a third party)[14].

2. Personal scope of the arbitration agreement (*locus standi*)

Due to the dispossession of the debtor, the trustee acquires the right to dispose of and to manage the estate: the extent of such "transfer" will vary depending on the jurisdiction (and depending on the reorganization procedure) but is a core feature of collective insolvency proceedings. It follows that the bankrupt debtor may not enter into any arbitration agreement in a way that would bind the estate. Does it also entail that the pre-existing arbitration agreement is not binding upon the estate?

In England, the 1996 Arbitration Act (Art. 107(1) N°46) amended section 3.4.9 of the 1986 Insolvency Act:

> "[...] (2) If the trustee in bankruptcy adopts the contract, the arbitration agreement is enforceable against the trustee [...].
> (3) If the trustee in bankruptcy does not adopt the contract [...] (a) the trustee with the consent of the creditors' committee, or, (b) any other party to the agreement, may apply to the court which may, if it thinks fit in all circumstances of the case, order that the matter be referred to arbitration in accordance with the arbitration."

The issue is thus to determine whether a pre-existing arbitration agreement is binding upon the debtor and/or the estate. This is a question of *locus standi*, i.e. of the personal scope of the arbitration clause. It is not to be mixed up with another issue, namely whether the debtor or the estate is entitled to the substantive rights subject of the arbitration or is empowered to assert such rights. In principle, this second issue is governed by the *lex concursus*.

On the contrary, it is the law governing the arbitration agreement which will determine which persons are bound by this agreement. As already mentioned, Article 178 (2) PILA edicts a substantive rule of private international law: the arbitration agreement will be valid if it conforms either to the law chosen by the parties or the law governing the subject matter of the dispute or Swiss law. Thus, the estate will be bound by the arbitration agreement if either of such three laws validates the "transfer" of such clause from the debtor to the estate. Practically, more often than not, the arbitrator will be led to recognize the transfer resulting from the bankruptcy law.

- The adjudication of bankruptcy does not void an arbitration clause[15].
- Many insolvency laws enable the trustee in bankruptcy to elect either to reject or to perform contracts which the debtor had entered into prior to the

---

[14] Cf. *A. Bucher*, Droit international privé suisse, tome 2, N° 195 and following, especially 197, p.85.

[15] See FTD 59 I 177; FTD November 15, 1961 unreported cited by *P. Jolidon*, Commentaire du concordat suisse sur l'arbitrage, Berne, 1984 (ad Art. 4, N°823, p. 141); Cantonal Court of Jura, October 8, 1981, BASA 1983 (3), p. 27, Cantonal Court Wallis, July 9, 1986, BASA 1987, p. 203.

adjudication of bankruptcy. If the trustee elects to reject such contracts, the arbitration clause will remain binding upon the estate[16]. The rejection should operate with respect to the substance of the arbitration, a matter possibly governed by the *lex concursus*, but not to the arbitration agreement.

- In the "Clear Star Limited" case, the Federal Tribunal confirmed implicitly that the estate becomes bound by the pre-existing arbitration agreement[17].

Swiss law permits the parties to an arbitration agreement to stipulate that such arbitration agreement is personal and cannot be transferred or assigned[18].

Does this personal nature of the arbitration clause exclude its "transfer" to the estate? Obviously, the arbitrator will have to construe the exact intent of the parties: it is permissible for the parties to exclude arbitration if one of them becomes insolvent. However, lacking an agreement of the parties, the presumption will be that, in spite of the non-assignable clause, the arbitration clause will survive the bankruptcy. Usually, the intent of the parties is to forbid the assignment of rights and obligations and does not concern the dispute resolution. Furthermore, the "dispossession" is not an actual transfer of rights in most jurisdictions.

In the above cited "Clear Star Limited" April 9, 1991 decision, the Federal Tribunal had an opportunity to determine this issue but left it open. A Swedish estate in bankruptcy assigned its contractual rights against two Polish entities to a Guernsey Company (Clear Star). Clear Star filed an ICC request for arbitration against the two Polish entities. The initial agreement between the Swedish bankrupt debtor and one of the two Polish respondents stipulated a prohibition to assign or to subcontract without the prior agreement in writing of the other party. The Swiss Federal Tribunal held that: *"If no right was arising for Clear Star from the arbitration clause because there was a complete prohibition to assign, the Arbitral tribunal rightfully held that it had no jurisdiction [...]; if the arbitration clause [...] is interpreted according to the framework of the prohibition to assign [...], which concerns all the claims, the arbitration clause will actually be personalized in function of the initial parties and thus not be assignable"*[19].

The Federal Tribunal noted that Clear Star Limited had been founded especially to initiate the arbitration, just a few days prior to the disputed

---

16 Separability of the arbitration agreement (Art. 178 (3) PILA); see FTD 59 I 177.

17 FTD April 9, 1991, 117 II p. 94; Revue de l'arbitrage (Paris) 1991, p. 709, note *P.Y. Tschanz*; cf. *J. Werner*, Jurisdiction of Arbitrators in Case of Assignment of an Arbitration Clause, Journal of International Arbitration, 1991 p. 13.

18 FTD 16 October 2001, BASA 2002, p. 97, and comment *M. Scherer*, p. 109.

19 FTD April 9, 1991, Revue de l'arbitrage 1991, p. 709 (714). See also in the United States *Apollo Computer vs. Berg* 886 F 2d 469 (1st Circuit 1989) and commentary by *W.W. Park*, The Arbitrability Dicta in *First Options vs. Kaplan*: What sort of Kompetenz-Kompetenz has crossed the Atlantic? Arbitration International 1996, pp. 137, 147-148.

assignment. Clear Star was not a creditor acting as a representative of the estate but as a third party assignee who had acquired an asset by virtue of an ordinary assignment of claim made by the estate. The Swiss Federal Court holds logically that the estate could not legitimately subrogate Clear Star into the arbitration agreement which was personal and non-assignable: the Clear Star decision does not expressly decide whether the arbitration agreement did bind the estate itself. In fact, *a contrario*, it does confirm that the arbitration agreement did bind the estate: otherwise, the issue of subrogation could not have arisen.

In conclusion, the dispossession of the debtor confers to the estate the legal standing to act in the stead of the debtor with respect to his assets and liabilities. The adjudication of bankruptcy does not terminate *de plano* the arbitration agreements binding the debtor and such arbitration agreements remain valid and may bind the trustee in bankruptcy and, possibly, the debtor himself (for instance with respect to assets and liabilities which are not included in the bankruptcy)[20].

B. *Subject-matter arbitrability*

1. Generalities

Article 177 (1) PILA provides: "*any dispute involving property can be the subject matter of an arbitration*".

Where the arbitral tribunal has its seat in Switzerland and one of the parties is not domiciled in Switzerland (Art. 176 (1) PILA), this Swiss substantive rule of international private law determines arbitrability ("Arbitrability" is the heading of Article 177 PILA).

This purely substantive determination of arbitrability excludes any conflicts of laws: arbitrability will only depend on the fulfilment of the Swiss law requirements. In principle, a Swiss arbitrator will not take into consideration any further prohibition of or restriction to arbitrability. Substantive Swiss law has no more standing to be applicable than any other law. Subject to different rules (such as Art. 35 "General Rule" of the ICC Rules of Arbitration), the law of the likely place of enforcement has no title either to determine arbitrability.

> "The legislature having selected the criterion for arbitrability which is dependant on the nature of the dispute and not on the law governing such dispute, has determined that there is, in principle, no case in which restrictions and prohibitions to be found in foreign law with respect to arbitrability should be taken into account. It is, as some authors opine, clear that an arbitral tribunal sitting in Switzerland, in the framework of an international arbitration, does not have jurisdiction to hear a dispute in a property matter where declaring the dispute arbitrable would be incompatible with public policy. In fact, the latter notion does not have the same meaning for all the authors (Swiss of

[20] For instance, because such assets and liabilities are not located in the country where the bankruptcy was declared.

Foreign Public Policy for *Bucher*; only Swiss International Public Policy for *Poudret* and *Lalive/Poudret/Reymond*)"[21].

Thus:

- All disputes involving "property" are arbitrable. A dispute shall involve property if the claims of at least one of the parties may be characterized as "economic". It is difficult to conceive a wider criterion.
- Disputes involving property will be arbitrable even where a municipal authority or court has exclusive jurisdiction over the dispute.
- Disputes involving property will be arbitrable although they should concern rights of which the parties could not freely dispose by way of settlement or otherwise.
- Matters involving public policy are arbitrable[22].

The arbitrator does not have to take into account the public policy of the country where the award is likely to be enforced: a refusal of enforcement is a risk which the parties have accepted[23].

A Swiss arbitrator must take into consideration the public policy which is reserved by Article 190 (2) (e) PILA. However, this is a very narrow exception:

> "An award is incompatible with material public policy where it violates fundamental legal principles of substantive law to such an extent that it is no longer compatible with the legal order and the recognized system of values; among such principles, one will find the binding character of a valid contract, good faith, the prohibition of misuse of law, the prohibition of discriminatory or confiscatory measures as a protection of incapacitated persons."[24].

Where arbitrability is being decided under Swiss law, "foreign" laws calling for their own application may be taken into consideration only under the conditions set by Swiss law. The matter is highly debated. In principle, such

---

21 SFTD June 23, 1992, *Fincantieri Navali*, Revue de l'arbitrage, Paris, 1993, 4 p. 691, 3.c, pp. 693-694).

22 SFTD April 28, 1992, c.5, BASA 1992 pp. 368 and ff. (377): Applicability of Article 85 (81) of the Rome Treaty by the arbitrator, at least where a European law (Belgian) governs the contract. Compare in France: Paris, September 20, 1995, *Matra*, Revue de l'arbitrage 1996 p. 187, note *D. Cohen* (regarding bankruptcy). Cf. *J.T. McLaughlin*, Arbitrability: Current Trends in the United States, Arbitration International, 1996, p.113, who quotes a decision of the Third Circuit Court of New York 1989, *Hayes & Co versus Merryl Lynch* and indicates (p. 134): "This is an important decision predicating that, in trustee initiated suits, arbitration agreements will be enforced, since it is unlikely that any trustee will be able to show that the policies behind the Bankruptcy Code "trump" those contained in the FAA".

23 Above quoted April 28, 1992 SFTD; above quoted June 23, 1992 *Fincantieri* SFTD c.3d § 2 p. 67. The Swiss Federal Court will not quash an award because the arbitrator does not take into consideration foreign public policy; it does not forbid the arbitrator to take such foreign public policy into consideration, especially if this is predicated in the procedure chosen by the parties (cf. Art. 26 "General Rule" of the ICC Rules for instance).

24 The Swiss Federal Tribunal uses repeatedly this definition, for instance, in SFTD June 11, 2001, *UEFA*, BASA 2001 (3), pp. 566 (570) (2d) to define public policy as a ground to set aside an award (Art. 190 (2) (e) PILA).

laws will limit arbitrability of a dispute only if they protect some interests that would pass the test of public policy as defined above. If Swiss law ignores such interests or does not grant such interests sufficient importance to limit arbitrability, an arbitral tribunal sitting in Switzerland, cannot restrict its jurisdiction under a "foreign" law, even if it is the *lex causae* or the law of the likely place of enforcement. Thus, the *lex concursus* will have only a very limited role if any when it comes to arbitrability.

2. Subject-matter arbitrability in bankruptcy matters

The above principles lead to the conclusion that a party's bankruptcy will generally not exclude arbitrability.

The very core of insolvency issues may not be subject to arbitration. For instance, arbitrators will not have jurisdiction to adjudicate the bankruptcy (i.e. to initiate the insolvency proceedings), to appoint the trustee, to verify and accept the creditor's claims, etc. This is not necessarily an issue of subject matter arbitrability. First, such issue will never be submitted to arbitrators because often there will be no arbitration agreement. Second, such issues are not "disputes" which could be settled by a court having jurisdiction "ensuring" equal treatment of the parties and the right of the parties to be heard in an adversarial procedure[25]. These are matters of debt collection, more specifically collective enforcement proceedings. In such proceedings, municipal courts will act more as enforcement agencies than as judges determining a dispute.

On the contrary, arbitrators will not be barred from deciding on disputes involving bankruptcy law issues. In particular, they will have jurisdiction to adjudicate substantive disputes arisen while a party is subject to bankruptcy. For instance, the creditors may not file individual actions against the debtor or the estate: they must file their claims with the trustee. However, if the trustee rejects the claim, the arbitrators may rule on a challenge of the schedule of claims. Likewise, if the trustee accepts the claim and a third party creditor objects, arbitrators will have jurisdiction to determine on the action by a creditor to challenge the admission of another creditor into the schedule of claims[26].

In other words, the prohibition of individual actions requires the filing of the claims in order for the trustee to have a general overview of the bankruptcy of the estate and to verify the claims; it does not at all impose any dispute

25 Art. 182 (3) PILA: "Whatever procedure is chosen, the arbitral tribunal shall ensure equal treatment of the parties and the right of the parties to be heard in an adversarial procedure".

26 See *R. Briner*, in International Arbitration in Switzerland, *S. Berti*, ed, Kluwer 2000, ad Art. 177 N° 14: "On the other hand, private law disputes regarding claims in bankruptcy procedures, e.g. regarding the existence and grounds of claims which have given rise to debt collection proceedings as well as regarding claims according to which certain assets are not to be taken into consideration bankruptcy and attachment matters, etc. are arbitrable". On the distinction between bankruptcy actions *stricto sensu* and ancillary proceedings arising during the liquidation of the estate, see SFTD 125 III 108 (concerning the exclusion of bankruptcy matters in the Lugano Convention).

resolution method when it comes to ascertaining the existence, quantum, etc. of the claim itself. Truly, in most jurisdictions, "the creditor who challenges the schedule of claim ... must initiate his action against the estate in front of the bankruptcy judge" (Art. 250 LP). However, at least in Switzerland, such a jurisdictional provision regards the local competence rather than subject matter competence. As a matter of fact, even under Swiss domestic law, jurisdiction clauses are admissible and no public policy consideration is at stake, in particular not the equal treatment of the creditors[27].

The same reasoning leads to admit arbitrability of actions to include or exclude assets from the estate[28]. An arbitrator may also determine on the voidance of fraudulent transactions filed by the estate and on exceptions of the same characterization: at least, in Switzerland, such actions are foreseen by bankruptcy laws but, under Article 177 (1) PILA's view, they are directly involving property[29]. A set-off exception is also arbitrable. The French Courts have a contrary view: they hold it as contrary to public policy to hand down an award which would be an executory decision (condamnation) against the estate itself[30].

Swiss law does not either exclude arbitration to determine in which class of creditors ("pecking order") a claim should be accepted. Arbitrators may also determine whether certain claims have to be paid directly from the estate rather than to be included in the schedule of claims[31].

Thus, arbitrators may entertain disputes relating to the claims made on behalf of the estate itself, to the diversion of some assets from the general execution (i.e. from the estate), and, obviously, to all contestations relating to the verified

---

27 SFTD 100 II 319, esp. factual part, lit. C, last paragraph, p. 322. Furthermore, in Switzerland, such action may be settled, which shows that the parties have the free disposition of their rights. A fortiori, they may thus submit their disputes to arbitrators.

28 SFTD 56 III 233. The proprietary actions (Art. 242 LP) of third party against the estate seem of mixed nature: they involve substantive and bankruptcy laws. In principle, they should thus be arbitrable.

29 Furthermore, at any rate, Art. 289 LP does not reserve the bankruptcy Court's jurisdiction but grants jurisdiction to the Court of the respondent's domicile. This is to say that it is not a typical bankruptcy proceeding. In fact, the parties may settle on such kind of actions. Accord: "the *actio pauliana* does not purport to determine on a dispute relating to the use of force, compulsion or dispossession of movable or immovable assets". Such action is thus not reserved by Art. 16-5 of the Brussels Convention": European Union Court of Justice, March 26, 1992, *Reichert* (second case / case C.261/90). *Contra*: *J.L. Chenaux*, Un survol de l'action révocatoire en droit international privé suisse, Revue suisse de jurisprudence 1996, p. 232, esp. III. For a detailed review, see *J.F. Poudret*, S. *Besson*, Le droit comparé de l'arbitrage international, *Bruylant*, LGDJ, *Schulthess*, 2002, No 363, p. 326, and N° 994, p. 327.

30 Cour d'appel de Paris, February 27, 1992, Revue de l'arbitrage 1992 p. 590, note *P. Ancel*. There is no such prohibition of executory awards against the estate under Swiss law.

31 Cf. SFTD 106 III 121 : The Federal Court held that the characterization of a debt as binding the estate itself is a substantive law matter rather than a debt collection matter. See also ICC award 4415, Clunet, 1984 pp. 952 especially 954, note S.J.

claims (whether the dispute arises between the trustee and a creditor or between two creditors).

The trustee may void, set aside or otherwise declare without effects upon the bankruptcy estate certain transactions (undue preferences, fraudulent transactions such as donations, granting of security for already existing liabilities, discharge of claims in kind rather than in cash, payments of debts which have not come to term). The trustee's actions to set aside are arbitrable as they involve property. There is no doubt that the trustee may enter into an arbitration agreement in this connection. However, would the trustee be bound by an arbitration clause agreed by the debtor? The trustee is not acting out of contract but exercising statutory causes of action arising out of bankruptcy law[32].

The trustee is in fact attempting either to deny the performance of a contract ("exceptio pauliana") or to claim the refund of a performance under the contract ("actio pauliana"). Such voidance actions or exceptions do not "belong to the debtor" and do result from the bankruptcy laws[33].

Their purpose is, however, to prevent any fraudulent connivance or preference when performing a given agreement: although there does not seem to be Swiss authority in this respect, we do not see why the arbitrator should decline jurisdiction if the arbitration clause is sufficiently broad to cover such actions and exceptions, for instance if its scope is "all the disputes in connection with a contract".

Arbitrating those various actions does not impugn on the equal treatment of the creditors. Truly, such kind of actions do produce effects *vis-à-vis* third parties, namely all the creditors. Litigation might be a more prudent course to follow as it would afford publicity, possibly third party intervention and avoid the difficulties of multi-party arbitration. However, such kind of practical considerations would not be sufficient to exclude arbitrability, especially as, of necessity, the trustee will always be informed. Thus, the trustee will be in a position to protect the interests of the estate. The arbitrator will also have to ascertain, if necessary *sua sponte*, that there is no undue connivance between the parties. In conclusion, the arbitrators will have jurisdiction but will have to take the existence of the bankruptcy proceedings into consideration.

III. Effects of Bankruptcy on the Arbitration Proceedings

The declaration of bankruptcy will produce effects both as to procedure and as to substance.

---

32 *V. Lazic*, Insolvency Proceedings and Commercial Arbitration, Kluwer 1998, footnotes 67, 68, 69 p. 200 citing several German, Dutch and American court decisions holding that the trustee should not be compelled to arbitrate claims relating to preferential transfers.

33 Although they might also exist without any declared bankruptcy to void certain fraudulent transactions made by an insolvent debtor (cf. for instance Art. 1167 French Civil Code).

A. Procedural Effects

1. Stay of proceedings

In international arbitration, the parties may shape the arbitral procedure. Where the parties have not determined the procedure, the arbitral tribunal shall determine such procedure to the extent necessary, either directly or by reference to a law or to arbitration rules. Whatever procedure is chosen, the arbitral tribunal shall ensure equal treatment of the parties and the right of the parties to be heard in an adversarial procedure (Art. 182 PILA). The Swiss PILA does not further determine the arbitral procedure: party autonomy commands subject to the only exceptions of the equal treatment of the parties and the right to be heard.

The PILA neither mentions the possibility of suspending the proceedings nor does exclude it. However, stays appear to be in principle contrary to the goal of arbitration: the brief of the arbitrator is to foster an expeditious resolution of the dispute, not to keep it in abeyance. Thus, a stay might be mandatory only if it is imposed either by public policy, by the equal treatment of the parties or their right to be heard. On 14 May 2001, in the Fomento Case[34], the Swiss Federal Tribunal held that the arbitrators must stay the arbitration if the very same case is already pending between the parties before municipal courts (whether in Switzerland or elsewhere). This highly controversial decision thus extends to arbitration the *lis alibi pendens* exception (under strict conditions) which is applicable before Swiss courts (Article 9 PILA). Whether arbitrators would have to stay the proceedings because the very same action should be pending before a bankruptcy court should usually lead to a negative answer but is to be decided upon a case-by-case basis: usually, the bankruptcy courts do not rule on substantive rights[35].

In France, "*the stay of the individual action of creditors in bankruptcy matters [...] is imposed both by domestic and international public policy*"[36].

In Switzerland, Article 207 LP provides: "*Save for urgency cases, civil proceedings to which the bankrupt debtor is a party and which have some influence on the state of the estate are stayed. Such proceedings may be resumed, in case of ordinary liquidation, only ten days after the second assembly of the creditors* [...]". This is a mandatory provision of Swiss law[37].

---

34 English translation by *Charles Poncet* in BASA 2001, p. 555.

35 The same issue may also arise in the framework of the *res judicata* exception, namely if a party argues in front of the arbitrators that a bankruptcy judge has already finally decided the case.

36 1st Civ. March 8, 1988, *Thinet*, R. Arb., 1989, P. 473 (474) note *P. Ancel*; see also Com. February 4, 1992, *Saret*, R. Arb., 1992, p. 663, note *J.H. Moitry*; in United States, cf. *J.O. Harwood*, Bankruptcy Arbitration and the Unwilling Debtor, Dispute Resolution Journal, December 1993, pp. 28 and ff., especially note 6. See also Art. 1465 NCPC "renvoyant pour l'arbitrage interne" to the Art. 369, al. 3 NCPC. See also *V. Lazic*, op. cit., p. 243 and ff. and references to the situation in the United States and England.

37 Geneva Court of Justice, November 6, 1987, La Semaine Judiciaire (Geneva) 1998, p. 167.

However, the issue is not whether national bankruptcy laws, should it be Swiss law, should mandatorily impose a stay of proceedings. It is whether an arbitrator sitting in Switzerland has authority to proceed with an international arbitration without any stay if bankruptcy has befallen one of the parties or both of them. Thus, the arbitrator must stay the arbitration proceedings only if public policy considerations so command[38].

However, the purpose of Article 207 LP is to grant the trustee the necessary time to study the files of the debtor (very often voluminous and badly kept), to examine if he should resume certain proceedings or abandon them (in bankruptcy liquidations, the trustees often find that the debtors initiated or continued litigations and arbitrations without any hope of success, just in order to postpone the inevitable). In sum, it is necessary to give the receiver the time necessary to acquire a global overview of the debtor's assets and liabilities: it is the only possibility for the estate to take the necessary decisions with a view to an optimal realization.

The bankruptcy may have some substantive effects on the litigation or arbitration: the trustee will need some time to decide whether the estate will perform or void certain contracts, avoid some transactions (preferences, fraudulent transactions, etc.) in general to apprise himself of the general situation.

Such grounds are not *per se* sufficiently compelling to justify a mandatory stay:

- Before municipal courts, the procedural effects of insolvency proceedings are in principle governed by the *lex fori* rather than by the *lex concursus*[39]. Likewise, an arbitral tribunal will apply the *lex arbitri*.
- Bankruptcy laws know of exceptions to the stay of proceedings. Certain litigations will continue in spite of the bankruptcy or it will be within the discretion of the courts to grant or refuse a stay (for instance, in Switzerland, the administrative proceedings, Art. 207 (2) LP).
- The Swiss Federal Tribunal stated *obiter* that a Swiss bankruptcy may not necessarily cause a stay of civil proceedings before foreign courts: such doubt about a mandatory stay does show that this is not a matter pertaining to public policy[40].

---

[38] SFTD September 7, 1993, *Fincantieri* (2nd decision of Federal Tribunal in this case), BASA 1994, p.248, c. 1c, p. 251: "the appellants rely on "the criminal proceeding will keep the civil proceeding in abeyance"... (such a doctrine) would be mandatory in the setting aside proceeding, in the field of international arbitration, if it was part of public policy".

[39] See Règlement 1346/2000 of the Council of the European Union of May 29, 2000.

[40] SFTD 93 III, 84, C. 3, p. 89: "A decision will be void if it is inconsistent with provisions which are taken in the public interest or with respect to an undetermined number of third parties and, thus, mandatory. Art. 63 of the bankruptcy ordinance (stay of certain decisions) is not a part of such provisions because the way to verify a claim against the debtor which was already pending in a Court at the time of the bankruptcy will concern only a limited group of persons, namely the creditors members of the bankruptcy's estate".

Thus, there is no reason to impose a mandatory stay to the arbitrators.

A stay will be compulsory only if its refusal would be a violation of due process, for instance because it would prevent the trustee from putting his case (for lack of time to prepare the files). In other words, the stay will be mandatory only where the continuation of the proceedings would either be contrary to the equality of the parties or constitute a denial of a proper hearing to the trustee. This is not to say that an arbitrator may not further find it fit to stay the arbitration in view of the circumstances. In practice, the interest of both parties may justify a stay. The solvent party may want to revisit his own position, especially if he suspects that the liquidation of the bankruptcy will generate a minimal dividend[41].

In sum, public policy will only command the observance of due process, for instance make it mandatory for the arbitrators to ascertain that the estate is informed of the arbitration and is in a position to assume its defence. *Obiter*, the Federal Tribunal pointed out that the possibility to stay an arbitration arises when "*the legal existence or the authority of a party is at stake and when the parties agree on a suspension*"[42].

The Federal Tribunal predicates its decision on a reference to Schlosser who, precisely, is of the same opinion[43].

The solution proposed here is flexible. It allows the arbitrators to preserve the legitimate rights of both parties and not to accept certain manoeuvres, such as

---

According to this decision, the only public policy rule is the equal treatment of the creditors.

41 It is our experience that a creditor will oppose a stay only if he has obtained security (especially third party's guarantees, for instance insurance policies) or if the bankruptcy was "organized" in order to circumvent arbitration. In the other cases, the estate's adverse party prefers to suspend in order to negotiate with a new partner, namely the trustee. Furthermore, if the trustee decides to proceed with the arbitration, the arbitration costs will become debts of the estate itself, which is an important element of decision for both parties. *F. Mantilla Serano* (International Arbitration Insolvency Proceedings, Arbitration International, 1995, pp. 51 and ff, p.56 last §) cites an arbitral procedural order which suspended an international arbitration with the consent of the parties: in that case, the interest at stake had been divided by ten (foreseeable dividend) while the arbitration costs remained the same (the ICC will compute the arbitration costs on the basis of the claim and not on the foreseeable dividend).

42 *Fincantieri* decision N°2 (cited above), BASA 1994 p. 248, c1b p. 250.

43 *P. Schlosser*, Das Recht der internationalen privaten Schiedsgerichtsbarkeit, second edition, Tübingen, 1989, N° 663, p. 492. This author is suggesting to apply, by analogy, to the arbitral tribunal the provisions relating to the suspension of proceedings before municipal courts, taking into consideration the discretion of the courts. "Such discretion can of course not be utilized in such a way that the persons who become in charge will not enjoy a right to be equitably heard". See in France Cour de cassation 1ère Chambre civile February 5, 1991, *Almira*, Revue de l'arbitrage 1991 p. 625 (627): "The superior principle of adversarial procedure, indispensable for an equitable proceeding, made it compulsory for the arbitrators to search to what extent the impossibility to act which had struck one of the parties, suspended the time limit which was resulting from the arbitral rules".

bankruptcy and other insolvency proceedings meant to stay arbitral proceedings[44].

In conclusion, the arbitrator should rely on the arbitral procedure rather than on the *lex concursus* to decide whether there is a case for a suspension of the arbitration. A stay will be mandatory only if there are considerations of procedural public policy (the existence of which the Federal Tribunal acknowledged).

2. Other procedural effects resulting from the bankruptcy

2.1 Notifications

In arbitration, it is the claimant's responsibility to ascertain the address of respondent for the purpose of notification to the other party. Subject to suspicion of fraud, the arbitrators will not have to vet whether the parties have communicated the right address. However, an award handed down against a party without proper notice may be quashed (Art. 190 (2) (d) PILA) and may not be enforceable (Art. V 1b, New York 1958 Convention)[45].

The representation of the bankruptcy is a matter to be determined according to the *lex concursus*, practically the law of the seat of the debtor, the place where the bankruptcy is usually declared. However, the form of the notification remains a matter to be decided according to the *lex arbitri*. There is no need for a formal notification which may be required by the *lex concursus*[46].

2.2 Representation

Likewise, the arbitrators may ascertain that counsel for the debtor remains empowered to represent the estate after the bankruptcy has been declared. The applicable law is determined by the "closest connection" test. (In principle, the law of the domicile of the counsel rather than the *lex concursus*.)

2.3 Challenges

The estate might have legitimate grounds to challenge an arbitrator, especially the arbitrator originally nominated by the debtor who could lack the necessary independence. For instance, it might be the case if the debtor has a personal

---

44 As an example, Cour d'appel de Paris, January 12, 1993, Revue de l'arbitrage 1994, pp. 687, especially 692 and 693.

45 Cf. *F. Mantilla Serrano* op.cit. pp. 52-53 according to whom the notifications may continue to be made at the address initially indicated by the claimant (p. 53). However, due to the "dispossession", a notification to the debtor will not bind the estate: upon filing of the claim for verification, the estate might disregard the claim in spite of the award. Such a risk is not infrequent, especially when the bankrupt debtor is a company which is a part of a group: in such cases, the notifications will often be made (erroneously) at the group's headquarter rather than at the address of the trustee.

46 Cf. Cour d'appel de Paris May 3, 1988 *Demarti*, Revue de l'arbitrage 1989, p. 75 note *P. Ancel*.

interest to see the estate fail in the arbitration. It may also happen that an arbitrator has a conflict of interests due to his ties with the trustee.

2.4 Intervention

If the estate becomes a party to the arbitration, is it possible for the debtor to make an intervention into the arbitration, either voluntarily or because he is called by one of the parties? The debtor may have a personal vested interest therein: for instance, he may dispose of assets which are not included in the estate which may become subject to execution if the other party prevails. The dispossession of the debtor does not void the arbitration agreement: the possibility of intervention will thus depend solely on the *lex arbitri*[47].

2.5 Costs

Last, the arbitration costs may raise some difficulties: is it possible to order the estate to pay an advance or to pay a security for costs? If the estate decides to continue the arbitration, it becomes an ordinary party and the arbitration costs become its own debts[48]. As already indicated, it is possible to order an estate to pay security for costs. However, it does not seem permissible to order an estate to make a provisional payment on account of the final award, such as to post a bond guaranteeing the enforcement of the final award: this would be contrary to the equal treatment of the creditors, i.e. the creation of a security which does not result from any law[49].

B. Substantive effects

The adjudication of bankruptcy calls into possible application a new law, namely the *lex concursus*. Under several bankruptcy laws, as already indicated, the trustee may refuse to perform some contracts: rather than to carry out his specific performance, the trustee may elect that "*a claim the object of which is not a sum of money becomes a monetary claim of equivalent value*" (Art. 211 LP). The arbitrators will also have to determine the effect of bankruptcy on the validity and effects of securities (mortgages, pledges, loans), on compensatory and moratory interest (which may be suspended by the bankruptcy, Art. 209 LP), on the currency of the agreement, the possible voidance or termination of the contract, set-off, etc.).

---

47 Under Swiss bankruptcy law, the intervention of the debtor, at least accessory, seems permissible either in favour or against the estate (see *Jaeger*, Commentaire de la loi fédérale sur la poursuite pour dettes et la faillite, Payot, ad Art. 250 N° 1 p. 351). *Contra* : Geneva Court of Justice, May 30, 1975, La semaine judiciaire 1976, p. 333. Whatever the case, the *lex concursus* has no standing to determine the validity of an intervention.

48 At least in Switzerland. In France, the solution would be different.

49 Cf. ICC Award 6697 of December 26, 1990, *CASA*, Revue de l'arbitrage 1992, p. 135, note *P. Ancel* (seat Paris; Swiss governing law).

Under Swiss law, the arbitrator has more discretion than a judge: he will determine according to the rules of law chosen by the parties or, in the absence of such a choice, according to the rules of law having the closest connection with the case. It is impossible to be more specific: the arbitrator will certainly take into consideration the *lex concursus* but the extent of such consideration will depend upon the circumstances.

The parties to an arbitration agreement may also authorize the arbitral tribunal to decide *ex aequo et bono* (amiable composition; Art. 187 (2) PILA). The bankruptcy will not void such a clause. And the arbitrator will render an "equitable" award. However, he will not fail to take into consideration the equal treatment of the creditors.

In bankruptcy proceedings, the equal treatment of the creditors is the touchstone. To each creditor, the exceptions to this principle will mean a diminution of the common dividend. Thus, an arbitrator should always bear the following factors in mind:

- Territoriality (or universality) of a brankruptcy have no relevance as the arbitration is international (no *lex fori*)[50].
- Mortgage will in principle be valid if constituted in accordance with the laws applicable to the secured claim and to the *lex rei sitae*. Whether the trustee may avoid a mortgage is a matter which may call several laws into application, especially the law governing such chattels and the bankruptcy law. A subsequent voidance will in principle depend on such laws rather than on the *lex concursus*. Article 187 (1) PILA does not otherwise call for the application of the bankruptcy law.
- Public policy does not require an absolute equality of the creditors: in principle, public policy has no normative effect[51]. The equal treatment of the creditors is a rule common to all European laws. However, the exceptions and limitations are numerous and will vary from one country to the other: thus, an arbitrator will not necessarily apply the exact conception of the equal treatment of the creditors, as prevailing in the *lex concursus*.

---

[50] See however ICC Award 6057 of 1991, Clunet, 1993, p. 1017, note Y.D.

[51] See SFTD June 10, 1996, BASA 2000, p. 764, comment by *Ph. Schweizer,* Revue suisse de droit international et de droit européen 4/2001, p. 482.

Impecuniosity of the Parties and its Effect on Arbitration - An English Perspective

*Robert Hunter**

I. Introduction

The catalyst for the conference for which this paper is written is a German Federal Court of Justice decision,[1] which I shall call "*the Poor Plumber Case*". The case concerned what in England would have been an application under S.9 Arbitration Act 1996 for a stay of court proceedings in favour of an arbitration agreement.

The judgment proceeded on the factual basis that

> the claimant was unable, on account of his personal and his financial circumstances, to pay the advance on costs to the arbitral tribunal and the necessary costs of his legal representation in this dispute.

It was also material to the Federal Court's decision that in an arbitration the Client's costs would not otherwise be covered (e.g. by legal aid or insurance) whereas the claimant would be entitled to financial assistance to pursue court proceedings. On this basis, the German Federal Court rejected the defendant's application for a dismissal of the Court proceedings on the basis that the arbitration agreement was "incapable of being performed" ("*undurchführbar*"). As the Court expressly mentioned, this decision is consistent with the German arbitration law prior to the 1998 reform, under which a party was entitled to terminate an arbitration agreement for good cause ("*aus wichtigem Grund*") if the performance of the arbitration proceedings was shown to be impossible in

---

* Solicitor, Lovells, Frankfurt am Main.

1 BGH Judgment of September 14, 2000 - II ZR 33/00.

practice because a party could not afford the cost of the arbitration proceedings. In the absence of deceit or bad faith, this entitlement to terminate existed even if the 'incapability of performance' of the arbitration proceedings originated in or was the fault of the terminating party.

The issue before the German Court raises profound questions about the nature of the agreement to arbitrate and in particular about the status of the parties' obligation under that agreement. As one commentator has observed,[2] the issue presents a collision between party autonomy and *pacta sunt servanda* on the one hand and a state's constitutional obligation to grant due process on the other. As I consider later, the collision may be more profound than that, since refusing a stay would infringe the respondent's right not to be sued in a national court.

This question cannot be seen as a purely German matter. § 1032 German Arbitration Act is drawn from Article 8(1) of the Model Law, and this in turn implements Article II of the New York Convention. The problem is therefore one which may potentially confront, in substantially identical form, all signatories to the New York Convention, whether or not they have adopted the Model Law.[3]

In the following paper, I consider:

- First, how the English Court would approach the facts of the Poor Plumber Case, and impecuniosity in arbitration generally.
- Secondly, the balance of such an approach with access to justice and Article 6 of the European Convention of Human Rights in particular.

Before embarking on this, I deal quickly with the effect of formal administration and insolvency proceedings on an arbitration.

Administration

The purpose of Administration is to preserve all or some of the undertaking of a company in financial difficulties as a going concern and avoid liquidation.

To further this purpose, a company in Administration has the benefit of a moratorium against legal proceedings. This means that no court or arbitration proceedings can be commenced or continued against it except with the consent of the administrator or the leave of the court (s 11(3)(d) of the Insolvency Act 1986). However, an administrator has the power to bring or defend any proceedings in the name of and on behalf of the company and may refer any matter concerning the company to arbitration (s 14(1)(b) of the Insolvency Act 1986, referring to schedule 1, paragraph 6).

---

2 *Wagner* zu LM § 1032 I ZPO, No. 11.

3 In England, the relevant provision is Section 9 Arbitration Act 1996, formerly contained in Section 1(1) Arbitration Act 1975.

Liquidation
After the presentation of a winding-up petition but prior to the grant of a winding-up order, the court may make an order staying arbitration proceedings against the company (s 126 of the Insolvency Act 1986). The liquidator may also be authorised by the court to bring or defend any action or legal proceedings, including arbitration (s 126 of the Insolvency Act 1986, referring to schedule 4, para. 6).

Once the winding-up order is made, no proceedings may be commenced and any proceedings to which the company is a party are suspended until the court orders otherwise (s 139(2) of the Insolvency Act 1986).

These provisions are not specific to arbitration (on the contrary, they affect both litigation and arbitration alike) and involve quite separate policy considerations to the issues in the Poor Plumber Case. I therefore do not consider them further in this paper.

I now turn to consider the interpretation of "incapable of being performed" under English law before looking at impecuniosity (short of liquidation) and arbitration in a wider context.

II. "Incapable of Performance"

The relevant provision of English law is Section 9 (4) Arbitration Act 1996, which obliges the English court to grant a stay of legal proceedings

> "unless satisfied that the arbitration agreement is null and void, inoperative, or incapable of being performed."[4]

This provision is one of the 'mandatory' provisions of the Act: i.e. it has effect notwithstanding any provision to the contrary and prescribes what the court must do (Section 4 (1) and Schedule 1 Arbitration Act 1996).

As mentioned already, the terminology of Section 9 derives directly from Article II of the New York Convention.

It appears that there was no discussion of the phrase "incapable of being performed" at the 1958 New York Conference itself.[5] The phrase was likewise subsequently incorporated into the UNCITRAL Model Law without comment or discussion.[6]

---

[4] There is one fine distinction between German and English procedural law in this respect. Whereas in Germany, the court accepting such a challenge must "reject the action as inadmissible", under English procedure, the court must stay the legal proceedings. This reflects the English position that the Court always retains ultimate jurisdiction but merely cannot exercise it save as allowed by the Act.

[5] *Albert Jan van den Berg*, The New York Arbitration Conference of 1958, 1981. At page 154 van den Berg states, "The Summary Records of the New York Conference of 1958 do not reveal any discussion regarding these words, nor have many courts interpreted them."

[6] *Aron Boches*, Commentary on the UNCITRAL Model Law on International Commercial Arbitration, 1990, p 45.

Van den Berg suggests that:

"The broad language...seems to have been provided upon the consideration that the Convention is to be applied in many different legal systems. Having regard to the "pro-enforcement bias" of the Convention, the words should be construed narrowly, and the invalidity of the arbitration agreement should be accepted in manifest cases only."[7]

He goes on to argue that the words "incapable of being performed" would apply to those cases where the arbitration cannot physically be set in motion; i.e. where the arbitration cannot take place even though the parties are willing to go forward with it. This appears to refer to more practical, or mechanical, aspects of the prospective arbitration proceedings. A number of possibilities as to when this may arise are then presented, such as where:

- the arbitral clause is too vaguely worded;
- other terms of the contract contradict the parties' intention to arbitrate; or
- the arbitral tribunal named in the agreement refuses to accept the arbitration.

Van den Berg's restrictive interpretation of the meaning of "incapable of being performed" is also the approach of the English courts. In two cases, the Court has held that a defendant's impecuniosity is not a ground upon which the court may reject an application for a stay of legal proceedings.

Both these decisions predate the 1996 Arbitration Act. They were made rather under its predecessor, the Arbitration Act 1975, by which the New York Convention was first enacted in England.

The wording of Section 1 Arbitration Act 1975 is in all material respects identical to Section 9 Arbitration Act 1996. I therefore first set out the English Court's interpretation of this wording before considering if any other provisions in the Arbitration Act 1996 might have affected the application of that interpretation.

1. The Common Law prior to 1996

The first case to come before the Court was *The Rena K.*[8] In an application for a stay of court proceedings, the defendants argued that the court should refuse to order a stay on the ground that the arbitration was "incapable of being performed" as the claimant's financial resources were such that, if an award was made against them, they would not be able to pay the full amount of it.

The Court (at first instance) rejected this submission, reasoning that it was clear above all from their context in the New York Convention that the words "incapable of being performed" referred only to the question of whether an arbitration agreement was capable of being performed up to the stage when it resulted in an award and did not extend to the question of whether, once an

---

[7] *Albert Jan van den Berg* (Fn. 6), p. 155.

[8] *The Rena K* [1979] 1 All ER 397.

award was made, the party against whom it was made would be capable of satisfying it.

This distinction between pre- and post-award almost invited later argument that impecuniosity affecting a party's ability to pursue arbitration pre-award should therefore constitute incapability of performance. Such an agreement duly came before the Court of Appeal only a few years later in the case of *Paczy v Haendler & Natermann*.[9]

The facts of *Paczy* closely resemble the Poor Plumber Case in many crucial respects:

- It concerned an application for a stay of legal proceedings to arbitration;
- The dispute concerned an ICC arbitration agreement with a corresponding obligation to pay an advance on costs;
- The claimant in the legal proceedings was an impecunious claimant who had been granted legal aid in the High Court. According to his own evidence, he was unemployed and dependant on unemployment benefit;
- Specifically, the claimant was unable to finance the ICC advance of costs, either with cash or by way of a bank guarantee.

Whereas in the Poor Plumber Case the German Court decided the question as a matter of public policy, the English Court of Appeal decided the case rather as a "simple" matter of construction of the relevant statutory provision.

The respondent argued for a narrow definition of the phrase "incapable of being performed", "*in the sense that circumstances have become such that it is impracticable to carry the agreement into effect and that it has become frustrated in law*". The claimant argued that the provision should be construed "*in a broad way so as to give it a sensible common sense practical effect*" and thereby include any case in which there was "*a real practical difficulty in proceeding*".

The Court of Appeal held that the narrow interpretation prevailed.

In reaching this decision, the Court of Appeal recognised that

> "in those circumstances the arbitration will never get under way, for the simple reason that the plaintiff will, owing to circumstances, fail to take the steps requisite to be taken by him as claimant."[10]

However, while at least one of the judges had sympathy for the claimant's position, the court unanimously found that the situation did not amount to "incapability of performance" and that it therefore could not refuse the respondent's application for a stay:

> "In my judgment, on the true construction of these words, "incapable of being performed" relates to the arbitration agreement under consideration. The incapacity of one party to that agreement to implement his obligations under the agreement does not

---

9 *Paczy v Haendler & Natermann* [1981] 1 Lloyd's Rep 302 (CA).

10 per Lord Brightman, *Paczy v Haendler & Natermann* [1981] 1 Lloyd's Rep 302 (CA), p. 308, 309.

> ... render the agreement one which is incapable of performance within the section any more than the inability of a purchaser under a contract for the purchase of land to find the purchase price when the time comes to complete the sale could be said to render the contract for the sale incapable of performance. The agreement only becomes incapable of performance ... if the circumstances are such that it could no longer be performed, even if both parties were ready, able and willing to perform it. Impecuniosity is not ... a circumstance of that kind.
> ... The plaintiff cannot rely on his own inability to carry out his part of the arbitration agreement as a means of securing a release from the arbitration agreement. The arbitration agreement remains an agreement which is perfectly capable of being performed if the parties are themselves capable of performing it, and to construe section 1 (1) in a way which would allow a plaintiff or claimant in arbitration proceedings to say, "I am unable to perform any part of the arbitration agreement, therefore the arbitration agreement has become incapable of performance, therefore the stay on the proceedings in the Court of law should be lifted" ... is quite contrary to the effect and the policy of the section."[11]

Whilst not expressed in the judgment, the decision in *Paczy* equates "incapable of performance" with the doctrine of frustration in English law.[12] Frustration enables a contract to be discharged when something occurs after its formation which renders it physically or commercially impossible to fulfil the contract or radically transforms the nature of the obligation.

The applicability of the contractual doctrine of frustration to arbitration was expressly considered by the House of Lords in *The Hannah Blumenthal*[13], (a case concerning delay rather than impecuniosity). In its judgment, the House of Lords (following the rationale of its judgment two years earlier in *Bremer Vulkan*, which is considered below) held that "*there can be no doubt that an agreement to refer a dispute to arbitration can in theory, like any other contract, be discharged by frustration*".[14] However, consistent with the principle of mutual obligation it had laid down in *Bremer Vulkan*, the court rejected the argument that one party's delay had frustrated the arbitration agreement. The fact of such a delay failed to satisfy the two usual requirements applicable to any claim of frustration, namely:

- There must have been some outside event or extraneous change of situation, not foreseen or provided for by the parties at the time of contracting, which either makes it impossible for the contract to be

[11] per Buckley LJ, *Paczy v Haendler & Natermann* [1981] 1 Lloyd's Rep 302 (CA), p. 307, 308.

[12] Such an equivalent of terminology was assumed by the Alberta Court of Appeal in *Kaverit Steel and others v Kone Corporation and Others*, following *Paczy*.

[13] *Paal Wilson & Co A/S v Partenreederei Hannah Blumenthal, The Hannah Blumenthal* [1983] 1 All ER 34 (HL).

[14] per Lord Brandon, *Paal Wilson & Co A/S v Partenreederei Hannah Blumenthal, The Hannah Blumenthal* [1983] 1 All ER 34 (HL).

performed at all, or at least renders its performance something radically different from what the parties contemplated then they entered into it; and

- This event or change of situation, and the consequences of it, must have occurred without the fault or default of either party to the contract.[15]

Impecuniosity would also fail to satisfy these two tests, on the basis of the same reasoning as applied by Lord Justice Buckley to the question of "incapability of performance", quoted above. It cannot properly be said that a party's inability to perform is a change of circumstance extraneous to the contract making it "impossible for the contract to be performed at all or at least [rendering] its performance something radically different",[16] since the arbitration agreement itself is capable of performance irrespective of the parties' ability or willingness to finance the arbitration.[17]

Another argument speaks very strongly for this narrow approach to interpretation. As the court in *Paczy* held, treating impecuniosity as a ground of inability of performance raises considerable administrative problems: how is the court to assess the financial resources of the party; what test is to be applied, short of insolvency; at what date is the test to be made; once declared "inoperable", does the arbitration agreement become operable again if the party's circumstances change, and with what effect? It is surely more satisfactory to

---

15 per Lord Brandon *Paal Wilson & Co A/S v Partenreederei Hannah Blumenthal, The Hannah Blumenthal* [1983] 1 All ER 34 (HL). It has been stated in a later judgment that the requirement that the frustrating event should not be due to the act or election of the party seeking to rely on it is "the essence of the doctrine" of frustration and that, since the effect of frustration is to "kill the contract" and discharge the parties from further liability under it, the court will as a matter of policy keep its application within very narrow limits. (Bingham LJ in J. *Lauritzen A.S. v Wijsmuller B.V (The Super Servant Two)*, [1990] 1 LLR 1).

16 *Hannah Blumenthal* (Fn. 13), p. 43. See also the Indian Supreme Court decision in *V/O Tractorexport v Tarapore and Co (India no. 1)*, January 1971, a case specifically on Article II.3 of the New York Convention, where the Supreme Court held that the unavailability of foreign exchange to cover the necessary costs of arbitration (e.g. for the payment of travel expenses of witnesses abroad and so on) was not a sufficient reason for refusing to stay court proceedings in favour of arbitration in Moscow on the ground of incapability of performance.

17 There is an exception to this general rule of objective impossibility in the concept of frustration in relation to contracts of personal performance. It is beyond the scope of this paper to discuss in full whether an arbitration agreement could be said to be such a contract. While such an agreement contains some aspects which might be said to be personal, it is submitted that it properly should not fall within such a category of contracts; not least, as a general rule an arbitration agreement may be assigned along with the underlying substantive contract. The exception of personal contracts to the rule of frustration was mentioned in Hannah Blumenthal (Fn. 13), but the House of Lords appears to have assumed that it did not apply to arbitration agreements.

restrict the court's intervention to cases of actual administration or liquidation, as outlined at the beginning of this article.

In this context, it is also worth considering that arbitration agreements are usually contained in commercial contracts which include either a unilateral right by one party to terminate the agreement in the event of the other falling into financial difficulties often short of insolvency or *force majeure* clauses giving the parties mutual releases in events significantly broader than those circumscribed by the English doctrine of frustration: they will often contain both. Subject to the discussion above about the contractual nature of the obligation, there is no reason why such clauses should not apply also to arbitration agreements contained within such a contract. If so, they should where appropriate be relied on; conversely, where they do not apply, there is even more reason not to imply more extensive terms.

I mention here one additional hurdle for a claimant seeking to resist a stay: the burden is on the claimant to prove the vitiation of the arbitration agreement. Certainly on the basis of the ICC Rules, it is hard to see how assertion merely of an inability to pay the advance, without more, can be said to amount to incapability of performance. Article 30 (2) provides for the advance to be adjusted at any time, and Article 30 (5) provides the Secretary General with a discretion, not a duty, to direct the tribunal to suspend work and to make a peremptory order for payment or dismissal.

However unlikely it is the ICC or a tribunal would conduct an arbitration without any advance, it would seem that an impecunious claimant must first argue its position with the ICC before it can begin to argue impossibility with a court.

At first sight, *Paczy* (both on its own terms and by analogy to the doctrine of frustration) gives a straightforward and definitive answer to the Poor Plumber case under English law: that is, impecuniousness of a claimant is not a ground of "incapability of performance" for the purpose of Section 9 Arbitration Act 1996 and Article II New York Convention.

Moreover, it has been cited with approval in a number of foreign courts in support of a narrow interpretation of "incapable of performance".[18]

However, it is necessary to consider in more detail two particular aspects of the decision:

- First, whether any doctrines of English law other than frustration could apply in such circumstances; and
- Secondly, whether the position would be different if both parties were impecunious (as was suggested in the Poor Plumber Case).

---

[18] *Dupont Scandinavia AB v Coastal (Bermuda) Limited* in the Court of Appeal of Bermuda (9.11.88); *Bakri Navigation Co Ltd v Glorious Shipping SA* in the Federal Court of Australia (5.6.91); *Kaverit Steel and others v Kone Corporation and others* in the Alberta Court of Appeal (16.1.91).

2. Can impecuniousness constitute any other ground of avoidance of an arbitration agreement?

The *Bremer Vulkan* case established the principle that the court has no inherent jurisdiction to intervene in an arbitration when justice so requires; the powers of the court are statutory in origin and there is no statute which permits such intervention. This precedent is preserved through Section 81 (1) Arbitration Act and the principle specifically enacted in Section 1 (c) of the Act.[19]

Any attempt by a claimant to defeat an arbitration clause must therefore fall within Section 9.

3. If impecuniousness alone does not constitute "incapability of performance", can it otherwise fall within Section 9?

Section 9 Arbitration Act lays down two further grounds of invalidity in addition to inoperability of performance: if the arbitration agreement is "null and void", or if it is "inoperable". Could the circumstances of the Poor Plumber Case fall within either of these other two grounds?

In *Paczy*, the claimant argued that the respondent had repudiated the agreement. The basis for this was that, given its own inability to proceed with the arbitration, the *respondent* was under an obligation to initiate the proceedings, and in correspondence the claimant had requested the respondent to do so. By commencing the arbitration, the erstwhile respondent would then have come under the obligation to fund the initial ICC advance, failing which the arbitration would not proceed. The claimant argued that this failure was itself 'repudiatory conduct' entitling it to proceed to ligitation.

It is not clear from its judgment in *Paczy* whether the Court of Appeal's consideration of this particular line of argument forms part of the Court's reasoning on the question of "incapable of being performed" or whether it comprises a quite separate ground of invalidity which was also dismissed.

Repudiation is part of the English common law of contract. A repudiatory breach of contract occurs where one party by words or conduct evinces an intention not to perform, or expressly declares that he is or will be unable to perform, obligations under the contract in some material respect. The innocent party can then discharge itself from the remainder of the contract and claim damages.

It is both interesting and significant that in the Poor Plumber Case the German Federal Court took into account an almost identical argument in its own reasoning. Indeed, it appears to take it one very large step further:

> "In this dispute, the arbitration agreement was "incapable of being performed" ("*undurchführbar*") because the claimant could not have paid for the cost of the arbitration proceedings and the payment of the costs was not otherwise provided for.

---

[19] See *Mustill & Boyd*, Compendium, p. 55.

> It is evident from the fact that the claimant would not have been able to afford the costs of pursuing his claim before the state courts that he was also unable, on account of his personal and his financial circumstances, to pay the advance on costs to the arbitral tribunal and the necessary costs of his legal representation in this dispute. The claimant submitted an affidavit of means[20] on 1 August 1996. Even the defendant is proceeding on the basis that the claimant is impecunious.
> There is no indication that the defendants could have removed this "incapability of performance" of the arbitration proceedings (stemming from the claimant's impecuniousness) or that they would have been prepared to do so. *The defendants did not claim that in the interests of the performance of the arbitration they would have advanced to the claimant the claimant's costs of the arbitration proceedings as well as the claimant's necessary attorney's costs.* ... It appears that the defendants were themselves impecunious as they had themselves submitted an affidavit of means on 6 May 1997 and 6 February 1998. The defendants' business liability insurance policy would only have covered its own costs of defending the arbitration proceedings; the claimant's costs of the proceedings would have remained uncovered." ... [Author's emphasis]

This implies that under German law, where a claimant is impecunious but a respondent wishes to rely on an arbitration agreement, the defendant is obliged to prefund not only the tribunal's costs but also the Claimant's necessary legal costs. The apparent rationale is that in such circumstance the respondent must assume the role of the provider of legal aid. To an English eye, this is an extraordinary proposition.

The first question under English law is whether repudiation, being a contractual concept is applicable at all to an arbitration agreement. The starting point for any such analysis is an understanding of the nature and extent of the obligations contained within an agreement to arbitrate.

Certainly until the enactment of the 1996 Act, the leading case on this question was the House of Lords' decision of 1981 in *Bremer Vulkan Schiffbau und Maschinenfabrik v South India Shipping Corporation.*[21] This case concerned the question whether a party was entitled unilaterally to terminate an arbitration in mid-proceedings where the claimant party had delayed so much in pursuing the arbitration that a fair hearing was no longer possible.

In the course of considering this question, the House of Lords held that an arbitration agreement should indeed be approached by reference to the traditional doctrines of the law of contract. The arbitration agreement was itself "*a self-contained contract collateral or ancillary to [the principal commercial] agreement itself*" which expressly incorporated by operation of statute the "*rules, regulations, etc*" of the Arbitration Act. There could also be implied into it other terms, whether express (as would be the case of, for instance, incorporation of the ICC Rules) or by necessity.

---

[20] Under German enforcement procedure (§807 ZPO), this is only necessary where a debtor has already claimed that he has insufficient assets to satisfy a judgment against him.

[21] *Bremer Vulkan Schiffbau und Maschinenfabrik v South India Shipping Corporation* [1981] All ER 289 (HL).

As with other contracts, the arbitration agreement comprised "unperformed primary obligations" which

> "may be brought to an end by frustration, or at the election of one party where there has been a repudiatory breach of that agreement by the other party."

The House of Lords held that those primary obligations included a mutual obligation on the parties

> "to co-operate with the other in taking appropriate steps to keep the procedure in the arbitration moving, whether he happens to be the claimant or the respondent in the particular dispute."[22]

Because they held that this duty was mutual, the House of Lords rejected the respondent's argument that the claimant's delay in failing to apply for directions amounted to a repudiatory breach: since the respondent was itself equally in breach of its own duty to apply for directions, it could not rely on the claimant's breach of the same duty.

The relevant aspect of the decision for present purposes is the underlying philosophy that the obligations of the arbitration agreement are inherently contractual and therefore subject to the contractual doctrines of repudiation and frustration.

In *Paczy*, the claimant based its argument on the *Bremer Vulkan*, arguing that, in view of its own inability to commence the arbitration by reason of its impecuniosity, there was an obligation on the defendants to initiate the arbitration or at least to offer to provide the whole of the advance required under the ICC arbitration rules to enable the claimant to proceed with his claim.

With reasoning diametrically opposed to that of the German Federal Court in the Poor Plumber Case, the English Court of Appeal roundly rejected this argument. Although proceeding on the assumption that ordinary contractual principles applied to the construction of the arbitration agreement, Brightman LJ called it "a fantastic assertion" that there should be imposed on a defendant an obligation to come to the financial rescue of a plaintiff to enable him to prosecute his claim. He added that "it cannot be possibly said that the defendants have been guilty of any repudiatory conduct." Buckley LJ, too, held that he could:

> "... see no justification for the suggestion which has been made, that the defendants were in this case under any obligation themselves to initiate the arbitration proceedings on account of the plaintiff's difficulties in initiating them."

However, the *ratio* of *Paczy* on this issue must be treated cautiously for the following reason.

In reaching their conclusion on the issue of repudiation, both judges considered carefully the provisions of the ICC Rules at that time in force in order to ascertain the precise nature of the obligation to pay the advance:[23]

---

[22] per Lord Diplock, *Bremer Vulkan Schiffbau und Maschinenfabrik v South India Shipping Corporation* p. 298.

[23] presumably the 1975 Rules.

> "It is clear from the ICC rules that it is the duty of the claimant to formulate his claim in the first instance. At that stage he does not have to find the deposit. It is then for the respondents to put in their defence, and it is only after that stage has been reached that any question of finding the deposit arises. It is for the arbitration court to decide by whom the deposit shall be paid, and if the deposit is to be paid partly by one party and parlty by another, to decide in what proportions it is to be paid. It is for the parties to abide by whatever directions that court gives in that respect. It has been suggested by [the claimants] that the defendants here are under an obligation to provide the whole of the deposit because of the plaintiff's inability to provide any part of it and because the defendants have entered into the arbitration agreement (cl. 12 of the contract). I can see no good basis ... of that submission. Still less do I think it can be said that the defendants in failing to offer to provide the deposit have been guilty of a repudiatory breach of the arbitration agreement *when ... they have not in fact been asked to provide any part of it by anybody*." [Author's emphasis]

It follows from these judgments that the position might be different where the respondent *was* at the time of its application for a stay in breach of a specific contractual obligation or tribunal direction in relation to the proceedings.

For instance, suppose that at the time of the application to the court for a stay, the respondent was already itself in breach of a current positive obligation to pay a share of the advance or take some other step in the proceedings, would it then be in repudiatory breach such that it could not then rely on the arbitration agreement? On the basis of *Bremer Vulkan*, this is at least arguable.[24]

Should such an argument in fact succeed, it is worth asking under which, if any, ground within Section 9 of the Arbitration Act and Article II of the New York Convention a repudiated arbitration agreement would fall.

The effect of the acceptance of a repudiatory breach is not that the contract is "rescinded" (as, for instance, in the case of misrepresentation), nor does it terminate the contract. The contract rather continues, with the "innocent" party absolved from further performance of his obligations under the contract and the primary obligations of the repudiating party converted to obligations in damages.

It is therefore submitted that the effect of such repudiation would not render the arbitration agreement "incapable of being performed", nor would the agreement be "null and void", but it would rather be "inoperable".

It is then necessary to consider whether the contractual analysis in *Bremer Vulkan* has survived the coming-into-force of the Arbitration Act 1996.

While Section 9 Arbitration Act 1996 is in all material respects identical to Section 1 Arbitration Act 1975, under which *Paczy* was decided, the 1996 Act

---

[24] We know of no authority on this under English law but see *Société TRH Graphics v Offset Aubin*, Cour de Cassation, 19.11.91, cited in *Craig, Park, Paulsson*, International Chamber of Commerce, Arbitration, 3rd ed., 2000 at page 270 where the French court accepted jurisdiction in relation to a claim by a claimant who had abandoned arbitration proceedings and commenced the legal proceedings after the respondent had refused to pay its share of the advance in the ICC proceedings.

has arguably brought about a fundamental change in the nature of the primary obligations of the parties under an arbitration agreement. Specifically, the mutual obligation of rather limited scope which was implied by the House of Lords in the *Bremer Vulkan* case has now become an express and substantial duty in Section 40 of the 1996 Act:

> (1) The parties shall do all things necessary for the proper and expeditious conduct of the arbitral proceedings.
> (2) This includes –
> a. complying without delay with any determination of the tribunal as to procedural or evidential matters, ...

Lord Mustill considers the effect of this section in his erudite commentary on the Arbitration Act.[25] As he says, the obligation in the section is a "*complete novelty, for it not only reverses the decision in the Bremer Vulkan case, which was directly concerned only with a possible duty of the claimant to press ahead with his claim, but also has a much wider subject-matter, since it imposes a mandatory general duty to take part in the 'proper' conduct of the arbitration spontaneously, without waiting for an order from the arbitrator.*"

Moreover, as he continues, Section 40 "*may be novel not only in what it says but in what it does*". Previous arbitration statutes have only elaborated or modified the obligations which would otherwise flow from the essentially contractual nature of the relationships in an arbitration. However,

> "Whether section 40(1) is of the same character seems to us far from clear. It is at least possible that section 40(1) creates duties which are independent of contract, ... that is, that they are 'statutory duties' of the type familiar in the field of public law."[26]

As Lord Mustill acutely observes, this lack of clarity about the nature of the duty in turn creates uncertainty in the remedies available for its breach. Apart from the power to dismiss a stale claim, the only statutory sanction for an aggrieved opponent is to apply to the tribunal for directions, and the only provision for reimbursement of losses is for wasted costs.[27]

Putting this now into the context of the repudiatory argument in *Paczy*, the essential question is whether, as Lord Mustill puts it, "*the shadow of a contractual relationship underlying the whole of the rights and duties of the parties and the arbitrator in the conduct of the reference*" continues to exist behind the statutory regime.[28]

As Lord Mustill says, while this has "an apparent plausibility" since the non-mandatory aspects of the relationship are consensual, "to equiparate the elements of this consent with a contract in the full sense does, however, seem to us impossible". Certainly, in relation to the specific duties of Section 40, there are serious problems with such an argument, not least because the existence of

---

[25] *Mustill & Boyd*, Commercial Arbitration, 2nd ed., 2001; Compendium, p. 63.
[26] *Mustill & Boyd*, (Fn 25), p. 36.
[27] *Mustill & Boyd*, (Fn 25), p. 63.
[28] *Mustill & Boyd*, (Fn 25), p. 64.

the statutory obligation in Section 40 leaves little if not no scope for implying contractual terms, and because there is no ground for supposing that Parliament contemplated a parallel set of remedies, differently founded, in relation to the same general obligations."[29] If that is the case, the appropriate cause of action would be for breach of statutory duty, for which repudiation is not an available remedy.

Even if there is no contractual element in the Section 40 duty itself, the obligation may still retain a separate contractual nature where the arbitration agreement itself stipulates relevant express duties of the parties (either directly or through the incorporation of a set of rules). For instance, where the parties have agreed the ICC Rules, the obligation to pay the advance on costs in equal shares in Article 30 (3) of the Rules might still be regarded as a *contractual* obligation and therefore capable of repudiation, but the question is undecided.

By way of summary, it is submitted that:

- The 1996 Act has no effect on the decision of *Paczy* as regards the narrow construction of the words "incapable of performance".
- In the light of the 1996 Act, it is questionable whether the doctrine of repudiation is still applicable to arbitration, at least as regards the existence of any general implied right on a party (per *Bremer Vulkan*) to proceed with the reference, although failure to perform an express obligation in an arbitration agreement may still amount to repudiation, disentitling the respondent from obtaining a stay under Section 9.

4. What if both parties are insolvent?

I now turn to the second aspect of the *Paczy* decision which requires particular consideration.

The discussion so far has been based on the impecuniosity of one party to the arbitration agreement. As I have demonstrated above, it is clear under English law that such circumstance alone is not sufficient to amount to "incapable of being performed" for the purposes of Section 9 Arbitration Act 1996 or Article II of the New York Convention.

What is the position if *both* parties to the arbitration agreement are impecunious? For convenience, I shall call this circumstance "*double-impecuniosity*".

There was suspected double-impecuniosity in the Poor Plumber Case, although this does not seem to have been central to the German Federal Court's decision, which proceeded on the basis that the claimant was entitled to proceed with his court proceedings unless the respondent pre-funded not only the arbitration costs but also the claimant's own necessary legal costs.

---

[29] op cit, p. 64.

However, it is possible that double-impecuniosity might have had an effect on the decision in *Paczy*.

There was no suggestion in *Paczy* that the respondent (a German company) was impecunious. Moreover, both judges of the Court of Appeal reasoned on the basis that under the agreed application of the ICC Rules, the burden was on the claimant to deposit at least part of the deposit at an early stage of the proceedings. Referring to this obligation, and the claimant's inability to perform it, Lord Brightman analysed the issue as follows:

> "The true analysis of the situation will be that the claimant is incapable of performing an obligation which is incumbent upon him if the arbitration is to proceed, *but the respondent to the arbitration on the other hand will be capable of performing his obligations under the rules applicable to the arbitration once the arbitration commences.* In such circumstances ought the Court to express itself as satisfied – and that is the wording of the Act – that the arbitration agreement is incapable of being performed? I think the answer to that question is quite plainly No."[30] [Author's emphasis]

The formulation of the issue in this way begs the question: What if the respondent will demonstrably *not* be capable of performing his obligations under the rules applicable once the arbitration commences?

To answer this question, it is necessary to look at the issue from the point of view of both of the common law doctrines we have already examined: frstration and repudiation.

5. Frustration

As we have already seen, in *Paczy* it was held that "incapability of performance" must relate not to one of the parties but to the arbitration agreement under consideration. For this reason, the incapacity of one party to the agreement to implement his obligations under the agreement does not render the agreement one which is incapable of performance: the agreement only becomes incapable of performance if the circumstances are such that it could no longer be performed, even if both parties were ready, able and willing to perform it.[31]

It is submitted that this is correct as a matter of construction, since the wording clearly relates the requirement of incapability objectively to the agreement and not to the parties' ability to perform it. As already observed, this construction equates closely to the contractual doctrine of frustration, summarised above in the quotation from the *Hannah Blumenthal*.

If this is correct, it would follow that it is immaterial to the question of incapability of performance whether just one or both parties to an arbitration agreement are impecunious.

A possible exception to this is if the cause of the double-impecuniosity lay in a common event. Such a circumstance would certainly be narrowly construed.

---

[30] *Paczy v Haendler & Natermann* [1981] 1 Lloyd's Rep 302 (CA), p. 309.

[31] per Buckley LJ (Fn. 30), p. 307.

As Lord Radcliffe said in *Davis Contractors v Fareham Urban District Council*:[32]

> "... it is not hardship or inconvenience or material loss itself which calls the principle of frustration into play. There must be as well such a change in the significance of the obligation that the thing undertaken would, if performed, be a different thing from that contracted for."

If it could be said that an event affected not only each of the party's ability to perform but also the actual nature of the arbitration envisaged by the agreement, that could arguably constitute frustration. However, in such a case, the impecuniosity would be an inevitable consequence of - and not the ground for - the frustration, so in reality it would not be a true exception to the principle proposed above.

6. Repudiation

A more fruitful ground of argument in relation to double-impecuniosity might be found in the field of repudiation (to the extent, of course, that there is still scope at all for the application of this doctrine to arbitration agreements).

In accordance with the general contractual principles of repudiation, an 'innocent' party faced with repudiatory contract from its partner must elect either to accept the repudiation or to affirm the contract. The innocent party, by electing to affirm the contract, leaves the primary obligations of the parties unchanged.

Putting this choice into the arbitration context, the 'innocent' party faced with the repudiatory conduct of its partner in instigating court proceedings may either accept the repudiation and take part in the court proceedings or affirm the arbitration agreement and apply for a stay under Section 9 Arbitration Act 1996. In the case of a double-impecuniosity, the repudiating party (i.e. the party commencing legal proceedings) could argue that a respondent who is itself unable to perform its obligations under the arbitration agreement should not be not entitled to rely on the claimants' own repudiatory breach. Considerable weight would be given to such argument by the House of Lords' judgment in *Bremer Vulkan*, where it was central to the decision refusing dismissal of the arbitration that, since both claimant and respondent were in breach of their contractual obligations to one another to apply directions to the tribunal, neither party could rely on the other's breach as giving him a right to treat the primary obligations of each to continue with the reference as brought to an end.[33]

The respondent could of course assert that it was not yet in breach of any obligation to pay an advance or take any other step. However, the claimant could counter any such argument in turn by asserting the doctrine of anticipatory

---

32 [1956] A.C. 696.

33 per Lord Diplock, *Bremer Vulkan Schiffbau* und *Machinenfabrik v South India Shipping Corporation* [1981] All ER 289 (HL), p. 298.

breach: i.e. that if at the time of the application for a stay he could prove the respondent would be unable to perform its future obligations to fund the arbitration costs when they fell due, that too would repudiatory conduct which should disable the respondent from affirming the arbitration agreement. Such an argument would be consistent with Lord Brightman's caveat to his judgment in *Paczy*, quoted above.

This falls far short of the implication in the judgment of the German Federal Court in the Poor Plumber Case that the respondent has a duty to prefund the arbitration costs and the claimant's legal costs if it wishes to assert the arbitration clause.

Even in its much more limited potential application, such an argument would be faced with a number of difficulties, in particular:

- Is the analysis of repudiation applicable at all under the Arbitration Act 1996?
- Even if it is, can the claimant actually prove the respondent's impecuniosity such as to constitute an anticipatory breach (short of an actual insolvency, which would suspend all legal proceedings anyway)? Even if the respondent were impecunious, would that necessarily prove a present intention not to perform the arbitration agreement? Might it not still be *possible* that funding might be achieved some other way?

In this context, it should be noted that arbitration agreements are usually contained in commercial contracts which include either a unilateral right by one party to terminate the agreement in the event of the other falling into financial difficulties often short of insolvency or *force majeure* clauses giving the parties mutual releases in events significantly broader than those circumscribed by the English doctrine of frustration: they will often contain both. Subject to the discussion above about the contractual nature of the obligation, there is no reason why such clauses should not apply also to arbitration agreements contained within such a contract. If so, they should where appropriate be relied on; conversely, where they do not apply, there is even more reason not to imply more extensive terms.

III. Impecuniosity, Section 9 Arbitration Act and Public Policy

As indicated at the beginning of this paper, the staying of arbitration proceedings pursuant to a Section 9 application despite a claimant's impecuniosity also has constitutional implications.

While these were not considered in, e.g. *Paczy*, which was decided purely on a question of interpretation of the statute, they are more likely to be raised now that the United Kingdom has enacted the European Convention on Human Rights by the Human Rights Act of 1998.

Article 6 of the ECHR entitles everyone to a fair and public hearing within a reasonable time by an independent and impartial tribunal established by law.

One element of this guarantee is the right to access to court. Section 6(1) of the Act makes it unlawful for a public authority to act in a way incompatible with a convention right, and the definition of a public authority includes any court or tribunal.

A party to an arbitration agreement who cannot pay the advance to the tribunal and faces a decision such as in *Paczy*, particularly where he would be entitled to legal aid before a court, might well argue that such a decision was in conflict with Article 6 of the ECHR and the right to a fair trial.

On the basis of the Poor Plumber Case, the German view is clearly that in such a situation the parties should be forced to submit to the claimant's jurisdiction. However, the question arises whether the *Paczy* decision is really a denial of justice in this sense.

The European Court of Human Rights (ECHR) has itself taken the view that where parties have freely consented to arbitration, they have waived their right to access to court under Article 6(1) on the basis that an arbitration agreement is seen to amount to a renunciation of the right to have a dispute dealt with by an ordinary court:

> "In Contracting States' domestic legal systems, a waiver of this kind is frequently encountered......in civil matters, notably in the shape of arbitration clauses in contracts......The waiver, which has undeniable advantages for the individual concerned as well as for the administration of justice, does not in principle offend against the Convention ..."[34]

It would therefore appear that the ECHR is reluctant to find that Article 6(1) has not been waived where the parties have agreed to arbitrate, unless there is manifest evidence of undue influence or duress.

Such a position is consistent with the treatment of express choices of jurisdiction in private international law. While availability of legal aid may be a legitimate ground of argument in deciding *forum non conveniens*,[35] *forum non conveniens* arguments are not sufficient to justify a stay in favour of an express choice of jurisdiction clause, on the basis of *pacta sunt servanda*.[36] The House of Lords has recently held[37] that where an applicant is relying on a contractual right not to be sued in a jurisdiction by reason of an exclusive jurisdiction clause or an arbitration clause then, absent some special circumstance, he has "by reason of his contract a legitimate interest in enforcing that right not to be sued in that jurisdiction". Similar considerations would apply to a stay, which is the "obverse" of an anti-suit injunction.[38]

---

[34] ECHR judgment of 5 February 1980, *Deweer v Belgium*, No. 6903/75, para. 49 with further references = (1980) 2 EHRR 439; see also European Commission of Human Right, admissibility decision of 17 May 1995, *Lundgren v Sweden*, no. 22506/93.

[35] *Connelly v RTZ Corp. plc* [1998] A.C. 854; *Carlson v Rio Tinto plc* [1999] C.L.C. 551.

[36] See *Dicey & Morris*, 13th ed. (2000), Sweet & Maxwell, para. 12-114 and 12-117.

[37] *Turner v Grovit and Others*, [2001] VKHL 65, per Lord Bingham at paras. 24 – 27.

[38] per Lord Bingham (Fn 45), p. 25.

It could be argued that different policy considerations should apply in relation to a purely domestic dispute. Indeed, on its face, Section 86 (2) (b) of the Arbitration Act 1996 contains an additional provision giving the court discretion to allow a stay of proceedings in relation to a domestic arbitration not only for the three grounds in Article II of the New York Convention and Section 9 of the Arbitration Act, but also where "there are other sufficient grounds for not requiring the parties to abide by the arbitration agreement". Such a discretion would defeat any strict reliance on *Paczy* and open up the possibility of arguments such as prevailed in the Poor Plumber Case.

However, the domestic arbitration provisions of the Arbitration Act 1996 (sections 85 to 87) have never been implemented. The reason for this is that they arguably conflict with the requirement for equal treatment under Community law and for that reason it is unlikely they ever will be given force. There is accordingly no difference in treatment between international and national arbitrations for the purpose of Section 9.[39]

While we are not aware of an English decision specifically on the question of Article 6 ECHR and Section 9 of the Arbitration Act, an analogy may be made to the provision of security for costs.

Section 38(3) of the Arbitration Act 1996 provides that, unless such power is expressly *ex*cluded in the arbitration agreement, a tribunal may order the claimant to provide security for costs. The Act does not specify the basis on which a security for costs order should be granted, and it therefore appears that the tribunal will have a broad discretion in choosing how to deal with any such application.

The most usual way for a tribunal to enforce an order for security for costs is to stay the arbitration proceedings until the security is provided. If the claimant fails to comply with a time limit for such provision, the tribunal can make

---

[39] It should be noted that the situation is different in relation to consumer contracts. Sections 89 to 91 of the Arbitration Act 1996 extend the Unfair Terms in Consumer Contracts Regulations 1994 (now 1999) to all agreements to arbitrate which involve consumers, irrespective of the law applicable to the contract, provided the claim exceeds a stipulated amount. The Regulations apply to any term in a contract between a seller or supplier and a consumer where the term in question has not been individually negotiated. Clause 4.1 of the Regulations defines an 'unfair term' as one "which causes a significant imbalance of the parties' rights and obligations under the contract to the detriment of the consumer." Illustrations of such terms in Schedule 3 of the Regulations include terms "binding the consumer to terms with which he had no real opportunity of becoming acquainted before the conclusion of the contract" and terms "excluding or hindering the consumer's right to take legal action ... particularly by requiring the consumer to take disputes exclusively to arbitration..." In one reported case, the court rejected an application by a building company for a stay under Section 9 of the Arbitration Act against a legal proceeding brought by a consumer on the basis that in the particular circumstances of the case the arbitration agreement was "unfair" in the light of these two factors.

peremptory order under the Arbitration Act, failure to comply with which would empower it to dismiss the claim. Specific provision for this is made in Section 41 (6) Arbitration Act. It is to be assumed that the effect of such dismissal is not to render the agreement null and void, inoperable or incapable of being performed as otherwise the purpose of the provision would be illusory.

The policy which underlies security for costs is to correct the manifest injustice which may result from a defendant having to spend substantial sums to defeat a claim, particularly a bogus claim, from an impecunious claimant without otherwise having any prospect of recovering those costs when he is successful. Section 38(3) of the Act was carefully considered in the parliamentary papers for the Arbitration Act, which recommended to Parliament that "*the power to order security for costs is an important one, and should be given to arbitrators ...* "[40] Moreover, the provision of a procedure for security for costs by a national legislature has been regarded as a "legitimate aim" by the European Court of Human Rights.[41]

For the purposes of considering the public policy and constitutional aspects of due process, there is no difference in principle between a party on the one hand being prevented from pursuing a claim by reason of being obliged at the outset of a dispute to pursue an arbitration he cannot afford and on the other hand being prevented from pursuing that arbitration *in media res* by an order to provide security for costs which he cannot afford to fulfil. It follows that if the latter is constitutional, the former must be as well, the more so since it follows from a prior agreement of the parties.

It can therefore be concluded that:

- Under English law, a party to a valid arbitration agreement has a legitimate right not to be sued before a national court, and that determination of this right is *not* a question of appropriate forum;
- The effective loss of a right to proceed at all as a result of having made a choice of arbitration is not an infringement of a fundamental human right.

IV. Summary and Conclusion

In conclusion, under English law:

- Impecuniosity of either one or both parties to an arbitration agreement is not of itself a ground of "incapability of performance". The test and effect of impecuniosity are matters better left to the relevant provisions of the applicable insolvency law and any express agreement of the parties in the contract itself.
- There is no implied obligation on the respondent to legal proceedings when applying for a stay to arbitration to offer to fund the arbitration or initiate

---

[40] *DAC Report*, §367

[41] ECHR, judgment of 13 July 1995, *Tolstoy Miloslavsky v United Kingdom*, No 18139191, para. 61 et seq. 20 = EHRR 442, p. 61.

proceedings or take any step other than such as it is already obliged to take by reason of the arbitration agreement or a direction of the tribunal.

- The inability of a party to pursue an arbitration through its own impecuniosity is not a denial of justice or an infringement of Article 6 ECHR where it arises in the context of the party's chosen form of dispute resolution and as a consequence either of an express provision of the agreement or the directions of its chosen tribunal.

No Money, No Arbitration?
The United States Perspective on Impecuniousness and Arbitration Agreements

*D. Brian King**

Justice is open to all – like the Ritz hotel.

– Sir James Mathew[1]

I. Introduction

This paper explores, from the United States perspective, the effect of the impecuniousness of a party to an arbitration agreement on the validity and enforceability of that agreement. It examines the view of the courts in the United States towards the inability – or unwillingness – of a party to pay the costs of

---

* Partner, Freshfields Bruckhaus Deringer, Amsterdam.

1 Oxford Dictionary of Quotations 453 (4th ed. 1992) (Sir James (1830-1908), an Irish judge, was referring specifically to the justice system in England).

arbitration, as well as the situation where one of the parties to the arbitration agreement is the debtor in a bankruptcy proceeding.

The basic question posed is: does the impecuniousness or insolvency of a party provide a ground for voiding or otherwise declining to enforce an arbitration agreement? As will be shown, the answer in the United States is "possibly, but only rarely." This is indeed an eminently sensible position, as discussed below, since any significant "poverty exception" would create the potential for great mischief, in particular in the context of international commercial arbitration.

The legal culture and the norms underlying the legal system necessarily inform the way lawyers and judges approach difficult issues in the United States, as in other countries. Accordingly, this paper will begin with an introduction to some basic tenets of United States legal thinking, in particular as regards contractual interpretation and the enforcement of arbitration agreements. The conclusion drawn is that a strong policy exists in the courts of the United States in favor of the literal enforcement of agreements to arbitrate, and that this policy will be applied except in unusual cases where some powerful countervailing interest is present.

Next, this paper turns to the question of what might be called "party avoidance of arbitration" – *i.e.*, whether a claimant or respondent party may avoid an agreement to arbitrate on the ground of inability (or unwillingness) to pay the costs thereof. As shown by a review of the jurisprudence on this issue, courts have answered the question in the affirmative in a few cases, but these rulings uniformly arise in the consumer context, where special protections have historically been afforded in U.S. law.

Thereafter, this paper addresses the issue of what I have called "judicial avoidance of arbitration" – that is, whether, in the context of a bankruptcy proceeding, a court may refuse to enforce an arbitration agreement between the debtor and a third party. Here, the question with which the courts have grappled is the extent to which the strongly pro-arbitration bias of the Federal Arbitration Act conflicts with the objectives of the federal Bankruptcy Code. While the law in this area remains somewhat unsettled, the growing trend in the federal courts is to uphold arbitration agreements, at least where the dispute is not intimately intertwined with the insolvency proceedings.

Lastly, in Section V, a few conclusions on the general issue of impecuniousness and arbitration are offered, along with a tentative prediction concerning the likely future development of the law in this area. Here, the forecast is that any "poverty exception" to an arbitration obligation will remain quite limited under United States law.

II. United States Legal Thinking in General

The United States has a federal legal system, in which federal law and state law coexist and, not infrequently, overlap with respect to subject matter. The basic principle is that in case of conflict, federal law prevails; where federal law is silent or not inconsistent with state law, however, state law will be applied. Generally, in matters involving interstate and foreign commerce, federal law will take precedence over state law.

Conflicts can sometimes arise within the federal system itself. The federal court system is divided into thirteen "Circuits," each comprised of District Courts, which function mainly as trial courts, and a Court of Appeals. In the absence of precedent from the United States Supreme Court, the Circuit courts can and do take different and sometimes inconsistent positions. This is illustrated in Section IV.C, below, in the discussion of federal court decisions on the interaction between bankruptcy and arbitration.

With this structural background in mind, the present section briefly surveys a few of the basic tenets of legal thinking in the United States, as a backdrop to understanding the specific issues dealt with in the remainder of this paper.

A. The plain language rule

The prevailing rule in the United States is that contracts (and statutes) should be construed, in the first place, according to their plain language.[2] Generally, only where the terms of the contract are uncertain or ambiguous is recourse to extrinsic evidence of the parties' intent relevant or appropriate. Further, unlike certain continental legal systems, the concept of good faith does not play a central role in contract construction in the United States. Nevertheless, concepts grounded in reasonableness and equity – such as unconscionability, repudiation and waiver – can be raised as contractual defenses in appropriate factual circumstances. As will be seen, such defenses have been asserted in cases where courts have been asked to decide whether or not to uphold an arbitration agreement (*see* Section III, below).

In principle, then, the construction and enforcement of contractual clauses in the United States proceeds on the basis of "what you write is what you get." This implies, with respect to an arbitration clause, that the agreement to arbitrate means just what it says: the parties have agreed to arbitrate their disputes instead of going to court, and they will be held to that choice and the consequences thereof. This premise is further strengthened by the decidedly pro-arbitration policy that exists in United States law, to which this paper now turns.

---

2 *See*, in this regard, *J.D. Calamari & Joseph M. Perillo*, The Law of Contracts 148-50 (4th ed. 1998); see also *W.W.W. Assocs., Inc. v. Giancontieri*, 566 N.E.2d 639, 642 (N.Y. 1990).

B. Strong pro-arbitration policy

Prior to the early part of the 20th century, the courts in the United States were generally hostile to arbitration agreements.[3] This traditional hostility began to be reversed in 1925 with the passage of the Federal Arbitration Act ("FAA").[4] The FAA applies to cases involving either interstate or international commerce.[5] Its provisions on domestic arbitration (in Chapter 1 of the Act) make arbitration agreements enforceable in the federal courts; provide for a dismissal or stay of court proceedings where a valid arbitration agreement is invoked by a party; set out rules for the appointment of arbitrators and the provision of judicial assistance to arbitral tribunals; and provide for the recognition and enforcement of awards by the federal courts.[6]

Two additional chapters have been added to the FAA subsequent to its enactment. Chapter 2 implements the United Nations Convention on Recognition and Enforcement of Foreign Arbitral Awards (the "New York Convention"), which was ratified by the United States in 1970; and Chapter 3 implements the Inter-American Convention on International Commercial Arbitration (the "Panama Convention"), ratified by the United States in 1990.[7]

The purpose and effect of the FAA has been to establish a strong federal public policy in favor of the resolution of disputes through arbitration.[8] Beginning in about the 1960s, this Congressional mandate has been increasingly emphasized, and relied upon, by the courts. This trend began with the *Prima Paint* judgment of the Supreme Court in 1967.[9] A series of watershed decisions delivered by the Supreme Court in the 1980s and 1990s went even further, emphasizing in unequivocal language the strong federal policy favoring

---

3 See, *e.g., Red Cross Line v. Atlantic Fruit Co.*, 264 U.S. 109, 120-121 (1924) (reviewing the historical limitations on the enforcement of arbitration agreements).

4 9 U.S.C. §§ 1-307.

5 *Id.* § 1.

6 9 U.S.C. §§ 2, 3, 4, 5, 7 & 9. The provisions in Chapter 1 also apply to international arbitral awards to the extent not inconsistent with Chapter 2 or Chapter 3 of the FAA. *Id.* §§ 208, 307.

7 Notwithstanding the existence of the FAA, most states have their own arbitration acts. These apply to domestic arbitrations, *i.e.*, cases having no interstate or international aspect. State arbitration laws may also be applied where such an aspect exists, but only to the extent that they are not inconsistent with the provisions of the FAA. In this regard, see discussion in *Gary B. Born*, International Commercial Arbitration, Commentary and Materials 333-335, 349-358 (2d ed. 2001) (hereinafter "*Born*").

8 *See also Gilmer v. Interstate/Johnson Lane Corp.*, 500 U.S. 20, 24 (1991) (noting that the purpose of the FAA "was to reverse the longstanding judicial hostility to arbitration agreements").

9 *Prima Paint Corp. v. Flood & Conklin Mfg. Co.*, 388 U.S. 395, 402-404 (1967) (broadening the power of arbitrators to determine their own jurisdiction).

arbitration.[10] This pro-arbitration policy has been held to be particularly strong with respect to international contracts.[11]

Furthermore, the scope of issues that may be resolved by arbitration has gradually been extended by the United States Supreme Court. Two objectives appear to underlie this trend: to ensure proper enforcement of the Congressionally decreed policy in favor of arbitration; and, on a more practical level, to reduce the heavy caseload in the federal courts. Thus, over the years, courts in the United States have developed a very wide doctrine of subject-matter arbitrability, so that arbitration agreements by now may cover disputes arising out of virtually any domestic commercial transaction and every international transaction. In the 1985 *Mitsubishi* decision, for instance, the Supreme Court found statutory antitrust claims arising in the context of an international contract to be arbitrable, emphasizing the "emphatic federal policy in favor of arbitral dispute resolution."[12] Matters involving claims under the securities laws,[13] the Racketeer Influenced and Corrupt Organizations Act ("RICO"),[14] and the federal anti-discrimination statute,[15] as well as patent,[16] copyright[17] and trademark[18] disputes, are now included within the scope of matters that may be referred to arbitration.

One slight caveat must, however, be made regarding the "emphatic federal policy" in favor of arbitration embodied in the FAA.[19] As confirmed by the Supreme Court in the recent consumer challenge to an arbitration clause in the

---

10 See, *e.g.*, *Dean Witter Reynolds, Inc. v. Byrd*, 470 U.S. 213, 218 (1985) (holding that the policy underlying the FAA "requires that we rigorously enforce agreements to arbitrate" even if that results in separate proceedings in different fora); *Vimar Seguros y Reaseguros, S.A. v. M.V. Sky Reefer*, 515 U.S. 528, 541 (1995) (holding that the FAA reflects a strong, well-established policy in favor of arbitration); *Moses H. Cone Memorial Hospital v. Mercury Construction Corp.*, 460 U.S. 1, 24-25 (1983) (finding that doubt concerning an allegation of waiver should be resolved in favor of arbitration).

11 See *Mitsubishi Motors Corp. v. Soler Chrysler-Plymouth, Inc.*, 473 U.S. 614, 629 (1985) (noting that "concerns of international comity, respect for the capacities of foreign and transnational tribunals, and sensitivity to the need of the international commercial system for predictability in the resolution of disputes require enforce[ment of] the parties' [arbitration] agreement, even assuming that a contrary result would be forthcoming in a domestic context").

12 *Id.*

13 *Scherk v. Alberto-Culver Co.*, 417 U.S. 506, 513-520 (1974) (securities claims under international contracts); *Shearson/American Express, Inc. v. McMahon*, 482 U.S. 220, 238 (1987) (securities claims under international and domestic contracts); *Rodriguez de Quijas v. Shearson/American Express, Inc.*, 490 U.S. 477, 484-486 (1989) (same).

14 *Shearson/American Express Inc. v. McMahon*, 482 U.S. 220, 242 (1987).

15 *Circuit City Stores, Inc. v. Adams*, 532 U.S. 105 (2001).

16 35 U.S.C. §§ 294 & § 135(d).

17 *McMahan Sec. Co. v. Forum Capital Mkts.*, 35 F.3d 82, 89 (2d Cir. 1994).

18 *Necchi Sewing Machine Sales Corp. v. Necchi SpA*, 369 F.2d 579, 582 (2d Cir. 1966).

19 *Mitsubishi Motors Corp.*, 473 U.S. at 629.

Green Tree case (discussed in Section III.A.1, below), the purpose of the FAA is to put arbitration agreements "upon the same footing as other contracts."[20] Thus, arbitration agreements are no less favored – but likewise no more favored – than other contractual clauses. This means, with respect to the issues under discussion here, that defenses that might be raised against contractual clauses in general may also be raised, in principle, to attempt to void or otherwise avoid an arbitration agreement.

B. Other important policy interests

As will be seen from the case law reviewed in Section III, below, the foregoing tenets of United States law – plain language construction and a pro-arbitration bias – may sometimes in practice be tempered by other important policy considerations.

The federal and state courts in the United States, as in many countries, have traditionally been concerned to ensure that no party is denied a forum to vindicate its legal rights.[21] This perceived imperative, absorbed into the national consciousness as "having your day in court," has occasionally tempered courts' enthusiasm for arbitration clauses where enforcing them might prevent the vindication of legal rights. This is plainly one of the motivating factors for the *Green Tree* and *Gateway* decisions, discussed below in Section II.

In the same vein, a trend in United States jurisprudence, almost from the beginning, has been a certain solicitude for the interests of the individual – often euphemistically described as the "little guy" – particularly in cases involving confrontations with the government or with large corporations. In the modern-day United States, the consumer has typically played the role of the "little guy," and legislatures and courts have tended to be more solicitous where the rights and interests of consumers are involved.

Furthermore, as will be seen, the policies of debtor repose and centralization of assets that underlie the U.S. bankruptcy laws may also conflict, in some cases, with the enforcement of arbitration agreements. This is illustrated in the discussion in Section 0, below.

Finally, in understanding the topics under consideration here, the influence of occasional local parochialism cannot be wholly disregarded. This is, for example, evident in the *Gateway* line of cases, discussed in Section III.A, below, in which international arbitration – and the ICC in particular – received some very poor judicial press.

The various, and sometimes conflicting, policies and perspectives discussed above have all played a role in the courts' reaction to the question of

[20] *Green Tree Financial Corporation v. Randolph*, 531 U.S. 79, 89 (2000).

[21] Indeed, this interest underlies one of the more controversial aspects of United States legal practice – the permissibility of contingency fees – which are generally defended on the ground that they serve to make sure that even persons without means have access to legal process.

impecuniousness and arbitration. This paper now turns to that question, examining the courts' responses to an impecunious party's attempt to avoid an arbitration clause in an agreement.

II. Impecuniousness and arbitration

It is an unfortunate truth that a claimant or a respondent in arbitration proceedings is sometimes either unable or unwilling to pay the costs of those proceedings. Courts in the United States have, in a few cases, grappled with the question whether a party may circumvent an arbitration clause on that ground.

The issues raised in the case of a defaulting claimant and a defaulting respondent are slightly different. This paper will therefore begin by looking at the claimant who is unable or unwilling to pay the costs of arbitration, followed by a look at the case of the recalcitrant respondent.

A. Claimant's failure or inability to pay

When a potential claimant to an arbitration is either unable to pay or unwilling to incur the costs of arbitration, it may seek to vindicate its rights in the courts. At that point, the respondent may raise the arbitration agreement as a jurisdictional defense in order to have the court case dismissed. The issue posed is whether the clause may be avoided on some contractual (or other) basis.[22] In this regard, it is important to recall that arbitration agreements are equal but not superior to other kinds of contractual promises, such that the usual defenses to enforcement of contractual obligations can, in principle, be raised against arbitration agreements as well.[23]

(1) The *Gateway* saga and consumer's remorse

In recent years, courts in the United States have been confronted with the situation of the small-scale consumer attempting to vindicate his rights in the courts, where there is an arbitration clause in the underlying contract. In such a situation, the courts have faced the conflicting imperatives of the pro-arbitration jurisprudence delivered by the Supreme Court, and a concern for protecting the consumer and ensuring that access to justice is not denied.

This situation is illustrated by the "*Gateway* saga" – a string of relatively recent state court cases involving a supplier of mail-order computers, which examined the enforceability of arbitration clauses in consumer agreements.

---

22 See 9 U.S.C. § 3. To resolve the question of the validity of the clause in these circumstances in a domestic arbitration, the court should in theory look to state contract law; in international arbitration subject to the New York Convention, a court should in principle look to federal common law. In practice, however, there has been much diversity in lower court decisions. See *Born*, *supra* note 7, at 333-335.

23 See *supra* text accompanying note 20.

In *Brower v. Gateway 2000, Inc.*,[24] decided by a New York intermediate appellate court in 1998, the court was called upon to decide the validity of an ICC arbitration clause in an agreement to purchase a mail-order computer. Mr. Brower and his fellow plaintiffs had all ordered computers or software products from the manufacturer, Gateway, and brought a class action in state court for breach of warranty, breach of contract, fraud and unfair trade practices. The respondent, Gateway, sought to have the case dismissed from the courts by invoking the arbitration clause in the underlying contracts referring disputes to ICC arbitration; this clause appeared in the purchase agreement that was included in the sales documents shipped to the purchaser with the computer. According to the terms of that contract, it would become binding on the recipient of the mail-order computer unless the computer was returned within 30 days.[25]

The court was clearly concerned about the practicability of ICC arbitration for consumers living in New York. And indeed, the plaintiffs attempted to play the parochial card to its fullest extent, arguing that the ICC:

> was not a forum commonly used for consumer matters; and that because ICC headquarters were in France, it was particularly difficult to locate the organization and its rules. To illustrate just how inaccessible the forum was, [plaintiffs] advised the court that the ICC was not registered with the Secretary of State . . . efforts to locate and contact the ICC had been unsuccessful and . . . apparently the only way to attempt to contact the ICC was through the United States Council for International Business, with which the ICC maintained some sort of relationship.[26]

The plaintiffs further emphasized the costs of an ICC proceeding, arguing that the deposit on costs required by the ICC[27] was far in excess of the individual claims and that, should Gateway prevail on the merits, they could be compelled to pay its legal fees.

The court went along with the plaintiffs' reasoning, at least in part. Noting that the costs of arbitration under the ICC system appeared to exceed substantially the value of the products purchased, the court found that these

---

24 *Brower v. Gateway 2000, Inc.*, 676 N.Y.S.2d 569 (N.Y. App. Div. 1998).

25 *Id.* at 570. It is customary in the computer business that a consumer orders a computer (often on-line), not negotiating the specific terms of the agreement; the agreement then arrives with the product and becomes binding if the consumer retains the computer for 30 days. These agreements are variously referred to as "pizza-box" or "shrink-wrap" agreements, both terms referring to the packaging in which the agreements are normally contained.

26 *Id.* at 571.

27 The minimum cost for an ICC arbitration is US$ 5,000, consisting of US$ 2,500 for administrative costs and US$ 2,500 for the arbitrator's fees. See ICC Rules of Arbitration, App. III, Art. 4 (setting out schedule of costs).

costs were "excessive," "unreasonable" and "surely serve[] to deter the individual consumer from invoking the process."[28] Accordingly, the court, applying the contract law doctrine of unconscionability, vacated that part of the arbitration clause referring the dispute to ICC arbitration. Significantly, however, the court did not retain the case but rather sent it back to the lower court with the instruction to refer the matter to ad hoc arbitration under the terms of the FAA.[29]

The end result of the *Brower* decision was therefore a mixed bag both for arbitration and for the consumer. On the one hand, the consumer avoided an ICC arbitration clause. On the other hand, however, the court maintained the defendant's right to arbitrate. Moreover – and probably more significantly for Gateway – the court's decision allowed it to avoid the class action mechanism, which would have enabled all similarly situated purchasers to have their claims litigated before the state court. In arbitration, such consolidation of claims is generally not possible, and thus the consequence of the ruling was, effectively, to reduce Gateway's exposure substantially.

(2) The Supreme Court leaves a window

In 2000, the situation of the remorseful consumer reached the United States Supreme Court in the *Green Tree case.*[30]

The plaintiff in that case, Mrs. Randolph, had purchased a mobile home under a financing agreement with the Green Tree Financial Corporation, which agreement contained a clause referring disputes to *ad hoc* arbitration under the FAA. She later brought a class-action lawsuit in federal district court, arguing, *inter alia*, that the defendant financing company had violated the federal Truth In Lending Act by failing to disclose certain aspects of the lending arrangement. The defendant interposed the arbitration clause as a jurisdictional defense and sought the dismissal of the court action. Mrs. Randolph responded that the arbitration clause was unenforceable because it failed to disclose – and thus to warn consumers regarding – the potentially steep costs of an arbitration proceeding.[31]

In its decision, the Supreme Court upheld the arbitration clause in the underlying agreement, ruling that an arbitration agreement is not rendered unenforceable simply because it does not disclose the anticipated arbitration costs and fees. In reaching this conclusion, the Court reviewed the pro-arbitration policy of the FAA, noting that in deciding whether a particular

---

28 *Brower*, 676 N.Y.S.2d at 574.

29 *Id.* at 575. For a critique of this case, see *Hans Smit*, May an Arbitration Agreement Calling for Institutional Arbitration be Denied Enforcement because of the Cost Involved?, 8 Am. Rev. Int'l Arb. 167 (1999).

30 *Green Tree*, 531 U.S. at 79.

31 *Id.* at 89.

agreement to arbitrate is unenforceable, it was mindful of the FAA's purpose to reverse the longstanding judicial hostility to arbitration agreements and to place arbitration agreements on the same footing as other contracts.[32]

The court noted further that where a party seeks to invalidate an arbitration agreement on the ground that arbitration would be prohibitively expensive, that party bears the burden of showing the likelihood of incurring excessive costs. While acknowledging that the existence of high arbitration costs may well preclude a litigant like the plaintiff from effectively vindicating her rights, the court found that the plaintiff had failed to prove that the arbitration would, in fact, be prohibitively costly for her. The mere "risk" that the plaintiff would be saddled with prohibitive costs was, in the Court's view, too speculative to justify invalidating the arbitration agreement.[33] It accordingly ruled that the lower court had erred in deciding that the arbitration agreement's silence with respect to costs and fees rendered it unenforceable – thus upholding the arbitration agreement while leaving open the possibility of a different result in a future case where the consumer succeeded in proving that the cost of arbitrating would be "prohibitively expensive."[34]

While the Supreme Court delivered a decision in *Green Tree* that is essentially pro-arbitration, it nonetheless left a window open for claims of inability to pay as a defense to arbitration. In a case with different facts, where a party could indeed show that high arbitration costs would prevent it from vindicating its rights, a different result cannot be excluded.

(3) The *Gateway* saga continues

Subsequent to the Supreme Court's decision in *Green Tree*, another episode in the Gateway saga went even further than the *Brower* judgment, with the court voiding the arbitration clause altogether. *Licitra v. Gateway, Inc.*[35] involved the same computer manufacturer, Gateway, in a small claim proceeding brought by the purchaser of a personal computer before a New York state court, seeking refund of the purchase price. In its judgment, the court affirmed earlier case law that a binding contract can result where there is no signed written agreement between the parties, even where the buyer of the computer had seen the contract

---

[32] *Id.*

[33] The American Arbitration Association had filed an *amicus curiae* brief in this matter, arguing that an arbitration clause that is silent on the payment of fees is ambiguous and should be construed to preserve enforceability. It also drew the Court's attention to its Consumer Due Process Protocol, providing standards and procedures for the equitable resolution of consumer disputes (providing that consumers in small-claims arbitration incur no filing fee and pay only $125 of the total fees charged by the arbitrator). See *id.* at 95 (Ginsburg, J., concurring in part and dissenting in part).

[34] *Id.* at 91.

[35] *Licitra v. Gateway, Inc.*, 734 N.Y.S.2d 389 (N.Y. Civ. Ct. 2001).

(containing an arbitration provision referring disputes to the National Arbitration Forum) for the first time when he opened the box containing the computer.

The court then proceeded to recite a litany of perceived disadvantages of arbitration compared with the small claims procedure in the local courts, including: additional costs; a lengthier procedure; less opportunity to put on an oral case; the absence of a complete transcript; a possibly inconvenient venue for the consumer; charges for an interpreter; a stricter evidentiary standard; a possible costs award against the losing party; and more extensive written pleadings.[36] The court further noted that because consent to arbitration involves the waiver of a consumer's right to go to court, such consent must be "clear, explicit and unequivocal," which was less than evident on the facts of the case.[37] Based upon all of these considerations, the court found that it would be inequitable to deny the plaintiff the perceived cost and procedural benefits of the small claims procedure available in the state court, and thus held that the arbitration provision in the sales agreement was unenforceable.[38]

A similar result was reached by another New York state court in a 2002 decision involving a one-year cellular telephone service contract containing a clause referring disputes to arbitration seated in a different city. The court granted the defendant's motion to compel arbitration, but only to the extent that an arbitration forum could be agreed that would not create costs for the claimant that might be "unconscionable."[39]

The strand uniting all these state court decisions is that they involved consumers in disputes with large corporations. They are thus best understood as reflecting the tendency of the courts, and in particular the state courts, to protect the interests of consumers as the weaker party to a legal dispute. This tendency may have been further strengthened in the reviewed cases by a dislike of "boiler

---

[36] *Id.* at 394-396. In a remarkable, if tongue-in-cheek, display of local pride, the court also noted that it:

"must address a troubling issue. The computer industry and other courts have adopted the term 'pizza box' to describe the package in which the document containing the terms and conditions of the agreement is shipped. As a matter of law in the State of New York, such a container is not a "pizza box." No self-respecting New York pizza would be caught soggy in such a box. The container may pass as a "pizza box" in those parts of the world that think food from Domino's, Little Caesar's, Pizza Hut, and Poppa John's is pizza. In this Court's opinion such a classification cannot be recognized east of the Hudson River."

Id. at 391.

[37] *Id.* at 396.

[38] *Id.* at 396-97.

[39] *Martin Bank v. Worldcom, Inc.*, No. 122484/00, 2002 WL 171629 (N.Y. Sup. Ct. Jan. 24, 2002); see also *In the Matter of Arbitration between Teleserve Systems, Inc. and MCI Telecommunications Corp.*, 659 N.Y.S.2d 659 (N.Y. App. Div. 1997) (finding that a filing fee of US$ 204,000, *i.e.*, US$ 4,000 plus 5 per cent of amount claimed, was unreasonable, unjust, unconscionable and therefore unenforceable).

plate" contracts with respect to which the consumer has little actual choice.[40] The jury, however, is still out on whether the pro-consumer stance taken by the New York state courts would be endorsed in other state courts or on the federal level, given the caution displayed by the United States Supreme Court in the *Green Tree* case.

B. Respondent's Failure or Inability to Pay

The issues are somewhat different where it is the respondent in an arbitration that is unable or unwilling to pay the costs of the arbitration.[41] Faced with such a refusal, a claimant is faced with a choice between: (i) funding the arbitration entirely itself (with no guarantee of recovery); or (ii) taking its claim to an alternate forum, and arguing that the arbitration agreement is no longer binding.

The specific issue of the non-paying respondent does not appear to have been directly addressed by the courts in the United States, possibly because the vast majority of arbitrations in the United States are conducted under the American Arbitration Association's (AAA) Commercial Arbitration Rules for domestic cases. These rules require a filing fee from the party asserting claims or counterclaims, but do not specify which party shall make subsequent deposits, or in what proportion.[42] Thus, the Rules provide the institution or tribunal with discretion to apportion payments towards the advance differently in individual cases, and thereby avoid (or ameliorate) the problem of the recalcitrant respondent.[43]

In principle, however, where a respondent has defaulted on an obligation – under the arbitration agreement or the applicable arbitration rules – to contribute

40 Note, however, that two cases decided before *Brower* had upheld arbitration clauses in computer/software boxes ordered by mail. See *Hill v. Gateway, Inc.*, 105 F.3d 1147 (7th Cir. 1997); *ProCD, Inc. v. Zeidenberg*, 86 F.3d 1447 (7th Cir. 1996).

41 The latter situation is, indeed, more common in practice, sometimes based on purely tactical considerations.

42 See AAA Commercial Arbitration Rules, Article R-54 ("The AAA may require the parties to deposit in advance of any hearings such money as it deems necessary to cover the expense of the arbitration, including the arbitrator's fee, if any, and shall render an accounting to the parties and return any unexpended balance at the conclusion of the case."). Other mechanisms may also come into play. For example, the AAA has special Consumer Arbitration Rules under which the consumer's potential contribution is limited to about US$ 125. See *supra* note 33. Similarly, it is industry practice in certain business areas – such as employment disputes in the securities industry – that the employer pays the arbitration costs. See *Green Tree*, 531 U.S. at 94.

43 Even under the AAA's International Arbitration Rules, while the filing party must deposit an advance on costs when it files a claim, the tribunal retains discretion regarding which party is requested to make subsequent deposits and in what proportion. Article 33(1) of the International Arbitration Rules provides that "[w]hen a party files claims, the administrator may request the filing party to deposit appropriate amounts as an advance for the [arbitration] costs"; Article 33(3) further provides that "[d]uring the course of the arbitral proceedings, the tribunal may request supplementary deposits from the parties."

to the payment of the costs of arbitration, a claimant could invoke theories such as repudiation or waiver as a justification for resorting to the courts. The argument would be that the respondent has committed a material breach of the arbitration agreement, such that the claimant is no longer bound by that agreement. This would then open the way for the claimant to pursue its claim in the appropriate courts.[44] Such a theory would be consistent with ordinary contract law principles, which the United States courts have held to apply to arbitration agreements.[45]

(1) Waiver/repudiation as applied to arbitration agreements

In principle, under United States law, the right to arbitrate – like any other contract right – may be waived.[46] The elements of waiver are generally understood to be: (i) awareness of the contractual right at issue; and (ii) the voluntary relinquishment of that right.[47] A waiver may be implied from conduct and may occur prospectively. Repudiation, on the other hand, is generally understood as comprising words or actions evincing a refusal to comply with a contractual obligation.[48] Thus the two doctrines are similar and, in many cases, the same conduct may establish either or both. In the context of arbitration agreements, the courts in the United States have tended to focus on waiver rather than repudiation in assessing whether a party's conduct has had the effect of voiding an agreement to arbitrate.[49]

Case law establishes that the standard for finding a waiver of the right to arbitrate is high.[50] In *Moses H. Cone Memorial Hospital v. Mercury*

---

44 See, *e.g.*, *Yves Derains & Eric A. Schwartz*, A Guide to the New ICC Rules of Arbitration 320 (1998) (hereinafter "*Derains & Schwartz*") (noting that it could be argued that "a party that fails to pay its share of the advance on costs repudiates, or renounces, the arbitration agreement, thus entitling the other party to pursue its claims against the defaulting party in court").

45 See, *e.g.*, *Green Tree*, 531 U.S. at 89.

46 See, *e.g.*, *Moses H. Cone*, 460 U.S. at 24-25; see also *Born*, *supra* note 7, at 239.

47 See Black's Law Dictionary 1574-75 (7th ed. 1999); see also Restatement (Second) of Contracts § 84 (1981).

48 See Black's Law Dictionary 1306 (7th ed. 1999); *see also* Restatement (Second) of Contracts § 250 (1981).

49 In the international context, an impecunious party might further be able to argue pursuant to Article II(3) of the New York Convention that its inability to pay the costs of arbitration renders the arbitration clause "incapable of being performed" and thus negates the court's obligation to refuse jurisdiction in the face of an arbitration clause. But compare *Mangistaumunaigaz v. United World Trade, Inc.*, Civil Action No. 96-WY-1290-WD, Order on Pending Motions (W.D. Colo. Jun. 17, 1997), reported in XXVIa Yearbook on Comm'l Arb. 806-12 (1999) (in action to enforce award under New York Convention, rejecting contention that costs of arbitration prevented the respondent from being able to present its case).

50 The statutory basis for this argument, in cases falling under the FAA, is Section 3 thereof, which provides that where an arbitration clause exists, the court shall refer disputes to

Construction Corp., for example, the United States Supreme Court held that a "waiver of arbitration is not to be lightly inferred" and that, in cases of doubt, an allegation of waiver should be rejected.[51]

The question of whether there is a waiver is fact-driven and typically requires not only that the waiving party has taken actions inconsistent with the arbitration agreement, but also that these actions have prejudiced the other party. Mere delay in commencing arbitration, or even commencement of an action in the courts, will thus not be enough to constitute a waiver absent substantial prejudice to the counterparty.[52]

To provide one example, the issue of waiver was at the center of the medical malpractice claim in *Engalla v. Permanente Medical Group, Inc.*[53] In that case, Mr. Engalla and his wife had attempted to institute arbitration proceedings against his health maintenance organization ("HMO") in accordance with the arbitration agreement in the underlying medical insurance contract, which referred disputes to arbitration "designed, written, mandated and administered by" the HMO itself.[54] After much dilatory conduct in connection with the commencement of the proceedings by the respondent HMO – which knew that Mr. Engalla was terminally ill (allegedly as a result of negligence by the HMO doctors) – Mr. Engalla died before the tribunal was finally constituted. The HMO then moved to reduce the Engallas' original claim for non-economic damages by half, on the ground that Mr. Engalla's death required merger of the widow's loss of consortium claim into the wrongful death claim. At that point, the deceased's frustrated family filed a complaint in the Californian courts asserting the medical malpractice claim, and alleging fraud and waiver as a defense to the enforcement of the arbitration agreement. After an extensive discovery process in the lower courts, the case ultimately came before the Supreme Court of California.[55]

In examining whether the HMO had waived its right to arbitrate, the court noted that the appointment of the arbitrators had not occurred until 144 days after filing of the claim (three months longer than the 60 day maximum set in

---

arbitration on application of a party unless the applicant is "in default in proceeding with such arbitration." 9 U.S.C. § 3.

51 *Moses H. Cone*, 460 U.S. at 24-25; see also *Merrill Lynch, Pierce, Fenner & Smith, Inc. v. Lecopulos*, 553 F.2d 842, 845 (2d Cir. 1977) (finding that "under federal law the filing of an action in a district court is not a waiver of the right to arbitrate, at least not before the defendant has answered on the merits"); *Rush v. Oppenheimer & Co.*, 779 F.2d 885, 887 (2d Cir. 1985) (reaffirming that waiver of arbitration is "not to be lightly inferred"); see generally *Born*, *supra* note 7, at 240 ("doubt as to the existence of a waiver is resolved against finding a waiver, and the party seeking to establish waiver bears a heavy burden").

52 *Born*, *supra* note 7, at 239-242.

53 *Engalla v. Permanente Medical Group, Inc.*, 938 P.2d 903 (Cal. 1997).

54 *Id.* at 909.

55 *Id.* at 914-15.

the arbitration rules); that the complainants had repeatedly attempted to expedite the appointment; and that the HMO knew that the complainant was terminally ill but nonetheless delayed the process. For these reasons, among others, the court found that the respondent had engendered unreasonable or bad faith delays in the arbitral process – and had thereby caused substantial prejudice to the complainants. While acknowledging that waiver of the right to arbitrate should not be "lightly inferred," the court found that there was sufficient evidence in the facts of the case to support the widow's claim that the HMO had waived its right to arbitrate. The court remanded the case to the trial court to assess the merits of the claim.[56]

The sad case of the Engallas aptly illustrates the high standard of waiver generally applied in the United States and the fact-based nature of that inquiry. Mere dilatory conduct – and indeed even the initiation and initial prosecution of court litigation – is not enough to constitute a waiver.[57] However, truly abusive conduct, causing prejudice to the other party, may suffice to establish that a waiver has occurred.[58]

How could the doctrine of waiver be expected to play out in the context of an impecunious or otherwise non-paying respondent? While, as noted, that particular issue has not been specifically addressed in the reported cases, it seems likely that mere non-payment – especially if justified by impecuniousness – would not suffice to satisfy the high standard of waiver applied by the courts. A respondent's failure to pay may in many cases engender delay and may also prejudice the claimant by requiring it to pay more in order to keep the arbitration going. However, the delay is unlikely to be substantial, and the prejudice is temporary because the arbitrators can apportion the costs of arbitration at the end of the proceedings. Accordingly, it would not be expected that non-payment would rise to the level required to find a waiver by United States courts.

[56] *Id.* at 923.

[57] See, *e.g.*, *I.T.A.D. Associates, Inc. v. Podar Bros.*, 636 F.2d 75, 77 (4th Cir. 1981) (finding no waiver based on passage of time between instituting action and motion to compel arbitration, where no prejudice resulted to the other party); *Dunn Construction Co., Inc. v. Sugar Beach Condominium Ass'n*, 760 F. Supp. 1479, 1485-1486 (S.D. Ala. 1991) (finding no waiver of right to compel arbitration by failing to file until nearly four years after litigation began).

[58] See *Davis v. Continental Airlines, Inc.*, 69 Cal. Rptr. 2d 79, 87 (1997) (finding waiver of arbitration rights by failure to move to compel arbitration until six months after answering complaint, and participating in extensive discovery); *Doctor's Assoc., Inc. v. Distajo*, 66 F.3d 438, 455-57 (2d Cir. 1995) (waiver of arbitration rights by participation in extensive discovery).

(2) The arbitration rules revisited

Aside from the question of possible waiver, there is also a more specific question as to the effect of non-payment by a respondent within the arbitration procedure itself. Here, the applicable arbitration rules take center stage.

The arbitration rules of many international arbitration institutes provide either for the advance on costs to be shared equally between the parties or for each party to contribute in some measure to the advance on costs.[59] Such rules typically provide for the possibility for the other party to advance the non-paying party's share of the costs of arbitration.[60] This is the case, for example, under the ICC Rules.

Nevertheless, it is not always clear whether a respondent has an absolute contractual obligation to pay its share of the advance on costs. One might argue that even where a party feels that the claim against it is unjustified, it is contractually required to contribute to the advance on costs. After all, the advance on costs is intended to protect the arbitrator(s) and the continuation of the arbitral process – which the parties jointly agreed to follow, and by implication fund, in the event of a dispute. Furthermore, it is simply an advance, subject to the arbitrators' decision on allocation of costs at the close of the proceedings. This is indeed the position taken in the LCIA Rules, which provide in Article 24(3) that "[i]n the event that a party fails or refuses to provide any deposit as directed by the LCIA Court, . . . the party paying the substitute payment shall be entitled to *recover that amount as a debt immediately due* from the defaulting party" (emphasis added).

The position under other sets of Rules is, however, less clear. There is at least one recent published ICC award, in which the tribunal found the payment of the advance on costs to be a contractual obligation, and, accordingly, entered an award against the respondent for its unpaid share.[61] Nevertheless, ICC awards

[59] See, *e.g.*, ICC Rules of Arbitration, Art. 30(3) ("The advance on costs fixed by the Court shall be payable in equal shares by the Claimant and the Respondent."); UNCITRAL Arbitration Rules, Art. 41(1) ("The arbitral tribunal, on its establishment, may request each party to deposit an equal amount as an advance for the costs [of arbitration]."); LCIA Rules, Art. 24.1 ("The LCIA Court may direct the parties, in such proportions as it thinks appropriate, to make one or several interim or final payments on account of the costs of the arbitration.").

[60] See, *e.g.*, ICC Rules of Arbitration, Art. 30(3) ("any party shall be free to pay the whole of the advance on costs in respect of the principal claim or the counterclaim should the other party fail to pay its share"); AAA International Rules, Art. 33(3) ("If the deposits requested are not paid in full within 30 days after the receipt of the request, the administrator shall so inform the parties, in order that one or the other of them may make the required payment. ..."); UNCITRAL Arbitration Rules, Art. 41(4) ("If the required deposits are not paid in full within thirty days after the receipt of the request, the arbitral tribunal shall so inform the parties in order that one or another of them may make the required payment.").

[61] See Partial Award of 27 March 2001, reprinted in ASA Bulletin 285-293 (October 2001) (referring to ICC arbitration between a Panamanian company and a Swiss company).

have been inconsistent on this topic, with a recent unpublished award finding that a respondent does not have a contractual duty to pay its share of the advance on costs, precisely because of the substitution option provided by Article 30(3) of the ICC Rules.

Prominent commentators suggest, however, that a paying party is in any event entitled to claim back the monies advanced from the non-paying party. In this regard, it seems clear that arbitrators have the discretion to issue an interim measure ordering the unwilling party to compensate the party who has been funding the arbitration.[62]

Thus, although unlikely to amount to a waiver under United States law, a respondent's failure to pay may have consequences for it in the arbitration, depending upon the applicable arbitration rules. These may include an immediate award of the unpaid amount against the respondent party or, alternatively, an interim measures order compelling payment. In the latter case, enforceability is more uncertain and will depend on the law of the place where enforcement is sought.

(3) Conclusion: the state of the law

What, then, is the present state of the law in the United States regarding impecuniousness and arbitration? There is some case law permitting an impecunious claimant to avoid an arbitration agreement. However, in practice, the effect of this case law is likely to be limited. This is because the cases invalidating or modifying arbitration clauses based on the costs of the proceeding have all been decided in the consumer context, where courts have historically shown some solicitousness in protecting the interests of a smaller party. Such jurisprudence is therefore unlikely to be extended to other contexts, such as business-to-business disputes, or, even less, to international commercial disputes.

As to contractual defenses such as repudiation or waiver, the sad case of Mr. Engalla illustrates the very high standard typically applied by the courts with respect to waiver, requiring not only conduct inconsistent with the agreement to arbitrate but also prejudice to the other party. This high standard is entirely

---

62 In the context of ICC arbitration, it lies within a Tribunal's discretion to order a non-paying respondent to pay its share of the advance on costs as provided in Article 30(3) of the ICC Rules. See *Derains & Schwartz*, *supra* note 44, at 319-321; *D. Mitrovic*, Advance to Cover Costs of Arbitration, 7 ICC Bulletin 88, 89 (1996) (discussing an unpublished ICC award in which the tribunal found that it had the authority to order a non-paying respondent to pay its share of the advance on costs); *W.L. Craig*, *W.W. Park & J. Paulsson*, International Chamber of Commerce Arbitration 269 (3d ed. 2000). ("The party injured by an opponent's non-payment of the advance on costs may also seek interim relief from the arbitral tribunal by way of procedural order"). The author has recently obtained such interim relief on behalf of a client in an ICC case.

consistent with the strong federal policy in the United States in favor of upholding arbitration agreements.

IV. Judicial Avoidance of Arbitration in the Context of Bankruptcy

The problems caused by the impecunious litigant are further complicated where bankruptcy proceedings have been initiated in the United States. In such a case, a judge may decide to disregard an arbitration clause, even over the objection of one of the parties, and direct that the dispute be resolved in court instead. It is to this question that this paper now turns.

Presented first below is a short introduction to the bankruptcy laws in the United States. Thereafter, this paper reviews the case law regarding when an arbitration clause may be avoided in the context of bankruptcy proceedings.

A. The United States Bankruptcy Code

United States bankruptcy law is regulated by federal statute – the 1978 Bankruptcy Code ("Code")[63] – Chapter 7 of which covers liquidation and Chapter 11 reorganization. The broad purposes of the Code are to assemble and protect the assets of the debtor in one forum; to ensure a reasonably prompt and equitable distribution of assets among competing creditors, in line with the distribution priority rules set out in the Code; to provide repose from multiple litigations to the debtor; and, for Chapter 11 reorganizations, to preserve the "going concern" value of the enterprise.

The jurisdiction of the federal Bankruptcy Courts (an autonomous adjunct of the District Courts) is generally quite broad. In this regard, the Code grants the Bankruptcy Courts: (i) original and exclusive jurisdiction over "core" matters (defined as matters arising "under" the Code and "in" the bankruptcy, such as placing the property of the debtor under control of the bankruptcy court and the priority of distribution of assets); and (ii) original but non-exclusive jurisdiction over "non-core" matters (*i.e.*, matters "related to" bankruptcy, such as debtor claims against third parties).[64] This distinction is significant as it may affect the arbitrability of the dispute.

When bankruptcy proceedings are initiated by or against a debtor, the effect, under Section 362 of the Code, is that an "automatic stay" of all pending legal proceedings comes into effect. This is a broad suspension of judicial, administrative and arbitral proceedings against the debtor and the debtor's property, which in principle has extra-territorial effect. In practice, virtually all court actions that could affect the debtor are stayed by the filing of the bankruptcy petition; thus, a claimant in litigation before a court or arbitral

---

[63] 11 U.S.C. §§ 101-1330.

[64] 28 U.S.C. § 1334.

tribunal will be prevented from continuing existing litigation (or instituting new proceedings) unless and until the Bankruptcy Court grants a lifting of the stay. The stay may be lifted upon application of a party on a showing of good cause.

B. Effect of Bankruptcy on Arbitral Proceedings

As already noted, arbitration proceedings also fall under the automatic stay imposed by the Bankruptcy Code upon the institution of bankruptcy proceedings. Absent the lifting of the stay, the arbitration proceedings may in principle not continue.

Because the automatic stay has extra-territorial effect as a matter of United States law, it can affect ongoing arbitration proceedings seated in other countries. Any acts taken in violation of the stay are in principle void as a matter of United States law and the court can impose contempt or other sanctions against violators.[65] However, the punitive power of the court to enforce the stay will only extend to parties over whom the court has personal jurisdiction. Thus, in practice, international arbitrators will often have discretion concerning whether to discontinue proceedings in light of the stay. And indeed the practice of, for example, ICC tribunals shows diversity in this regard, with some tribunals taking the position that they are not bound by the stay.[66]

C. The Bankruptcy Code Meets the Federal Arbitration Act

So let us look at what happens when a United States court is confronted with parallel arbitration and insolvency proceedings. The primary question to be answered is under what circumstances the automatic stay will be lifted, since, if this does not occur, the disputed issues will be resolved in court and the arbitration clause will, effectively, be voided.

The first point to note is that there is an inherent tension between bankruptcy and arbitration law in the United States. This is because these sources of law reflect two conflicting federal policies: (i) the bankruptcy policies of providing repose to the debtor, consolidating assets and distributing them in accordance with the Code's distribution rules, which favor the centralized resolution of disputes in the Bankruptcy Courts; and (ii) the pro-arbitration public policy embodied in the FAA, which tends to lead to decentralized dispute resolution. This tension is clearly visible when Bankruptcy Courts are asked to lift the

---

65 11 U.S.C. §362(h); *In re Schwartz*, 954 F.2d 569 (9th Cir. 1992).

66 See generally *Fernando Mantilla-Serrano*, International Arbitration and Insolvency Proceedings, 11 Arb. Int'l 51 (1995). Notably, the United States courts have shown some willingness to respect international arbitration awards, notwithstanding a violation of the automatic stay. See, *e.g.*, *Fotochrome, Inc. v. Copal. Co.*, 517 F.2d 512, 516-18 (2d Cir. 1975) (allowing claim based on international arbitration award to be put forward in bankruptcy proceeding, despite fact that award was rendered after stay went into effect, where creditor was outside the personal jurisdiction of the Bankruptcy Court).

automatic stay and permit the resolution of claims in arbitration. To date, however, there is no definitive Supreme Court jurisprudence settling this question, and the lower court jurisprudence on the issue is both extensive and inconsistent.

The Bankruptcy Code was enacted by Congress long after the FAA, and it is established law in the United States that a later statute can modify an earlier one, if indeed that was Congress's intention.[67] The courts have thus tended to frame the issue as whether the Code implicitly modifies the FAA's command that arbitration clauses be enforced and, if so, to what extent.

The decisions of the lower federal courts regarding the lifting of the stay in favor of arbitration have tended to follow two lines. The first line holds that the decision whether or not to lift the automatic stay in order to refer a case to arbitration lies within the "sound discretion" of the bankruptcy judge.[68] The second line draws a distinction between "core" and "non-core" matters, finding that "non-core" matters should generally be referred to arbitration.[69]

A recent decision by the influential Second Circuit Court of Appeals in the *United States Lines* case may, however, offer additional clarity.[70] That case involved a class action of some 12,000 employees filing over 18,000 claims against a Trust representing insolvent ship-owners, mostly for asbestos-related injuries sustained by the employees while serving on ships in the debtors' fleet over the course of four decades. The proceeds of several insurance policies held by the debtors were the only asset available to satisfy these mass tort claims, and these policies contained arbitration clauses. The issue before the Second Circuit was whether to permit resolution of the Trust's claims against the insurers through arbitration, as the insurers had requested, or rather to annul the arbitration clause and try these claims in the Bankruptcy Court.

Noting that a dispute involving both the Code and FAA sometimes "presents a conflict of near polar extremes," the Second Circuit decided that in the context of bankruptcy proceedings, a Bankruptcy Court cannot override an arbitration clause in "non-core" matters; however, when a "core matter" is involved, the

---

67 See *Shearson/American Express*, 480 U.S. at 226-227 (holding that the mandate of the FAA may be overridden by a contrary federal statute, and finding that the courts must apply a balancing test in evaluating whether this has occurred). An interesting query, beyond the scope of this paper, is whether this same line of reasoning can be applied in respect of international obligations such as those imposed by the New York or Panama Conventions.

68 See, *e.g.*, *Zimmerman v. Continental Airlines, Inc.*, 712 F.2d 55, 56 (3d Cir. 1983) (holding that the Bankruptcy Code "impliedly modif[ied]" the Federal Arbitration Act and that the decision whether to require arbitration lies within the "sound discretion" of the bankruptcy court).

69 See, *e.g.*, *Hays & Co. v. Merrill Lynch, Pierce, Fenner & Smith, Inc.*, 885 F.2d 1149, 1158-62 (3d Cir. 1989).

70 *In re United States Lines, Inc.*, 197 F.3d 631 (2d Cir. 1999).

Court retains discretion to override an arbitration clause if enforcing the clause "would seriously jeopardize the objectives of the [Bankruptcy] Code."[71] Finding that the underlying insurance contract claims were "core" to the bankruptcy proceedings (as they directly affected the Bankruptcy Court's core function of asset preservation and allocation among creditors), and noting that "the bankruptcy court is the preferable venue in which to handle mass tort claims against an insolvent debtor," the Second Circuit ruled that the Bankruptcy Court had acted within its discretion in declining to refer those claims to arbitration.[72]

While the ultimate resolution in *United States Lines* was against the enforcement of the arbitration clauses at issue, this appears to have resulted from the case's unique factual situation, involving mass tort claims against an insolvent party with only one significant asset. Furthermore, the rule put forward by the Court was essentially pro-arbitration, calling for the enforcement of arbitration clauses even in "core" disputes, except where an arbitral resolution would seriously disrupt the bankruptcy proceedings.

The decision in *United States Lines* has recently been applied in *In re The Singer Company N.V.*[73] In *Singer*, the court reversed a decision of the Bankruptcy Court denying a creditor's motion to compel arbitration in a "core" dispute. In so doing, the Court held that a bankruptcy judge only has discretion to override an arbitration agreement, even in a "core" proceeding, where the dispute "presents issues premised on provisions of the Bankruptcy Code whose provisions conflict inherently with the arbitration policy."[74] Finding that not to be the case on the facts before it, the District Court remanded the matter to the Bankruptcy Court with the direction that the creditor's claim be referred to arbitration.[75]

What conclusions, then, are to be drawn regarding what this paper has termed "judicial avoidance of arbitration" in the context of bankruptcy? It must first be noted that the law in the United States remains somewhat unsettled, due to the absence of any Supreme Court precedent on the question of when a Bankruptcy Court may override an arbitration clause. That being said, the more recent jurisprudence – in particular the *United States Lines* and *Singer* cases – suggests that the Bankruptcy Court's discretion to do so is rather limited. Assuming that the trend laid out in those cases is followed by other federal courts, it is to be

---

[71] *Id.* at 640 (quoting Hays, 885 F.2d at 1161).

[72] *Id.* at 641.

[73] *In re The Singer Company N.V.*, No. 00 Civ. 6793 LTS, 2001 WL 984678 (S.D.N.Y. Aug. 27, 2001).

[74] *Id.* at *5. In this regard, the court noted that "not all core proceedings present inherent conflicts between the FAA and the Bankruptcy Code severe enough to support a finding ... that Congress intended to override the FAA's general policy of enforceability of arbitration agreements." *Id.*

[75] *Id.* at *7.

expected that the bankruptcy exception to arbitration will remain, but that its application will be relatively restricted.

V. Conclusions

In bringing this paper to a close, we return to the question posed in the title: is "no money, no arbitration" an accurate reflection of the state of the law in the United States? As shown in the body of this paper, the answer to this question is a qualified "no."

With respect to the issue of party impecuniousness, the case law in the United States provides only limited support for the thesis that inability or unwillingness to pay provides a valid ground for voiding an arbitration agreement. The cases that have so held have uniquely arisen in the consumer context, where special protections have historically been afforded. It seems unlikely that the cost exception to arbitration applied in the *Gateway* cases, and considered by the Supreme Court in *Green Tree*, would be extended outside the consumer context.

As to bankruptcy, recent judgments suggest that the existence of insolvency proceedings will only sometimes be an impediment to arbitration. While the law remains unsettled, if the judgment in *United States Lines* shows the way forward, then parties who wish to arbitrate their disputes against an insolvent party will have a good chance of lifting the automatic stay in "non-core" proceedings; in some federal circuits (and depending on the discretion of the judge), parties may also able to have the stay lifted in "core" proceedings.

It remains to emphasize that, from a practical perspective, any generalized "poverty exception" to the enforcement of arbitration agreements would create a great source of potential mischief, especially in the context of international commercial arbitration. By putting arbitration clauses into their agreements, commercial parties agree to exclude the competence of the national courts, and indeed this is often a primary reason for including such clauses in the first place. Were an inability or unwillingness to pay arbitration costs recognized as a general defense to the enforcement of arbitration agreements, then every party – including sophisticated commercial parties who surely knew what they were signing up for – would have the possibility to rush to their local courts when a dispute arose to seek avoidance of an arbitration agreement, quite possibly for dilatory or tactical reasons. At the very least, delay in the arbitral proceedings would result, costs would be increased, and the intention of the parties to avoid litigation in the national courts would be undermined.

These results are surely to be avoided. Fortunately, the approach taken thus far by the United States courts on the issue of impecuniousness and arbitration gives little reason to fear that such mischief would be condoned.

Bank-related Instruments to Secure the Right to Arbitration despite the Impecuniousness of a Party

Dr. Stefan Kröll, LL.M.[*]

I. Introduction

Arbitration has long since been the primary means of dispute resolution in international business transactions. This is in part due to the fact that the conclusion of an arbitration agreement provides for a certain predictability as to the dispute resolution process. The parties know from the conclusion of their contract in which forum potential disputes will be resolved and it is not for the claimant to engage in forum shopping. The various courts which would otherwise have jurisdiction are generally required under their national arbitration law or under Article II (3) New York Convention to decline jurisdiction if a party invokes the existence of an arbitration agreement.[1]

This obligation, however, only exists where the arbitration agreement is not null and void, inoperable or unenforceable. The latter may be the case where one

---

* *Rechtsanwalt*, Senior Researcher, R.I.Z. (European and International Law Center) Cologne.

1 See for example section 1032 ZPO (implementing Article 8 UNCITRAL Model Law); section 9 English Arbitration Act 1996; Article 7 Swiss PIL; section 3 US FAA.

of the parties lacks the necessary funds to initiate and participate in the arbitration proceedings. In a recent decision the German Supreme Court has held, that:

> "the arbitration agreement became inoperable, as the Claimant could not raise the costs for the arbitration proceedings and there was no other process established to provide for the costs".[2]

Concerning the non-enforceability of the arbitration agreement the ruling confirms a well established line of decisions of the German courts. The only difference is that under the old law the impecuniousness of a party only gave a right to terminate the arbitration agreement[3] while under the new law the agreement automatically becomes unenforceable without any further act of the party required.[4] However, the above cited statement also indicates that even under the new dogmatic approach, there might be chances to save the right to go to arbitration. As long as payment of the costs is ensured by other means the enforceability of the arbitration agreement will not be affected.

In the following it will be examined whether and by which bank related instruments parties can secure their rights to go to arbitration.

II. Arbitrating with impecunious parties

The availability and suitability of bank-related instruments to secure the right to go to arbitration depends to a certain extent on the situation in which they are meant to operate. The following table sets out the various scenarios where the impecuniousness of a party may become an issue.

---

2 See BGH ZZP 2001, 97, 98 („Im Streitfall ist die Schiedsvereinbarung undurchführbar gewesen, weil der Kläger die Kosten des Schiedsverfahrens nicht hat aufbringen können und auch nicht anderweit für Kostendeckung gesorgt gewesen ist")

3 See for example BGHZ 41, 104; 51, 79; 55, 344; 77, 65, 102, 199

4 For a critical evaluation of this change of approach see *Schlosser* JZ 2001, 260; *Walter*, ZZP 2001, 99, 101f; *Wagner* LM H. 2/2001 300, 302 et seq.

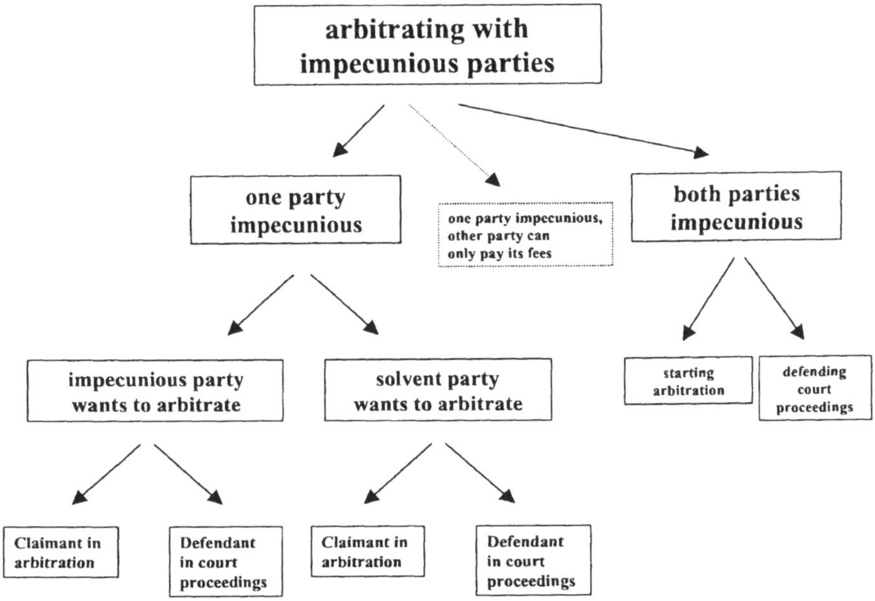

The first distinction to be drawn is whether both parties lack sufficient funds to arbitrate or only one. In the former situation unless funding can be provided for both parties there is always the threat that the arbitration agreement will be inoperable. In this regard it hardly makes a difference whether the impecuniousness is raised as a defence in arbitration proceedings or in court proceedings.

By contrast where only one party is impecunious there is always the possibility that the solvent party pays all the costs. In these cases it is, therefore, of considerable importance which party wants to arbitrate. If it is the solvent party the issue is primarily of ensuring reimbursement of the expenses made for the other party. If it is the impecunious party that wants to arbitrate the right to do so depends on whether it can ensure the necessary funding.

This may inter alia depend on its position in the proceedings, whether it is the claimant in the arbitration proceedings or whether it raises the arbitration agreement as a defence in court proceedings. Where it is the claimant in the arbitration proceedings it might be easier to get funding. Banks or other third parties may hope to be repaid from the amount awarded at the end of the arbitration. By contrast where the impecunious party is the defendant in court proceedings often no such prospects of additional funds exist so that outside funding will be nearly impossible to get unless secured already at an earlier time.

The position of the party in the proceedings may also be of relevance in those cases where the solvent party wants to arbitrate, which will be the primary focus of this article. This is particularly so where the solvent party can pay its costs of arbitration but not those of the other party which tries to rely on its impecuniousness to defeat the arbitration agreement.

III. Extent of coverage

The first question to be answered in determining the availability and suitability of bank-related instruments is which costs these instruments have to cover to ensure the enforceability of the right to go to arbitration. In its decision the Supreme Court stated very broadly that the arbitration agreement became inoperable "as the Claimant could not raise the costs for the arbitration proceedings". This includes the costs of the tribunal as well as the costs for legal representation in the proceedings.[5]

At first sight the undifferentiated reference to "costs of the arbitration proceedings" in this and earlier decisions appears to imply that the arbitration agreement will only be enforceable if all costs of the impecunious party in connection with the arbitration are borne. As a consequence also the bank related instruments would have to be drafted in a way that they cover all cost of the impecunious parties.

It is, however, submitted that the rationale underlying this jurisprudence does not support such an interpretation. In all its decisions the Supreme Court justified the disregard of the arbitration agreement with the need to ensure that the lack of sufficient funding should not deprive an impecunious party of an effective protection of its legal rights.[6]

This reasoning is based on two assumptions: first, that an impecunious party cannot effectively enforce its rights in arbitration and second, that effective protection is possible in court proceedings. Only in cases where both conditions are met can it be justified to deny the enforcement of an agreement freely entered into by the parties. Only then is it actually the arbitration agreement which "deprives" a party of its legal protection.

It is fairly obvious that an impecunious party will not be able to protect its rights properly in arbitration proceedings. Since there is no legal aid available[7] it will neither be able to pay its share for the advance on costs nor will it be able to pay for legal representation. While the latter may not in all cases prevent an effective protection of a party's rights, the inability to pay the advance on costs

---

5 See also BGHZ 51, 79, 82.

6 BGH ZZP 2001, 97, 99 "As the legislator has now expressly stated in § 1032 (1) ZPO n.v., the parties must– within the limits of §§ 226 242, 826 BGB – have the right to disregard the arbitration agreement where it becomes inoperable, since they would *otherwise be left without legal protection*" (emphasize added)

7 *Zöller/Philippi*, Zivilprozeßordnung, 23rd ed. 2002, § 114 para. 1.

will often de facto bar an impecunious claimant from bringing the claim. Under most rules the payment of the advance on costs is a prerequisite for effective initiation of the arbitration proceedings.[8]

While courts will in general only become active when the costs are paid, legal aid will often be available to ensure that the necessary payments can be made. In these cases the enforcement of the arbitration agreement would actually deprive a party of the opportunity to enforce its legal rights.

However, legal aid is by no means available in all cases. Sections 114 et seq. ZPO make the granting of legal aid dependent on the existence of a reasonable chance to win. Furthermore, foreign legal persons are completely excluded from legal aid while German legal persons must additionally prove that the non-enforcement of their claims would contravene public policy. In these cases, where no legal aid is available, there is no justification to deny the enforcement of the arbitration agreement in favour of court proceedings. The protection available in court proceedings will not be greater than that available in arbitration proceedings.

As consistently held by the Constitutional Court, the protection provided by the provisions on legal aid is sufficient to fulfil the constitutional right of access to justice.[9] There is no reason why the standard should be higher in arbitration. Consequently, to ensure the operability of the arbitration agreement, the banking instruments must at least provide the same protection as the provisions on legal aid, but need not provide more protection.

IV. Solvent party wants to arbitrate

In cases where the solvent party wants to arbitrate the primary function of bank related instruments is to keep arbitration an economically attractive alternative to litigation. From a purely legal perspective a solvent party can always ensure its right to arbitration by paying all costs involved even without having to rely on bank-related instruments. Economically, however, this often makes no sense. While in court proceedings at least the costs of the other side would be covered by legal aid, in arbitration proceedings the solvent party would have to bear all costs involved with no or little chance of recovering them. Consequently, the higher costs involved in arbitration would normally outweigh all other advantages of arbitration unless there are serious doubts as to the effectiveness and impartiality of court proceedings.

There are two conceivable ways in which the objective of maintaining the attractiveness of arbitration can be attained. Either the bank-related instruments can prevent that the other side becomes impecunious by ensuring the availability of sufficient funds so that the solvent party would not be forced to pay the costs

---

8 See section 7 (2), 8 DIS Arbitration Rules; Article 4 (4) (5) ICC Arbitration Rules; Article 1 (1) (f) LCIA Arbitration Rules.

9 See for example BVerfGE 9,124, 130 et seq.; 56, 139, 142; 78, 104, 118; 81, 347, 357.

of the other side. Or the instruments may be directed to ensure that the solvent party will be reimbursed at least for all payments it made for the impecunious side.

1. Solvent party is claimant in arbitration proceedings

There may be a number of reasons why proceedings are brought against an impecunious party, despite the non-availability of any assets for execution. The most obvious is where the award sought does not have to be enforced or is of a non-enforceable content. This is for example the case where declaratory relief is sought. Furthermore, the award may be a prerequisite for payment under an export guarantee scheme. Another reason may be that the award is binding on third parties that have sufficient funds for execution. For example, in the construction industry awards rendered between employer and main-contractor may under the contractual arrangements also be binding on the subcontractor.[10]

a) The potential instruments and the need for advance regulation

There are several conceivable banking instruments by which a claimant could in these cases ensure either that the otherwise impecunious respondent has access to sufficient funds for the arbitration proceedings or that payments made for such a respondent are repaid. To attain the former objective the parties may either agree on a cash deposit, a conditional loan or a bank guarantee securing the claims of the tribunal or the lawyers. To secure claims for repayment of respondent's part of the costs, which were pre-financed by claimant, a bank guarantee could be an appropriate means.

Irrespective of what means are used it should already be agreed upon well before the dispute arises. It is highly unlikely that any of these instruments can be agreed upon on an ad hoc basis once the dispute has arisen and one party has declared its impecuniousness.

- First, it will be very difficult if not impossible to find a bank which gives credit to an already impecunious party against which a claim is brought. Loans or the issuance of bank guarantees normally depend on the existence of sufficient assets of the main debtor. However, generally no such assets exist as otherwise the respondent could not invoke the unenforceability of the arbitration agreement. Unless this impecunious party raises a counterclaim it will also be unlikely to find a claims financing company to provide the necessary funding. As already mentioned before, even in a best case scenario there will be no further

[10] See for example the interpretation given to the arbitration clause in *Lafarge Redlands Aggregates Ltd v Shephard Hill Civil Engineering Ltd,* [2000] 1 WLR 1621 by the minority of the House of Lords.

funds available from which the financing company could be repaid for its financial engagement.

- Second, any newly devised instrument at the time of the dispute would require the cooperation of the respondent. It would be the impecunious party which would have to apply for credit or the issuance of a bank guarantee. It seems very doubtful whether a claimant could force the respondent to do so. The obligation to cooperate arising under the arbitration agreement probably does not extend to the respondent being required to apply for credit to arbitrate.

Consequently, the bank related instruments should preferably already be agreed upon at the time of contracting.

b) Cash deposit pledged to other side

A cash deposit pledged to the other party is a safe way to ensure that the depositing party has sufficient funds to arbitrate. It can be structured in a way to ensure

- first, that the money deposited is used for no other purpose than to finance the arbitration; and
- second, that other creditors of the depositing party do not have access to it.

The existence of the money in conjunction with the claimant's declaration that it may be used for the arbitration will prevent the other party from relying on its impecuniousness to frustrate the arbitration agreement.[11]

While it is in theory possible to structure the deposit and the pledge in an appropriate way there are two practical problems. Of these two problems, the minor one is that at the time of conclusion of the contract the parties do not know how much money will be needed for arbitration proceedings. It may well be that the amount finally in dispute is much larger than originally anticipated by the parties, so that the deposit is not sufficient to pay for arbitration proceedings in relation to the whole claim. In these cases it is always possible to bring a claim for only a part of the amount in dispute. The fact that the arbitration proceedings do not resolve the whole claim do as such not lead to the inoperability of the agreement. By far, the prevailing view is that even in these cases the agreement stays valid.[12]

---

[11] There are various different ways to attain these objectives either through a trust account or a blocked account in favour of the solvent party. For details on blocked accounts under German law see *Schimansky/Bunte/Lwowski*, Bankrechts-Handbuch, Vol. I, 2nd ed. 2001, §§ 36, 37.

[12] *Lonrho Ltd. v Shell Petroleum Co Ltd. et al* [1981] 2 All ER 456; Alberta Court of Appeal, 16 January 1992, *Kaverit Steel and Crane Ltd. et al. v Kone Corporation et al.*, XIV YBCA 643 (1994) 651 para 31; for a different view see the decision of the British Columbia Supreme Court, *Prince George (City) v McElhanney Engineering Services Ltd.*

The second problem, which is more serious, is that through the deposit a considerable amount of capital will be bound and cannot be used for other purposes. In particular, parties which already have a weak financial status at the time of contracting will probably not be willing or even not be able to set aside the necessary assets for the deposit. Consequently, a cash deposit pledged to the other side is hardly a practical solution. It is more likely that in those cases parties will either run the risk of not being able to arbitrate or employ another instrument that avoids the downsides of the cash deposit.

c) Conditional loan

The necessary funding for the arbitration proceedings could theoretically also be ensured by conditional loan.[13] Payment of the amount must be linked to two conditions: the starting of arbitration proceedings and the impecuniousness of the borrower. The first condition is necessary to avoid that the loan facility is used for other purposes. In combination with the special purpose mentioned it excludes any execution in the loan facility by other creditors of the impecunious party. The second condition is necessary to prevent the bank from possibly terminating the credit contract when it is actually needed, i.e. when the originally solvent party becomes impecunious. Generally the deterioration of the financial situation of the potential borrower gives the bank the right to unilaterally terminate the loan contract. This right does not, however, not exist where the credit is granted specifically for such a situation.[14]

For opening the credit facility the bank will usually charge an arrangement fee, the amount of which depends on the likelihood of the usage of the credit and the prospects of recovering the money once spent. When respondent makes use of the credit facility interest would have to be paid for the amount used. The repayment conditions of the credit and whether the respondent will actually make use of the loan is of no concern to the claimant in the arbitration proceedings. Respondent may also decide not to incur any costs for lawyers by defending the case itself.

d) Bank guarantee

In a comparable way the right to arbitrate or at least any claim for repayment can also be secured by a bank guarantee. These instruments can easily be structured in an way to reach either of the results. Like conditional loans they have the advantage over cash deposits that the amount of capital bound is much

---

and Al Sims and Sons Ltd., 30 December 1994, 6 ADRLJ 315-320 (1997); further cases cited by *van den Berg*, The New York Convention of 1958 – Towards a Uniform Judicial Interpretation, 1981, 162 et seq.

13 For details on loans see *Schimansky/Bunte/Lwowski*, Bankrechts-Handbuch, Vol. II, 2nd ed. 2001, §§ 75-77.

14 *Claussen*, Bank und Börsenrecht, 2. ed. 2000, § 8 para. 39.

lower.[15] Though a bank will only issue a guarantee where sufficient assets are available the principal is generally allowed to make other use of its assets. In return for the issuance of the bank guarantee he only has to pay a certain annual fee. The amount of this fee depends to a large extent on its credit standing and the relationship the principal has with its bank.

aa) Beneficiary – Secured claim

Guarantees generally operate in a way to ensure a specific payment claim against a party. In arbitration proceedings involving an impecunious party there are three conceivable claims which could be secured by the guarantee

- the tribunal's claim for legal costs and the lawyer's claim for payment;
- a claim for reimbursement of a third party providing the necessary funding; or
- a claim for reimbursement of the other party paying the complete costs for arbitration

Out of these three options the last one is the most likely to be chosen in practice. The other two require the cooperation of third parties and may even lead to additional costs beyond the opening commission of the bank guarantee.

The first option requires that the arbitral tribunal and the lawyers of the impecunious parties agree to work on the basis of a security given rather than on the basis of actual payment. Though this may well happen in practice,[16] the parties cannot be sure at the time of contracting that the third parties will actually cooperate once a dispute has arisen. Furthermore, at the time of issuance the beneficiary of the guarantee will in most cases not yet be known. It is rare and not advisable that the parties appoint their arbitrators or their lawyers at the time of contracting. Though at least under German law the beneficiary may originally be left open, [17] its final determination may require the cooperation of the respondent, which might no longer be willing to cooperate. The problem of the undetermined beneficiary might also arise in the context of the second option. It may not be clear at the time of contracting which third party will finance the proceedings. In addition the involvement of a third party, in particular that of another bank or any other financial institution, will normally lead to additional costs. The institution will charge the parties for the money lent. The existence of the guarantee will influence the decision whether a credit

---

15 *Nielsen*, Bankrecht und Bankpraxis, 2002, para. 5/231.

16 See for example the ICC practice reported by *Craig, Park, Paulsson*, International Chamber of Commerce Arbitration, 3rd ed. 200, p. 36 according to which the ICC does not insist on actual payment of the full amount of the advance on costs but accepts bank guarantees for 50 % of the advance on costs.

17 *Canaris*, Bankvertragsrecht, 3rd ed. 1988, para. 1123.

or loan is given and will probably lower the fees to be paid. It does in general, however, not lead to a complete exclusion of further costs.

Problems in conjunction with the third option may only arise where the claimant is not so solvent as to pre-finance the whole proceedings. Even where a company liability insurance exists that covers the costs necessary for legal actions it will at least be doubtful whether it will also cover the costs of the other side. However, in these rare cases it should not be too difficult to overcome these problems. Since the period of pre-financing will generally be limited it should be possible to get outside interim financing.

bb) Determination of the case of default

The determination of the conditions for payment under the guarantee leads to few difficulties. The reimbursement claim of the solvent party presupposes that payments have been made. Consequently proof of such payment should be required but should also be sufficient. The arbitrators usually inform the parties that the advance on costs has been paid and it is fairly easy to put the lawyer to be paid under the same obligation concerning payment of their fee. In light of these readily available documents proving the existence of the reimbursement claim, payment under the guarantee should be made dependent on the presentation of these documents.

Any additional requirement, however, would significantly deprive the guarantee of any practical value. In particular, should the beneficiary not be obliged to prove that the allegedly impecunious party is actually not capable of paying the costs. With the exception of the cases where the impecunious party has already formally declared insolvency such proof will be difficult to bring. It is also impracticable to make payment obligations dependent on the chances of success. Though legal aid will only be granted when there are such chances it is not appropriate to try to mirror that in the drafting of the bank guarantee.

cc) Amount of the guarantee

In determining the amount of the guarantee two conflicting interests have to be balanced. On one hand, the commission to be paid for the issuance of the guarantee is usually calculated as a percentage of its amount. Consequently, for keeping costs low, the smaller the amount the better. On the other hand, the amount should be high enough to cover all costs of the proceedings to avoid a situation in which the guarantee cannot fulfil its purpose. Irrespective of the fact that a party may normally bring partial claims the guarantee should be high enough to cover at least the major part of potential claims.

dd) Expiry date

A comparable dilemma as in relation to the amount in dispute exists in relation to the determination of the expiry date. On one hand it should not be too long since fees have to be paid until that time. On the other hand, it cannot be too short to avoid that the coverage is no longer available at the time the dispute arises. Guidelines for the determination of the expiry date can be the contractual or statutory prescription periods. After that time generally no claims can be brought. Consequently, it is also not necessary to provide security for proceedings started at a later date. It will, however, often be appropriate to have shorter time limits for the expiry of the bank guarantee.

There are several options in determining the relevant event to stop the expiry. It may be linked to the commencement of the arbitration proceedings, the payment of the full advance on cost or even a full demand accompanied by the necessary documentation. The latter situation has the disadvantage that the party seeking reimbursement under the guarantee will often have no influence on the time when the necessary documents are provided, in particular those proving payment to the other side's lawyer. To provide the greatest protection to the party paying all costs, the date of commencement seems to be the most appropriate date. By that time the party has done everything possible to start the arbitration and has lost the ability to influence when the advance on cost will be required, whether the other side will be able to pay it or not, and when the other side's lawyer will present their fees.

e) Practical evaluation

From a purely legal perspective, conditional loans and bank guarantees have the potential to provide adequate protection of the right to arbitrate and the reimbursement claim.[18] Nevertheless it appears doubtful whether they will be widely used in practice. They will only be issued where at the time of application the applicant has sufficient assets to secure the guarantee. Banks will generally not issue a bank guarantee if already at that time the applicant lacks the necessary funding. Furthermore, to actually ensure both parties the right to arbitrate two guarantees might be needed. At the time of contracting it is not clear which party will not be able to pay its share of costs. Consequently, to be on the safe side, both potential reimbursement claims have to be secured by a bank guarantee.

2. Solvent party is defendant in court proceedings

In general the same bank related instruments are available to protect the solvent party's right to arbitrate in those situations where the impecunious party has started court proceedings. Where these instruments ensure the availability of sufficient funding for the impecunious party no specific problems arise. Since sufficient funding is available the impecunious party cannot invoke the

[18] In relation to bank guarantees see also *Polkinghorne & Lehmkuhl*, International Business Lawyer, March 2002, Committee D News p. 26.

inoperability of the arbitration agreement and any court has to refer the parties to arbitration if the solvent party invokes the arbitration agreement.

Problems may, however, arise where the bank guarantee operates to secure the solvent party's right to be reimbursed for payments made for the impecunious party. According to the new dogmatic approach of the Supreme Court the impecuniousness of one party automatically leads to the inoperability of the arbitration agreement. Consequently, one could argue that from the moment the impecunious party starts court proceedings the solvent party can no longer rely on the arbitration irrespective of whether it declares later that it will bear the costs for the impecunious party.[19] It is, however, submitted that such an interpretation would be in violation of the parties' agreements. Where the parties when entering into their contract have already agreed upon bank-related instruments to provide for such a situation the impecunious party cannot later defeat their agreement unilaterally. It has an obligation first to ask the solvent party whether it is willing to pay the full costs before it can rely on its impecuniousness to defeat the arbitration agreement.

Apart from this, the situation is widely comparable to that described above with, however, two differences. First, the solvent party may be able to await the decision on legal aid. Often the application for legal aid precedes the action on the merits. In such a case where legal aid is not granted arbitration will not be less advantageous to the impecunious party than court proceedings. Therefore, the solvent defendant should be allowed to invoke the arbitration agreement without being required to undertake payment of claimant's costs in the arbitration proceedings.

The second difference relates to those cases where the solvent party can pay its own costs but not those of the impecunious party. Where the solvent party is the respondent and does not raise any counterclaims the chances of being able to get a claims financing company to pay the costs will be much lower than in cases where it is the claimant.

V. Impecunious party wants to arbitrate

At first sight it might appear unlikely than an impecunious claimant would like to rely on its right to arbitration. The proceedings may be more expensive and the claimant will not be entitled to legal aid. There are, however, situations were such claimant may have a justifiable interest in its right to arbitrate.

- It may well be that such claimant is afraid of not getting a fair treatment in the national courts having jurisdiction.

[19] See also BGHZ 51, 79, 83 where the Supreme Court held under its old approach that once an impecunious party had terminated the arbitration agreement by starting court proceedings any offer to pay the costs came too late to save the arbitration agreement.

- The court proceedings may take so long that by then the party may have gone bankrupt.
- Or a judgment rendered by the competent courts may not be enforceable in the country where the other side has assets.

Furthermore, the mere fact that a party is impecunious can by no means in itself justify the loss of the party's right to arbitrate. The impecuniousness may actually be the result of the other party's behaviour. For example, a seller may lack the necessary funds to arbitrate its claims against the buyer merely because the buyer never paid for the goods. To reward the buyer for its behaviour and to deprive the seller of its right to arbitrate but instead force him to bring the action at the buyer's place of business would be unfair.

1. Impecunious claimant

To enforce its right to arbitration an impecunious claimant will generally have to ensure that at least the administrative fee and the advance on costs will be paid. Under an ordinary arbitration clause the solvent respondent is under no obligation to help an impecunious claimant by providing the necessary funding. Though the arbitration agreement requires the parties to cooperate in the arbitration proceedings it does not entail the obligation for one side to pay the complete costs of the tribunal if the other party is not able to do so.[20]

Consequently, unless expressly regulated before the dispute arises, an impecunious claimant will have to rely on outside funding. It may try to convince its bank to give it a loan to finance the proceedings or find someone who directly finances the proceedings in return for a portion of the money awarded. There are cases where process financing institution have done so[21] but due to the lack of sufficient data on arbitration it may be much harder for an institution to arrive at a reasonable pricing of its services. The claimant may also sell its claim to a third party with the necessary funds to start arbitration.

Concerning the bank-related instruments to ensure the claimant's right to arbitration through cash deposits, conditional loans or bank guarantees the above made comments are largely applicable. However, particularly in connection with the use of bank guarantees the additional problem arises that the parties must contractually fix an obligation for the solvent party to make the necessary payments on behalf of the impecunious claimant. Even then a claimant may be obliged to go to the courts to enforce this obligation before being able to arbitrate.

---

[20] See BGHZ 102, 199, 202.

[21] This information is owed to *Jens Bredow*, Secretary General of DIS.

2) Impecunious party as defendant in court proceedings

To raise the defence of an arbitration agreement successfully in court proceedings, an impecunious party will probably have to give an undertaking that it is capable of paying its share of the advance on cost. As arbitration does not require representation by a lawyer the ability of paying its lawyer's fee should not have any influence on the decision. For the reasons mentioned above its position as a respondent in the arbitration proceedings will generally negatively affect its chances to find a third party to provide the necessary funds.

VI. Conclusion

So far parties' bank-related instruments have played a limited role in securing the right to arbitrate. Claimants may have received funding on an ad-hoc basis to bring their claim in arbitration or have sold their claims to a solvent party. In all these cases the right to arbitrate, however, depended on the unilateral decision of one party, financed the arbitration. Means to free the right to arbitrate from such a unilateral decision of one party and to make it an enforceable right for both irrespective of the other sides behaviour have not been employed.

It is without doubt theoretically possible to do so. The means exist and according to my information banks would have no problems in issuing the required guarantees. However, in the future the costs associated with these instruments will prevent their wide use in practice. They may be suitable for very specific cases where the right to arbitrate is considered to be of such an importance that it justifies the extra expenses. In general the transaction costs involved, however, make these bank-related instruments unsuitable. The instruments will be available only to parties which at the time of contracting are financially sound. Furthermore, since it is not known which party will at the time of dispute lack the necessary funds both parties would have to provide the necessary security.

Are there means – contractual or otherwise – to guard against an adverse impact of financial incapacity on arbitration? - Insurance-related instruments -

*Dr. Hubertus W. Labes**

I. The case

A recent decision by the German Federal Court of Justice[1] has permitted a party to an arbitration agreement to avoid arbitration and proceed to the state court because that party lacked the financial means to pursue its claims in arbitration. In fact, both parties to the arbitration in question were impecunious. It will be considered subsequently, whether insurance-related instruments provide a solution against such an adverse impact of financial incapacity on arbitration. Two statements of the Federal Court of Justice seem to open a window in that regard.

The first interesting statement of the Court is that the respondents did not claim that they would have advanced the claimant's costs of the arbitration including the lawyer's costs in order to carry through the arbitration procedure[2]. This indicates that a solvent party to a dispute will always have the possibility to pay for the entire procedural and lawyer's costs in order to assure the continuation of the arbitration procedure. De facto this is privately financed legal aid.

Legal aid indeed seems to be the important distinction for the Federal Court of Justice between arbitration procedures where an impecunious party cannot get legal aid, and state court procedures where the impecunious party - under certain circumstances - has the legal right to get aid to defray legal costs and advances

* Attorney-at-Law; Partner, Chiltington International

[1] BGH (III ZR 33/00), Judgment of 14 September 2000.

[2] Quote BGH: „Die Beklagten haben nicht behauptet, dass sie im Interesse der Durchführung des Schiedsverfahrens dem Kläger die auf ihn entfallenden Kosten des Schiedsverfahrens sowie seine notwendigen Anwaltskosten vorgestreckt hätten.“

on costs. One condition for getting this legal aid is according to paragraph 114 of the Code of Civil Procedure (*ZPO*) that the intended prosecution or defence of a lawsuit has adequate promise of success[3]. It is therefore important to precisely render the definition of "success" in this context[4].

The second important statement of the Federal Court of Justice referred to the respondent's employer's liability insurance (*Betriebshaftpflichtversicherung*) that would have taken over his costs of the arbitration procedure. Here the Court in theory confirmed another option to assure the continuation of the arbitration procedure, because the only reason why the Court did not acknowledge the existence of employer's liability insurance in this case was that this insurance would have only paid for the respondent's but not for the claimant's procedural and lawyer's costs[5]. This leaves the claimant without sufficient financial means to conduct arbitration proceedings.

Therefore, it indeed could be the insurance industry offering ways to avoid termination of the arbitration agreement and therefore avoid the closing of the arbitration procedure due to the impecuniosity of a party or both parties to arbitration. The following lines of business can be identified as possibly providing respective protection[6]:

- the employer's liability insurance mentioned already
- an insurance for bad debt losses (*Forderungsausfallversicherung*)
- an insurance for legal costs (*Rechtsschutzversicherung*)
- or some kind of process-financing (*Prozeßfinanzierung*)

II. Insurance Cover (Lines of business)

1. Process-financing organisations

There are various process-financing suppliers in Germany[7] - some of which are run by daughter companies of insurers - which sponsor lawsuits the claimant either can't or doesn't want to follow through if he has to fund them by himself.

---

3 Excerpt quote § 144 ZPO: „Eine Partei (...) erhält auf Antrag Prozesskostenhilfe, wenn die beabsichtigte Rechtsverfolgung oder Rechtsverteidigung hinreichende Aussicht auf Erfolg bietet und nicht mutwillig erscheint."

4 See below II. 1.

5 Quote BGH: „Die Betriebshaftpflichtversicherung der Beklagten hätte nur die von ihnen aufzubringenden Kosten der Rechtsverteidigung im Schiedsverfahren beglichen; die auf den Kläger entfallenden Kosten wären ungedeckt geblieben."

6 Apart from this catalogue there might be insurers offering cover even under further lines of business such as for example credit insurers which provide cover for bad debt losses however not covering any legal costs such as lawyer's fees, court fees, costs for expertise, costs for hearings of evidence etc.

7 acivo Prozessfinanzierung AG, Allianz ProzessFinanz GmbH, D.A.S Prozessfinanzierung AG, Exactor AG, First Pacific Risk Financing Ltd., Foris AG (the first on the market), Gepro GmbH, Juragent AG, Jurecon AG, Kapp Stiftung, Proxx AG, Roland Prozeßfinanz AG, Solvantis AG, etc.

A process-financing organisation will take over costs and risk of the lawsuit. Thus the claimant doesn't have to pay anything even if he loses his case. If a case is won, most of the process-financing organisations ask for a contingency fee depending on the costs and the risk of a case, others receive half of the actual profit, others less. Furthermore, process-financing organisations offer miscellaneous standards provided a partial victory or a settlement arrangement is gained and/or if the claimant also has to pay for parts of the lawsuit.

And, most importantly for the Federal Court of Justice case in question, process-financing organisations usually also finance arbitrations, mediations and other out-of-court negotiations or settlements.

But what are the conditions for obtaining process-financing? Inter alia, process-financing organisations require:

- that they must be convinced of the chances of success;
- that the opposing party is solvent, should this party lose the case.
- and a minimum value in dispute at least amounting in 50.000 EURO; some even require 200.000 EURO[8]. A maximum sum of claim normally does not exist.

In the case in question, the respondents installed heating and sanitary equipment pursuant to a construction contract concluded with the claimant. After a portion of the works had been completed, the claimant refused to provide security for the payment and the respondents stopped the construction work. That means, both parties in the Federal Court of Justice case were rather small parties, essentially on the "consumer" level and it is most likely that the value in dispute was less than 50.000 EURO.

But even if in this case the amount involved would have exceeded this minimum value in dispute, the overall problem can, needless to say, only be solved by process-financing organisations for all those disputes with a minimum value in dispute over 50.000 EURO.

The chances of success required by process-financing organisations also significantly affect the Federal Court of Justice case in question. For process-financing organisations, success means that the claim can be realised with a predominant probability of success by victory, partial victory or arrangement. The respective consideration needs to be done by the lawyer of the claimant.[9]

---

8 Allianz Profi: 100.000 EURO; DAS Profi: 50.000 EURO; Foris: 200.000 EURO.

9 Quotes: Allianz Profi: „Nach eingehender Prüfung der Unterlagen sowie der Sach- und Rechtslage kommt der Rechtsanwalt des Klägers zu dem Schluß, daß der Anspruch mit überwiegender Erfolgswahrscheinlichkeit realisiert werden kann"; DAS Profi: „Der Rechtsanwalt des Klägers beurteilt die Erfolgsaussichten der Klage und die Bonität des Gegners als gut"; Foris: „Der Anspruch verspricht in rechtlicher und tatsächlicher Hinsicht eine hohe Erfolgsaussicht. Anwalt und Mandant sind vom Erfolg überzeugt".

This definition of success differs from the definition within the legal aid system where success is an adequate prospect to prove conclusive pleading.[10]

As this has been mentioned before, these organisations review the case in order to verify the chances of success and will not give any support, when not convinced of the chances of success. Most of them may even withdraw from the contract if the prospects of success diminish substantially on account of altered circumstances.

A third reason is that process-financing organisations do not finance lawsuits against obviously impecunious debtors and they typically ask for a proof of solvency. Some process-financing organisations also bear the risk of solvency, such as the risk of proceedings costs, but none of them will finance lawsuits against obviously impecunious debtors. Some of those organisations even ask for a rating of the respondent's financial reliability. And no distinction is drawn for the case where a solidly solvent party suddenly experiences financial hardships, and the situation where an already impecunious party agrees to arbitration knowing that it cannot afford the advances.

The reason for this is obvious: the process-financing organisation does not want to run the risk of not being able to recover sums payable following a successful arbitration or court procedure.

Therefore, if – like in the Federal Court of Justice case – the claimant is without sufficient financial means and the respondents are not in a position to bear the costs of the claimant, the involvement of a process-financing organisation will not avoid the risk of a termination of the arbitration procedure.

2. *Legal insurance (Rechtschutzversicherung)*

Legal insurance, also called insurance for legal (litigation) costs or legal (litigation) expenses insurance and regulated in paragraphs 158 et seq. German Insurance Act (*VVG*), covers any legal costs encountered and, in case of a countersuit, pays as long as there is a reasonable chance of winning. It provides up-front finance for legal expertise and representation in order to protect rights and obtain justice especially for those parties who are deterred from taking legal action due to the costs of litigation in virtually any forum. Solicitors' fees, experts' costs and the cost of court hearings are generally covered by legal insurance. This also includes the costs of the opposing party if the outcome of a dispute is unsuccessful although the legal insurer confirmed protection prior to the procedure (*Deckungszusage*).

Legal insurance is usually purchased on an annual basis or for the period of a specific contract that is being concluded. For situations where a party to a dispute is contemplating a law suit or required to defend itself in litigation or arbitration without having adequate insurance to meet such costs then some

---

[10] *Thomas-Putzo*, ZPO, § 114: "hinreichende Aussicht, daß schlüssiges Vorbringen beweisbar ist".

insurers also offer "after the event" legal insurance. For this kind of cover the chances of success obviously are of a significant importance for the insurer in order to be able to confirm protection.

Legal insurance was first developed in the early 1920's at Le Mans, France. Accidents at this famous racing track gave rise to extremely complicated and long legal disputes. A whole range of insurance companies with varying interests was involved. Today legal insurance can be purchased for the entire family, for the job *(Arbeitsrechtschutz),* for traffic infractions *(Verkehrsrechtschutz)* and, for example, for tenancy disputes (*Mietrechtschutz*).

An Executive Board member of one of the biggest legal insurance providers in Germany confronted with the Federal Court of Justice case in question immediately asked: Why would two impecunious parties institute and proceed arbitration? The background of this question is of course that legal insurers do not step in if the claim is inconsiderate – and in the understanding of legal insurers it would indeed be a case of wantonness or abandon if a claimant is initiating arbitration procedure against an obviously impecunious party.

And when asked about a possible new source of revenue - having seen the Federal Court of Justice case - this Executive Board member stated that creating a specific insurance cover for cases like this would certainly not be interesting for his company due to the relatively small market and therefore an unattractive return on investment. This is despite the fact that especially legal insurers nowadays offer a lot of individual and unusual products, for example for prejudicial procedures such as pre-trial settlements or for extrajudicial procedures such as arbitrations and mediations.[11] The fact that legal insurance covers arbitration costs is included also in paragraph 5 sub-paragraph 1d General Conditions of Legal Insurance (*AVB für die Rechtsschutzversicherung*) according to which the insurer has to pay the costs of an arbitration procedure up to the costs which arise from a state court procedure within the first instance.[12]

Comparable to the process-financing organisations, although not with exactly the same definition for success, a precondition for a confirmed protection by the legal insurer is again the chance of success. In the same way as process-financing organisations, legal insurers, too, need a verification of the chances of success prior to the case. Again, it will typically be the lawyer of the claimant estimating. Provided the legal insurer and the claimant's lawyer are of different opinion regarding the chances, most of the insurance terms of legal insurers provide an expert arbitration procedure (*Schiedsgutachterverfahren*) to clarify the issue.

---

[11] AdvoCard Rechtsschutzversicherung AG; R+V Rechtsschutzversicherung AG and others.

[12] Quote § 5 Nr. 1d AVB für die Rechtsschutzversicherung: „Der Versicherer trägt die Gebühren eines Schieds- und Schlichtungsverfahrens bis zur Höhe der Gebühren, die im Falle der Anrufung eines zu-ständigen staatlichen Gerichts erster Instanz entstehen".

But as mentioned before, a procedure where the opposing party is not in a position to bear the costs to conduct state-court or arbitration procedures, or like in the case in question where both parties are without sufficient financial means, a legal insurer will definitely not confirm the protection due to the risk of not being able to recover sums payable following a successful court or arbitration procedure.

3. Employer's Liability Insurance (Betriebshaftpflichtversicherung)

Reference was made already to the statement of the Federal Court of Justice concerning employer's liability insurance and the fact that in the case at issue the Court defined an option to assure the continuation of the arbitration procedure. The Court did not accept the respondent's employer's liability insurance as an instrument to avoid termination of the arbitration procedure because the respective insurance company would not have been obliged also to bear the opposing parties procedural and lawyer's costs.[13]

Employer's liability insurance belongs like for example a fire insurance policy to the basic equipment of a company in Germany. The employer's liability insurance protects companies from third party claims for damages or comprehension; claims that might even threaten the subsistence of a company. The same protection for private persons – by the way – is granted by the personal liability insurance.

The duty of the employer's liability insurer to bear the costs of a legal procedure is standardised in the General Conditions of Employer's Liability Insurance.[14] Pursuant to paragraph 150 sub-paragraph 1 sentence 1 of the

---

[13] The decision of the Federal Court might have been dissimilar provided both parties to the case in dispute would have had agreed on an employer's liability insurance each bearing the costs of an arbitration procedure (see below III).

[14] Excerpt quote from the *Allgemeine Versicherungsbedingungen für die Haftpflichtversicherung – AHB*:

§ 3 (Beginn und Umfang des Versicherungsschutzes)

§ 3 II 3: Kommt es in einem Versicherungsfall zu einem Rechtsstreit über den Anspruch zwischen dem Versicherungsnehmer und dem Geschädigten oder dessen Rechtsnachfolger, so führt der Versicherer den Rechtsstreit im Namen des Versicherungsnehmers auf seine Kosten.

§ 3 II 4: Die Aufwendungen des Versicherers für Kosten werden nicht als Leistungen auf die Versicherungssumme angerechnet (vgl. aber Ziff. III 1).

§ 3 III 1: Übersteigen die Haftpflichtansprüche die Versicherungssumme, so hat der Versicherer die Prozesskosten nur im Verhältnis der Versicherungssumme zur Gesamthöhe der Ansprüche zu tragen, und zwar auch dann, wenn es sich um mehrere aus einem Schadenereignis entstehende Prozesse handelt. Der Versicherer ist in solchen Fällen berechtigt, durch Zahlung der Versicherungssumme und seines der Versicherungssumme entsprechenden Anteils an den bis dahin erwachsenen Kosten sich von weiteren Leistungen zu befreien.

German Insurance Act (*VVG*) the entitlement to refund costs involves all those costs which need to be spent as the circumstances may require.[15] This is the case if the costs according to paragraph 91 sub-paragraph 1 German Civil Procedural Law (*ZPO*) have been indispensable for an appropriate prosecution of an action or justification.[16] Included therefore are also the costs for the enforcement of the claim.

It is, however, questionable and a controversial issue within the German literature[17] if the employer's liability insurer is also obliged to take over the costs of an arbitration procedure. There are indeed several publications according to which the insurer cannot be forced to participate in arbitration and therefore bear his insured's costs. And even if the insurer agrees to participate in an arbitration procedure or the insurer even takes over the process, this does not necessarily mean that the insurer also has to adopt the costs.

By referring to an employer's liability insurance in its judgement without questioning the applicability to arbitration, the Federal Court of Justice in principle may already have acknowledged the employer's liability insurer's general obligation to take over the costs also of an arbitration procedure.

Though, if the insurer denies an obligation to bear the costs the insurer will have to draw his insured's attention to the missing commitment effect already at the point of institution of an arbitration procedure or even when the insured

---

§ 3 III 3: Falls die von dem Versicherer verlangte Erledigung eines Haftpflichtanspruchs durch Anerkenntnis, Befriedigung oder Vergleich an dem Widerstand des Versicherten scheitert, so hat der Versicherer für den von der Weigerung an entstehenden Mehraufwand an Hauptsache, Zinsen und Kosten nicht aufzukommen.

§ 5 (Obliegenheiten des VN, Verfahren)

§ 5 IV: Kommt es zum Prozess über den Haftpflichtanspruch, so hat der VN die Prozessführung dem Versicherer zu überlassen, dem von dem Versicherer bestellten oder bezeichneten Anwalt Vollmacht und alle von diesem oder dem Versicherer für nötig erachteten Aufklärungen zu geben. Gegen Mahnbescheide oder Verfolgungen von Verwaltungsbehörden auf Schadenersatz hat er, ohne die Weisungen des Versicherers abzuwarten, fristgemäß Widerspruch zu erheben oder die erforderlichen Rechtsbehelfe zu ergreifen.

§ 5 V: Der VN ist nicht berechtigt, ohne vorherige Zustimmung des Versicherers einen Haftpflichtanspruch ganz oder zum Teil oder vergleichsweise anzuerkennen oder zu befriedigen. (...)

§ 5 VII: Der Versicherer gilt als bevollmächtigt, alle zur Beilegung oder Abwehr des Anspruchs ihm zweckmäßig erscheinenden Erklärungen im Namen des VN abzugeben.

15 Excerpt quote from § 150 I Satz 1 VVG: "Aufwendung der Kosten den Umständen nach geboten".

16 Excerpt quote from § 91 I ZPO: "Zur zweckentsprechenden Rechtsverfolgung oder Rechtsverteidigung notwendig".

Explaining the subject of discussion: *Späte*, Haftpflichtversicherung, AHB-Kommentar, München 1993, § 3 Rdnr. 44 und § 5 Rdnr. 39; overview of the arguments: *Prölss*, Schiedsverfahren über Haftpflichtansprüche und Haftpflichtversicherungsschutz, in: VersR 1965, S. 101ff; *Sieg*, Bindung des Haftpflichtversicherers an Schiedssprüche und Schiedsgutachten in Haftpflichtverhältnissen, in: VersR 1984, S. 501ff.

informs his insurer that he intents to agree an arbitration clause with his client. This follows from the principle of the insurer's duty to be loyal with the insured. But this of course means that the insured needs to inform his insurance company about the existence of an arbitration clause either when signing the insurance contract or later when agreeing upon. An exception to this may be that the insured is regularly using arbitration clauses to the knowledge of his insurer.

A result from this uncertainty is that protection regarding a liability on the basis of an arbitration clause is one of the most frequently agreed supplemental inclusions in employer's liability insurance contracts.[18] And that is the only safe method also with respect to the issue resulting from the Federal Court of Justice decision. In order to have an undeniable obligation of the employer's liability insurer to take over the costs also of an arbitration procedure the insured needs to agree with his insurer on a corresponding supplemental inclusion.

But a major problem with respect to the Federal Court of Justice case still remains: Only one party to the arbitration in question purchased an employer's liability insurance and the corresponding insurance company was not obliged to bear the opposing parties procedural and lawyer's costs.

4. *Insurance for Bad Debt Losses (Forderungsausfallversicherung)*

This problem, however, might be solved by the owner of an employer's liability insurance with a supplement cover, a cover for irretrievable receivables by an insurance for bad debt losses, if so exists.

The main purpose of this line of business is to protect the insured when he claims from a damaging party that caused a loss but has no financial means, nor any insurance protection to compensate this loss. In this case the insurance for bad debt losses will pay the claim on behalf of this damaging party to the insured usually up to 1 Million EURO – even if the insured has been wilfully and knowingly damaged. Therefore, the insurance for bad debt losses covers all those claims the employer's liability insurance – and also the personal liability insurance by the way – normally pays for, if the insured would have caused the loss himself. For small claims, however, normally below 2 to 3.000 EURO, the cover is excluded and the insured has to accept respective retention.

The insurance for bad debt losses is a quite new product within the German insurance industry, established in 2000. There are some insurers that proactively try to offer such an insurance cover[19], however, the products significantly vary

---

[18] „Mitversicherung der Haftung auf der Grundlage von Schiedsgerichtsvereinbarungen abweichend von § 4 I 1 AHB".

[19] LVM-Versicherungen, R+V Versicherungen, Axa (Axa together with Roland Rechtsschutzversicherung also offers the financing of the enforcement of respective claims), Gerling Speziale Kreditversicherung (offers insurance for bad debt losses within an consumer credit insurance), Versicherungskammer Bayern, VHV Versicherungen, Haftpflichtkasse Darmstadt, Westfälische Provinzial, Cosmos Direkt, Debeka, etc.

from insurer to insurer. For example LVM (*Landwirtschaftlicher Versicherungsverein Münster*) offers this kind of insurance only in combination with personal liability insurance and not for commercial entities. Included in the insurance provided by LVM, however, are the costs of an enforceable court or arbitral award. R+V (*Raiffeisen und Volksbanken Versicherung*), the big public insurer in Germany, offers an insurance for bad debt losses also in combination with an employer's liability insurance and will pay immediately if the debtor owes money for more than three months. But R+V will not bear any legal costs. Hermes Insurance, the German credit insurer, offers protection for all amounts due from deliveries of goods and performance of services only.

III. Conclusion and consequence

As a conclusion and therefore an answer to the question raised in the heading to this article, if there are insurance-related instruments to guard against an adverse impact of financial incapacity on arbitration, it must be said that the insurance industry in Germany does unfortunately not yet provide an absolute solution against the termination of an arbitration procedure due to the impecuniosity of both parties to an arbitration.

A way out could be that both parties to a dispute agree on an employer's liability insurance each bearing the costs of an arbitration procedure for the respective insured. However, apart from the uncertainty described already with regard to the obligation of the employer's liability insurer to take over also the costs of an arbitration procedure, an employer's liability insurer typically will not stand up for the assertion of a third party claim by its own insured. That would be the task of a legal insurance protection. Therefore, it will customarily be only the respondent's but not the claimant's procedural and lawyer's costs the employer's liability insurer will pay for.

The key could have been an insurance cover combining employer's liability insurance and insurance for bad debt losses with the effect that the Federal Court of Justice would have had to acknowledge the existence of an insurance protection providing also the claimant with sufficient financial means to conduct arbitration proceedings. But even in case such a combination would exist, the preconditions for avoiding termination of an arbitration procedure like in the Federal Court of Justice case would be:

- That the respondent to the arbitration procedure needs to have bought an employer's liability insurance cover. As this has been mentioned earlier already, such a protection belongs to the basic equipment of a company. Therefore, it can be assumed that most German companies – even smaller companies – have purchased such an insurance cover.
- Due to the uncertainty regarding the obligation of the employer's liability insurer to take over also the costs of an arbitration procedure, the insured needs to agree with his insurer on a corresponding supplemental inclusion.

- And thirdly, the same party needs to buy insurance for bad debt losses to also avoid the opposing party's inability to bear its own costs within an arbitration procedure.

Apart from the problem that apparently no German insurer is offering an insurance for bad debt losses which covers the needs of the case in issue, it will be also rather exceptional for German companies to purchase such an insurance protection although bad dept losses covers tendered at present are comparable cheap. Hence, the combination of both lines of business - employer's liability insurance and insurance for bad debt losses - is not quite common in Germany nowadays. Thus, first of all the insurance industry needs to be convinced to create a new or supplement existing insurance for bad debt losses in order to provide protection as needed here in combination with an employer's liability (and/or personal liability) insurance. Secondly, it will be necessary to convince corporate bodies such as the parties in the Federal Court of Justice case to agree upon such an insurance for bad debt losses in addition to an employer's liability insurance, if they intent to use arbitration clauses in their contracts with business partners.

The Discussion

reported by
Marc-Oliver Heidkamp[*] and *Jens Wenzel, LL.M.*[**]

Morning Session, chaired by Professor Dr. Karl-Heinz Böckstiegel

After Professor *Böckstiegel*, President of the Deutsche Institution für Schiedsgerichtsbarkeit (*DIS*), had opened the discussion, *Hilmar Raeschke-Kessler*, attorney at the German Federal Supreme Court, stated that it should not be forgotten, that the German Federal Supreme Court (BGH) decided on a purely domestic situation when it held that impecuniosity renders the arbitration agreement inoperable. It might be that the Court simply did not think about the implications of its decision on an international level. *Mr. Raeschke-Kessler* informed the audience that the German Federal Supreme Court will soon have the opportunity to revisit its jurisprudence. At present, a case is pending involving ICC arbitration where a US defendant, claiming its own impecuniosity, relied on the ineffectiveness of the arbitration agreement. When the defendant did not participate in the arbitration proceedings, the arbitral tribunal issued an award in favour of the claimant. The American defendant then turned to the German courts to have the award set aside, but the Higher Regional Court of Berlin (*Kammergericht*) held that the arbitration clause was valid. Mr. Raeschke-Kessler doubted whether the Supreme Court will transfer the solution it adopted in its decision concerning the domestic case to the international level. Instead, *Mr. Raeschke-Kessler* assumed that the Federal Supreme Court will reverse its approach.[1]

Professor Wagner, University of Bonn, responded that he doubted whether the German Federal Supreme Court would change its position shortly after adopting the new concept. Though it was highly interesting to know the outcome of the pending case, *Professor Wagner* would be astonished if the Court walked away from its position right in the next case.

Dr. Siegfried H. Elsing from Hölters & Elsing, Düsseldorf, pointed out that the Federal Supreme Court's new approach would place Germany (possibly together with Austria) in isolation regarding international arbitration jurisprudence. He stressed, however, that this isolation was not a "splendid isolation", since it would rule out Germany as a seat for international arbitration. Next he addressed *Professor Wagner's* prediction that even if the arbitration clause specifically addressed the issue of impecuniosity, the arbitration agreement would still be inoperable. *Dr. Elsing* took a more optimistic view, at

---

[*] Law Center for European and International Cooperation, Cologne.

[**] Research Assistant, Institute for Banking Law, University of Cologne.

[1] The Federal Supreme Court has since rejected the appeal without a decision on the merits. (Ed. note)

least as far as international economic arbitration is concerned. He expected that the German courts would consider such an agreement fair and lend their support to enforce it. A possible way to generally overcome the isolation mentioned by *Mr. Raeschke-Kessler* could be to regard such a stipulation as implied in every arbitration agreement unless the parties rule it out in express terms.

Concerning this fear of isolation *Professor Wagner* replied that, in the first place the human animal did not like isolation and that second there was still a strong argument against any impact of impecuniosity on arbitral proceedings: As long as bankruptcy had not been filed a party may not rely on its lack of money. Concerns that the impecuniosity concept might give leeway for strategic behaviour should, however, not be overestimated. It could be prevented by imposing a high burden of proof. *Professor Wagner* pointed out that no arbitration law could make a poor party rich. The mere insistence on the principle of "*pacta sunt servanda*" and hence that arbitration agreements are binding in any case would not bring a practical solution to the issue. Especially it was not acceptable to *Professor Wagner* that the parties might bargain away the right to any recourse be it in an arbitral or state court forum and that it was often not even the poor party, but the other one who relied on impecuniosity. He acknowledged that *Dr. Elsing* had a strong case when stating that well informed business parties may regulate the situation of a possible later impecuniosity already in the arbitration agreement. To *Professor Wagner's* contention, this view is, however, limited to clauses specifically negotiated by the parties and may not be applied to boiler plate clauses.

Dr. Marc Blessing from Baer & Karrer, Zurich, stressed the relevance of the issue by presenting an example from his practical experience. He mentioned an ICC arbitration dispute in which a local Chinese court voided an arbitration clause that provided for ICC arbitration in London. The arbitration clause had been concluded by a German and a Chinese party to a construction contract. The latter claimed that it would not be able to pay the expenses of these proceedings. The Court accepted this contention and thereby assumed its competence to decide on the counterclaims of the Chinese party. On the merits of the case the Court ordered the German party to make restitution of all payments received by applying Chinese bankruptcy provisions, which stipulate that all payments made within the 12 months prior to the declaration of bankruptcy are recoverable.

Professor Wagner pointed out that the concept of impecuniosity would not deprive the solvent party of the possibility to have the dispute settled by arbitration as long as it was willing to pay for the costs. This argument would also have invalidated the Chinese court's reasoning in the case referred to by *Dr. Blessing*.

Andrew Burr, Atkin Chambers, London, raised the question what implications would arise from the reasonable suspicion that the underlying claim would concern money-laundering. He further inquired if other jurisdictions adopted the same view as the British where legal aid for arbitration was not available. He concluded by mentioning the tendency in Britain towards rendering an interim award for breach of contract if one of the parties failed to pay for the agreed arbitration proceedings.

Concerning the issue of legal aid for arbitration proceedings *Professor Wagner* sees little chance that States would be willing to fund arbitration proceedings with public money as the advantage of arbitration for the state court system is that the workload of the state courts is eased which in turn alleviates the costs for the state courts. Besides there was little thought about arbitration on a political level. For politicians the way to save money was rather mediation.

Mr. Detlev Kühner, International Chamber of Commerce, Paris, confirmed that there was a growing number of demands for security for costs in ICC cases. These requests are, according to Article 23 ICC Arbitration Rules, regarded as a provisional matter. Art. 23 ICC Arbitration Rules offered the possibility to render an interim award ordering a party to pay. The yardstick for an affirmative provisional award, however, was very high, which was stressed by the fact that eighty per cent of the requests for security for costs are rejected. With regard to insolvency he remarked that arbitrators often turned to the ICC board for advise on this matter. *Mr. Kühner* pleaded for a *de facto* suspension of proceedings in case one of the parties enters insolvency. *Mr. Kühner* emphasised that due to economic slowdown the question may gain higher practical relevance in the near future.

With regard to *Mr. Kühner's* intervention *Professor Wagner* proposed that Sec. 240 German Code of Civil Procedure should at least be factually applied to arbitration, as well as the provisions on bankruptcy. The provision of Sec. 240 Code of Civil Procedure stipulates, that proceedings (before state courts) shall be suspended if a party is declared insolvent, until insolvency rules allow for a resumption or until insolvency proceedings have ceased.

Laurent Lévy from Schellenberg Wittmer, Geneva, referred to the notion of impecuniosity and doubted whether it could be clearly distinguished from bankruptcy in the legal sense. The primary purpose of bankruptcy regimes was to secure equal treatment of all creditors. In many jurisdictions a trigger event for the declaration of bankruptcy was the party's inability to pay. Impecuniosity and bankruptcy might thus intervene at precisely the same moment in time, so that the scope of application of impecuniosity concept was limited.

With regard to *Brian King's* presentation *Professor Gaillard* from Shearman & Sterling, Paris, pointed out that in the United States arbitration clauses were often agreed to evade the consequences of possible class actions, which leave parties in uncertainty as to the consequential costs. To overcome the problems arising from impecuniosity of a party to an arbitration agreement *Professor Gaillard* made three suggestions: Firstly, costs should more often be awarded to the winning party, secondly more cases should be administered by a sole arbitrator instead of a panel of three arbitrators and thirdly, the availability of legal aid should be extended to arbitration. *Mr. King* from Freshfields Bruckhaus Deringer, Amsterdam, expressed his consent with *Professor Gaillard's* statement regarding class actions.

Robert Hunter from Lovells, Frankfurt, expressed the hope that the German Federal Supreme Court would be encouraged to take a comparative approach to the issue when deciding the forthcoming appeal mentioned by Mr. Raeschke-Kessler. He pointed out that in England there was a noticeable trend in the House of Lords to adopt such an approach where English law appeared to be in isolation, referring by way of example to the *Kleinwort Benson* and *Fairchild* cases in which the judgments had expressly taken into account German jurisprudence.

Professor Böckstiegel joined *Mr. Hunter* in saying that the German Federal Supreme Court should also adopt a comparative approach and hopefully would do so in the upcoming decision on the pending case mentioned by *Mr. Raeschke-Kessler* in the beginning.

Afternoon Session, chaired by Hilmar Raeschke-Kessler, LL.M.

Mr. Raeschke-Kessler opened the discussion following the afternoon session asking whether there was an offer for products for financing arbitration on the Paris or London insurance market.

Mr. Hunter replied that, while there was an established market for legal expenses insurance in England, he very much doubted this would cover the risk of interim funding of the legal costs of an impecunious party in the circumstances of the decision by the Federal Supreme Court. *Professor Gaillard* gave the same assessment for the insurance market in Paris.

Mr. Raeschke-Kessler further inquired whether third party financing of arbitral proceedings entailed an obligation for disclosure. It was *Dr. Kröll's*, Law Center for International and European Cooperation, Cologne, opinion that there was no basis for such an obligation to disclose third party financing.

With regard to a "secondary market" for arbitration claims, i.e. third parties financing the claims, *Mr. Lévy* outlined three practically relevant constellations: First, the case of process financing that seems available also for arbitrations. Second, the case of bank insolvencies; due to the fact that insurance for the case of bankruptcy is mandatory for banks, there would usually be someone willing to finance the arbitration involving an insolvent bank. Third, in case of export trade secured by public insurers like COFACE or Hermes, the insurers usually want bankruptcy to be declared first, before they will finance arbitration proceedings. *Mr. Lévy* further stated that in other cases banks did usually not finance an arbitration at the request of the trustee in bankruptcy. Therefore, the bankrupt's estate itself was often used to finance arbitration by prior liquidation of assets.

Asked about his experience *Dr. Lionnet* gave the perspective of a counsel for a multinational company. Arbitration proceedings were always initiated with the consent of the company's insurer. A problem linked to the impecuniosity of the opposing party was never an issue.

Mr. Raeschke-Kessler thanked all speakers and participants of the conference for their valuable contributions and closed the discussion.

Appendix

Bundesgerichtshof (Federal Court of Justice), Judgment of 14 September 2000 - III ZR 33/00

Headnote:

The respondent is barred from relying on an arbitration agreement in proceedings before the state court if the court finds the arbitration agreement is incapable of being performed (in this case: because the claimant is insolvent). Termination of the arbitration agreement is not required.

Facts:

Pursuant to a construction contract concluded with the claimant, the respondents installed heating and sanitary equipment. After a portion of the works had been completed, the claimant refused to provide security for the payment. The claimant also rejected a proposal by the respondents to waive the arbitration agreement concluded between them. The respondents abstained from pursuing their claims before an arbitral tribunal because of the costs involved.

In the present case, the claimant sued for damages resulting from allegedly faulty works. Referring to his insolvency, he had expressly terminated the arbitration agreement in writing.

In defence to the claim, the respondents invoked the arbitration agreement.

The LG (Regional Court) Dresden and the OLG (Higher Regional Court) Dresden held the claim to be inadmissible.

Grounds:

Pursuant to Sec. 1032 sub. 1 ZPO (Code of Civil Procedure/version of 1998), a state court, seized with a claim which is subject to an arbitration agreement, must reject the claim as inadmissible unless the court determines that the agreement is null and void, inoperative or incapable of being performed.

Under the new arbitration law, termination of the arbitration agreement is not required.

In this case, the claimant was without sufficient financial means to conduct arbitral proceedings. The respondents were not in a position to bear the costs of the claimant, as they, too, were insolvent.

By way of exception, the claimant was not barred in this case from relying on his insolvency due to his prior contradictory behaviour. By relying on the arbitration agreement to ward off the claims of the respondents but filing his claim against the respondents in the state courts, the claimant did not act in bad faith, but merely made use of the procedural means at his disposal.

The same would have applied under previous law, since the claimant had validly terminated the agreement by notice of September 10, 1997. Under previous law, it was common cause that both parties were entitled to terminate the arbitration agreement for good cause, in particular if a party was not able to bear the costs of the arbitral proceedings. This also applies if the party terminating the agreement has caused the inability to perform the agreement itself, or if the inability to perform the agreement existed from the outset, since otherwise such a party would be prevented from seeking legal redress.

The judgments of the LG Dresden and the OLG Dresden were vacated and referred back for decision to the LG Dresden.

Leitsatz:

Die im Prozess vor dem staatlichen Gericht erhobene Schiedseinrede des Beklagten ist unbegründet, wenn das Gericht entsprechend dem Klägervortrag (hier: wegen Mittellosigkeit des Klägers) feststellt, die Schiedsvereinbarung sei undurchführbar; einer Kündigung der Vereinbarung bedarf es nicht.

Tatbestand:

Mit "VOB-BAUVERTRAG" vom 22. Februar 1996 beauftragte der Kläger die Beklagten mit Heizungs- und Sanitärinstallationen. Ferner schloss er mit den Beklagten am selben Tag eine Schiedsvereinbarung.

Nachdem die Beklagten Teilleistungen erbracht hatten, verlangten sie von dem Kläger gemäß § 648 a BGB Sicherheitsleistung, was dieser jedoch verweigerte. Die Beklagten regten daraufhin mit Schreiben vom 12. April 1996 an, auf die Schiedsvereinbarung zu verzichten und damit eine Auseinandersetzung vor den ordentlichen Gerichten zu ermöglichen. Mit Schreiben vom 17. April 1996 lehnte der Kläger indes ab. Die Beklagten sahen aus Kostengründen davon ab, das Schiedsverfahren durchzuführen.

Im vorliegenden Rechtsstreit nimmt der Kläger die Beklagten auf Schadensersatz und auf Erstattung von Kosten für die Beseitigung von Mängeln in Anspruch. Die Beklagten hätten den Spülkasten einer Toilette nicht ordnungsgemäß angeschlossen. Dadurch sei ein Wasserschaden entstanden. Ferner hätten die Beklagten veraltete Thermostate eingebaut und die Anschlüsse der Heizkörper falsch montiert. Unter Hinweis auf seine Zahlungsunfähigkeit hatte der Kläger die Schiedsvereinbarung mit Schreiben vom 10. September 1997 aus wichtigem Grund gekündigt; er wiederholte diese Kündigung mit Schriftsatz vom 4. Juni 1999.

Die Beklagten erheben gegenüber der Klage die Einrede der Schiedsvereinbarung. Die Kündigung des Klägers sei unzulässige Rechtsausübung. Die Beklagten rechnen hilfsweise mit Werklohnansprüchen auf.

Die Vorinstanzen haben die Klage für unzulässig erachtet. Mit der Revision verfolgt der Kläger sein Klagebegehren weiter.

Entscheidungsgründe:

Die Revision ist begründet; sie führt zur Aufhebung der vorinstanzlichen Urteile und zur Zurückverweisung der Sache an das Landgericht.

I. Das Berufungsgericht hat im Wesentlichen ausgeführt:

Die Klage sei unzulässig, weil die Beklagten wirksam die Einrede des Schiedsvertrages erhoben hätten. Die mit der Klage geltend gemachten Ansprüche unterfielen der Schiedsvereinbarung, die durch die Kündigungen des Klägers vom 10. September 1997 und vom 4. Juni 1999 nicht hinfällig geworden sei. Es sei schon zweifelhaft, ob ein wichtiger, zur Kündigung berechtigender Grund in dem Sinne vorgelegen habe, dass sich die wirtschaftlichen Verhältnisse des Klägers nachträglich verschlechtert hätten. Der Kläger habe bereits bei Abschluss des Schiedsvertrages die Kosten eines Schiedsverfahrens nicht aufbringen können und es hätten nur vage Aussichten bestanden, dass sich daran etwas ändern könne. Entscheidend sei aber, dass sich der Kläger durch die Kündigung der Schiedsvereinbarung in treuwidriger Weise zu seinem früheren Verhalten in Widerspruch gesetzt habe. Während er sich wegen der

eigenen Ansprüche die Vorteile des staatlichen Verfahrens nutzbar mache, habe er gegenüber der Werklohnforderung der Beklagten auf der Schiedsvereinbarung bestanden. Daran müsse er sich nach dem Grundsatz von Treu und Glauben festhalten lassen.
Der Kläger könne nicht einwenden, die Beklagten handelten ihrerseits arglistig; sie erhöben die Einrede des Schiedsvertrages, obwohl sie die zur Durchführung des Schiedsverfahrens notwendigen finanziellen Mittel nicht hätten. Die Beklagten hätten nachgewiesen, dass ihre Betriebshaftpflichtversicherung die auf sie entfallenden Kosten des Schiedsverfahrens übernehmen werde.
II. Die Erwägungen des Berufungsgerichts halten in einem entscheidenden Punkt der rechtlichen Prüfung nicht stand. Die von den Beklagten erhobene Einrede der Schiedsvereinbarung greift nicht durch. Dabei kann offenbleiben, ob in diesem gerichtlichen Verfahren die §§ 1025 ff ZPO in der Fassung des Gesetzes zur Neuregelung des Schiedsverfahrensrechts (Schiedsverfahrens-Neuregelungsgesetz - SchiedsVfG) vom 22. Dezember 1997 (BGBl. I 3224) oder - gemäß Art. 4 § 1 Abs. 3 SchiedsVfG - das bisher geltende Recht anzuwenden ist.
1. Das Gericht hat gemäß § 1032 Abs. 1 ZPO n.F. eine Klage, die in einer Angelegenheit erhoben wird, die Gegenstand einer Schiedsvereinbarung ist, als unzulässig abzuweisen, sofern der Beklagte dies vor Beginn der mündlichen Verhandlung zur Hauptsache rügt, es sei denn, das Gericht stellt fest, dass die Schiedsvereinbarung nichtig, unwirksam oder undurchführbar ist. Hier ist die Einrede der Schiedsvereinbarung unbegründet, weil die Schiedsvereinbarung undurchführbar gewesen ist (§ 1032 Abs. 1 letzter Halbsatz dritte Alternative ZPO); einer Kündigung des Schiedsvertrages bedurfte es nicht.
Der Gesetzgeber des Schiedsverfahrens - Neuregelungsgesetzes hat das nach bisherigem Recht im Falle der Undurchführbarkeit des Schiedsvertrages bestehende Kündigungserfordernis (Senatsurteil BGHZ 102, 199, 202 m.w.N.) nicht übernommen. Auch den Gesetzgebungsmaterialien ist, soweit ersichtlich, nichts dafür zu entnehmen, dass die Undurchführbarkeit der Schiedsvereinbarung im Wege der Kündigung geltend gemacht werden müsste (vgl. die Begründung der Bundesregierung zum Entwurf eines Gesetzes zur Neuregelung des Schiedsverfahrensrechts BT-Drucks. 13/5274 S. 37 f). Es ist deshalb davon auszugehen, dass im Prozess die Schiedseinrede des Beklagten schon dadurch zu Fall gebracht werden kann, dass das Gericht entsprechend dem Klägervortrag feststellt, die Schiedsvereinbarung sei undurchführbar.
a) Im Streitfall ist die Schiedsvereinbarung undurchführbar gewesen, weil der Kläger die Kosten des Schiedsverfahrens nicht hat aufbringen können und auch nicht anderweit für Kostendeckung gesorgt gewesen ist.
Dass der Kläger aufgrund seiner persönlichen und wirtschaftlichen Verhältnisse außerstande gewesen ist, den Kostenvorschuss für das Schiedsgericht und die Kosten einer im Streitfall erforderlichen anwaltlichen Vertretung im Schiedsverfahren zu bestreiten, ergibt sich bereits daraus, dass er die Kosten seiner Rechtsverfolgung vor dem staatlichen Gericht nicht hat aufbringen können. Der Kläger hat am 1. August 1996 die eidesstattliche Versicherung abgelegt. Auch die Beklagten gehen davon aus, dass der Kläger vermögenslos ist.
Es besteht kein Anhalt, dass die Beklagten die in der Mittellosigkeit des Klägers begründete Undurchführbarkeit des Schiedsverfahrens hätten beheben können und dass sie dazu bereit gewesen wären. Die Beklagten haben nicht behauptet, dass sie im Interesse der Durchführung des Schiedsverfahrens dem Kläger die auf ihn entfallenden Kosten des Schiedsverfahrens sowie seine notwendigen Anwaltskosten (vgl. hierzu BGHZ 51, 79, 82) vorgestreckt hätten (vgl. Senatsurteile BGHZ 77, 65, 69 und 102, 199, 202 f sowie vom 10. März 1994 - III ZR 60/93 - NJW-RR 1994, 1214, 1215; s. auch BGHZ 55, 344, 353). Sie dürften selbst vermögenslos gewesen sein. Denn sie haben am 6. Mai 1997 und am 6. Februar 1998 die eidesstatt-

liche Versicherung abgelegt. Die Betriebshaftpflichtversicherung der Beklagten hätte nur die von ihnen aufzubringenden Kosten der Rechtsverteidigung im Schiedsverfahren beglichen; die auf den Kläger entfallenden Kosten wären ungedeckt geblieben.

b) Dem Kläger ist es nicht ausnahmsweise verwehrt, sich auf die Undurchführbarkeit der Schiedsvereinbarung zu berufen, weil er sich schikanös, treuwidrig oder sittenwidrig verhalten hätte (§§ 226, 242, 826 BGB - vgl. BGHZ 41, 104, 108 f). Zwar war es widersprüchlich, dass der Kläger gegenüber dem Werklohnanspruch der Beklagten die Einrede des Schiedsvertrages erhoben, seinen eigenen Schadensersatzanspruch aber vor dem staatlichen Gericht eingeklagt hat. In dieser bloßen Nutzung prozessualer Mittel lag aber noch kein gegen die vorgenannten Generalklauseln verstoßender Rechtsmissbrauch, der es rechtfertigen könnte, den Kläger an der - aus finanziellen Gründen undurchführbaren - Schiedsvereinbarung festzuhalten und damit praktisch rechtlos zu stellen. Die Beklagten andererseits werden durch den hiermit eröffneten Rechtsweg zum staatlichen Gericht nicht unbillig belastet (vgl. Senatsurteil BGHZ 77, 65, 69 f).

2. Auch nach dem Schiedsverfahrensrecht alter Fassung können sich die Beklagten nicht auf die Schiedsvereinbarung berufen, weil der Kläger diese mit Schreiben vom 10. September 1997 wirksam gekündigt hat.

Für das Schiedsverfahrensrecht alter Fassung ist anerkannt, dass die Parteien berechtigt sind, die Vereinbarung aus wichtigem Grund zu kündigen, wenn sich die Durchführung des Schiedsverfahrens praktisch als unmöglich erweist, insbesondere, weil eine Partei die Kosten des schiedsgerichtlichen Verfahrens nicht aufbringen kann. Die Kündigungsbefugnis ist - mit Ausnahme schikanösen, treuwidrigen oder sittenwidrigen Verhaltens (§§ 226, 242, 826 BGB) - auch dann gegeben, wenn der Kündigende die Undurchführbarkeit des Schiedsverfahrens selbst verursacht oder gar verschuldet hat; denn ihm darf der Rechtsschutz nicht völlig abgeschnitten werden (BGHZ 41, 104, 108 f; Senatsurteile BGHZ 77, 65, 66 f und 102, 199, 202; vgl. auch Senatsurteil vom 11. Juli 1985 - III ZR 33/84 - NJW 1986, 2765, 2766; Stein/Jonas/Schlosser, ZPO 21. Aufl. 1994 § 1025 a.F. Rn. 43 unter Hinweis auf Art. 6 EMRK; Maier in MünchKomm, ZPO 1992 § 1025 a.F. Rn. 34; Musielak/Voit, ZPO 1999 § 1025 a.F. Rn. 9; Zöller/Geimer, ZPO 21. Aufl. 1999 § 1029 Rn. 82; Schwab/Walter, Schiedsgerichtsbarkeit 6. Aufl. 2000 Kap. 8 Rn. 11). Das muss im Grundsatz auch dann gelten, wenn der Kündigende - wie im Streitfall der Kläger - bereits bei Abschluss des Schiedsvertrages die Kosten eines Schiedsverfahrens nicht aufbringen kann und nur ungewisse Aussichten auf ausreichende Einkünfte bestehen. Wie der Gesetzgeber in § 1032 Abs. 1 ZPO n.F. jetzt ausdrücklich festgelegt hat, müssen sich die Parteien im Falle der Undurchführbarkeit des Schiedsverfahrens - in den Grenzen der §§ 226, 242, 826 BGB - stets von der Schiedsvereinbarung lösen können, da sie sonst rechtsschutzlos stünden. Soweit der Senat in seinen früheren Entscheidungen das Kündigungsrecht an zusätzliche Erwägungen - insbesondere zur wirtschaftlichen Lage des Kündigenden - geknüpft hat, entsprach dies den damaligen Fallgestaltungen; das Erfordernis, effektiven Rechtsschutz zu gewähren, sollte und darf dadurch nicht in Frage gestellt werden.

III. Hiernach waren die vorinstanzlichen Urteile aufzuheben und die Sache zur anderweiten Verhandlung und Entscheidung an das Landgericht zurückzuverweisen (§§ 565 Abs. 1, 538 Abs. 1 Nr. 2 ZPO; vgl. BGHZ 16, 71, 82; BGH, Urteil vom 22. November 1994 - XI ZR 45/91 - NJW 1995, 1225, 1227; Urteil vom 11. Juli 1996 - IX ZR 304/95 - NJW 1996, 3008, 3009).

Schriftenreihe der August Maria Berges Stiftung für Arbitrales Recht

Herausgegeben von Dr. Hubertus W. Labes

Band 1 August Maria Berges – Ausgewählte Schriften zum Schiedsrecht. Herausgegeben von der August Maria Berges Stiftung für Arbitrales Recht. 1998.

Band 2 Iris Koch: Außergerichtliche Streitbeilegung im japanischen Wirtschaftsverkehr unter besonderer Berücksichtigung der Schiedsgerichtsbarkeit. 2000.

Band 3 Hans-Claudius Scheef: Der einstweilige Rechtsschutz und die Stellung der Schiedsrichter bei dem Abschluß von Schiedsvergleichen nach dem deutschen und englischen Schiedsverfahrensrecht. Eine rechtsvergleichende Untersuchung. 2000.

Band 4 Dominik Lentz: Die internationale Wirtschaftsschiedsgerichtsbarkeit in der Russischen Föderation. Darstellung und Analyse anhand der Praxis des internationalen Handelsschiedsgerichts bei der Handels- und Industriekammer der Russischen Föderation. 2000.

Band 5 Torsten Lörcher: Neue Verfahren der internationalen Streiterledigung in Wirtschaftssachen. Verfahren vor dem Internationalen Seegerichtshof, WTO-Panelverfahren, ICSID-und WIPO-Schiedsverfahren. 2001.

Band 6 Julia Tief: Discovery und Informationspflichten der Parteien in der Internationalen Schiedsgerichtsbarkeit. Ein deutsch-amerikanischer Vergleich. 2000.

Band 7 Richard Happ: Schiedsverfahren zwischen Staaten und Investoren nach Artikel 26 Energiechartavertrag. Eine Studie zum Wandel der Streitbeilegung im Investitionsschutzrecht unter den Bedingungen einer globalen Weltwirtschaft. 2000.

Band 8 Jörn Schämann: Schiedsgerichte unter staatlicher Kontrolle. Das englische Recht und das UNCITRAL-Modellgesetz. 2001.

Band 9 Jana Dominique Jaeger: Die Umsetzung des UNCITRAL-Modellgesetzes über die internationale Handelsschiedsgerichtsbarkeit im Zuge der nationalen Reformen. 2001.

Band 10 Michael Kronenburg: Vollstreckung ausländischer Schiedssprüche in den USA. Die Rechtsprechung US-amerikanischer Gerichte. 2001.

Band 11 Jan-Michael Ahrens: Die subjektive Reichweite internationaler Schiedsvereinbarungen und ihre Erstreckung in der Unternehmensgruppe. 2001.

Band 12 Klaus Peter Berger: Arbitration Interactive. A Case Study for Students and Practitioners. 2002.

Band 13 Daniel Paul Simms: Das Recht der Schiedsgerichtsbarkeit in Irland. 2002.

Band 14 Johann von Pachelbel-Gehag: Das reformierte deutsche und schwedische Schiedsverfahrensrecht. Eine vergleichende Betrachtung unter Berücksichtigung des UNCITRAL-Modellgesetzes über die internationale Handelsschiedsgerichtsbarkeit. 2002.

Band 15 Volker Nienaber: Die Anerkennung und Vollstreckung im Sitzstaat aufgehobener Schiedssprüche. 2002.

Band 16 German Institution of Arbitration (ed.): Financial Capacity of the Parties. A Condition for the Validity of Arbitration Agreements? Based on a Conference organized by the German Institution of Arbitration (DIS) on November 29th 2002 in Berlin. 2004.